W9-CLM-470

THE SOCIAL WORLD OF IMPRISONED GIRLS

A Comparative Study of Institutions for Juvenile Delinquents

By Rose Giallombardo

This study explains why adolescent female inmates form courtship, marriage, and kinship ties with other inmates to cope with the rigors of imprisonment. It describes how these ties are formed and to what extent the social and behavioral patterns of these relationships mirror their heterosexual and familial counterparts in the community.

Comparative in its approach, the book provides a comprehensive survey of female correctional institutions differing in size, organizational structure, and modes of operation, showing how deprivational aspects of incarceration influence the social behavior of the inmates. Based on direct observation, questionnaires, interviews, and official records, the empirical findings are then compared with relevant literature on male and female prisons to provide a greater understanding of prison communities that will hopefully lead to significant and urgent reforms.

The Social World of Imprisoned Girls is intended specifically for sociologists interested in criminology, delinquency, and social organization, as well as for professional correctional personnel. It will also be useful to laymen wishing a more penetrating view of the aspects of daily prison life that the media may overlook.

THE SOCIAL WORLD
OF IMPRISONED GIRLS

ROSE GIALLOMBARDO

The Social World of Imprisoned Girls

A COMPARATIVE STUDY OF INSTITUTIONS FOR JUVENILE DELINQUENTS

A WILEY-INTERSCIENCE PUBLICATION

JOHN WILEY & SONS, New York · London · Sydney · Toronto

CARNEGIE LIBRARY
LIVINGSTONE COLLEGE
SALISBURY, N. C. 28144

Copyright © 1974, by John Wiley & Sons, Inc.

All rights reserved. Published simultaneously in Canada.

No part of this book may be reproduced by any means, nor transmitted, nor translated into a machine language without the written permission of the publisher.

Library of Congress Cataloging in Publication Data:
Giallombardo, Rose.
  The social world of imprisoned girls.

  "A Wiley-Interscience publication."
  Includes bibliographical references.
  1. Delinquent girls—United States. 2. Reformatories for women—United States. I. Title.

HV9104.G5.   365'.42   74-3318
ISBN 0-471-29735-6

Printed in the United States of America

10 9 8 7 6 5 4 3 2 1

365.42
G 431

ACKNOWLEDGMENTS

The research reported in this book was supported by Public Health Service Research Grant No. MH14993, National Institute of Mental Health, (Center for Studies of Crime and Delinquency). I am grateful to the staff members of this center for their cooperation.

I am indebted to the state directors of youth services who facilitated my entry into Eastern, Central, and Western institutions, and to the superintendents of these institutions for their cooperation in all phases of the research. My greatest debt, however, is to the inmates and the staff members of these institutions—without their willing cooperation, this study would not have been possible.

I also express my thanks to several research assistants for their help on various aspects of the project. Ann Cordelia did an excellent job of abstracting the file data at Eastern and also helped with the coding of the questionnaire data. General research assistance in connection with the Eastern questionnaire and file data were provided by Patrick Malloy and Giorgio Piccagli. My special thanks to Louise Rehling of the Computation Center at the University of Chicago who assumed responsibility for computer programming and helped with the coding of the Central and Western questionnaire and file data. Finally, special mention must be given to Birdie Reeve for her patience, skill, and diligence in typing the manuscript.

ROSE GIALLOMBARDO

102403

CONTENTS

THE SOCIAL WORLD
OF IMPRISONED GIRLS

The Research Task

PREVIOUS RESEARCH. Scholars who have attempted to explain the emergence of a social system among adult male prison inmates generally conclude that the formal prison regime not only facilitates the existence of the informal social system but also directs its organizational form. However, these researchers have failed to examine the possible relationship between the structure of the external culture from which the inmates are drawn and the internal world fashioned by prisoners.

Previous accounts of adult male prisons have explained the emergence of the inmate culture in terms of current functional theory, interpreting the inmate social system as a response to the deprivations found within prison.[1] The most important responses include (1) a sharp cleavage between the staff and the inmates that opposes staff values and emphasizes loyalty to fellow inmates; (2) an inmate world that, although not a "war of all against all," is nevertheless notable for violence, struggles for power, and involvement in illicit activities; (3) the emergence of social roles defined in the argot of the prison community.

While the prisoner cannot completely eliminate the deprivations of imprisonment, a cohesive system with group allegiance as its dominant value can provide a reference group through which the inmate can reinstate his self-image or in some sense neutralize the effects of its loss.

1

This conclusion was derived from case studies of single institutions. No assessments have been made of several adult prisons simultaneously for comparative analysis. Further, we are only beginning to understand the variability among prisons as they may be affected by organizational goals and the composition of staff and inmates. Recent systematic studies of socialization in male prisons by Wheeler and Garabedian call into question the solidary opposition model of inmate culture even within single institutions.[2] They found that prisoners varied in their support of the inmate culture according to length of time served and type of prisoner.

A recent interpretation suggested by Schrag[3] and Irwin and Cressey[4] views inmate culture as somehow imported into the prison world from the external world through the inmates' preprison experiences, social identities, and cultural backgrounds. However, the external world is important only in providing the particular cultural elements that the inmates learned before entering prison. But because individuals who enter prison are not a random sample of the population and their values and attitudes do not comprise a random sample of elements of outside culture, prison culture differs from outside culture, particularly in increased hostility, violence, and traffic in illicit goods. However, at one point Schrag returns to the functional argument that the social organization develops to provide solutions to problems caused by incarceration:

> Juxtaposed with the official organization of the prison is an unofficial social system originating within the institution and regulating inmate conduct with respect to focal issues, such as length of sentence, relations among prisoners, contacts with staff members and other civilians, food, sex, and health, among other things.[5]

Roebuck points out that Irwin and Cressey do not demonstrate that their three prison subcultural groups exhibit behavior patterns common and peculiar to them either in or out of prison.[6]

THE IMPACT OF EXTERNAL CULTURE ON INMATES' SOCIAL SYSTEM. My study of the Alderson prison for women produced findings that suggest a different approach to explaining the existence of inmates' informal social system.[7] Although the deprivations of imprisonment were felt keenly by the female prisoners, their social roles as defined in argot differ in structural form and in the sentiment attached to them from male prisoners' roles. The twenty argot roles that existed in this prison community were consistent with sex roles in outside society. Moreover, unlike the social system of male prisoners, homosexual alliances took the form of marriages; together with the family groups and other kinship ties, these structures integrate female inmates into a social system and represent an attempt to create a substitute universe within the prison.

The female inmate community consists of a large network of loosely structured nuclear families, matricentric families of varying sizes, and other kinship dyadic configurations or family fragments. These structural units are linked by filaments of kinship ties to other inmates through overlapping membership by at least one of the family members. The vast majority of inmates in this prison are engaged in homosexual relations within or without a prison marriage, and the formation of kinship ties among the inmates tends to establish an equilibrium between sexual relations and casual unstable and unregulated contacts.[8] The sexually neutral kinship system represents a predictable structure of social relationships wherein an inmate may turn for help. In contrast, the homosexual marriage alliance, although foremost in the lives of the inmates, is an unstable structure.[9]

The remarkable differences between inmate cultures formed by males and females may be understood in these terms: The prison inmate social system is not an intrinsic response to the deprivations of imprisonment, although the deprivations of imprisonment may be important in precipitating inmate culture. Nor can inmate culture be viewed as a mere reflection of the values and attitudes inmates bring into the prison world. The evidence reported thus far indicates that the adult male and female inmate cultures *are* a response to the deprivations of prison life, but the *nature* of the response in both prison communities is influenced by the differential participation of males and females in the external culture. The culture that emerges within the prison structure may be seen to incorporate and reflect the total external social structure; that is, the way in which roles are defined in the external world influences the definitions made within the prison. General features of the cultural definitions and content of male and female roles in American society are brought into the prison setting, and they function to determine the direction and focus of the inmate cultural system.[10] They are the features concerned with the orientation of life goals for males and females; cultural definitions of passivity and aggression; acceptability of public expression of affection displayed toward a member of the same sex; and perception of the same sex with respect to the "popular" culture—that is, the stereotype of women as untrustworthy and self-orientation because of her orientation to the marriage market.

The family group in female prisons is singularly suited to meet the inmates' internalized cultural expectations of the female role; it serves the social, psychological, and physiological needs of the adult female inmate. Together, the prison homosexual marriage and the larger kinship network provide structures wherein the female inmate may express herself during incarceration.

The cultural orientation of males in our society precludes legitimate marriage and family groupings as a feasible alternative solution for male prisoners; the serious adoption of a female role is contrary to the definition of the male role as masculine.[11] Thus family groups do not emerge in the male prison or training school. In their argot, "fags" and "punks" are held in derision by the vast majority of male inmates, who consider these individuals to have sacrificed their manhood; but the homosexuality of "wolves" is considered a temporary adjustment to sexual tensions. The absence of sentiment and the aggressive behavior of the "wolf" is consistent with the cultural definition of the masculine role, and thus homosexuality loses the taint of femininity that male homosexuality tends to carry in civilian society.

Consistent with the cultural definition of the female as nonaggressive, the roles of violence that emerge in the male prison are notably absent among female inmates. In fact, the behavioral expectations associated with the females' argot roles are consistent with the differential cultural definitions ascribed to male and female roles in our society. For example, a role resembling the structure of the "right guy" who is such a dominant figure in the male prison does not emerge in the female prison. Concepts such as "fair play," and "courage," which are consistent with the concepts of endurance, loyalty, and dignity associated with the right guy, are not meaningful to the female. Although the norm of inmate loyalty exists in the female prison world, the popular culture of women as untrustworthy is imported into the prison world and serves both to neutralize many deviant acts and to furnish the rationale for their commitment.

In short, the *system* of roles and statuses is imported into the prison setting, not merely the values and attitudes of the individuals who enter the prison world. The importance attached to the female role, marriage ties, and family groups can be understood in these terms as salient elements of prison culture in the female prison but not in the male prison. The deprivations of imprisonment may provide necessary conditions for the emergence of an inmate social system, but they are not in themselves sufficient to account for the structural form such systems assume in adult female and male prisons.

RECENT STUDIES OF THE SOCIAL ORGANIZATION OF THE FEMALE PRISON. In the voluminous literature on the female prison and its inmates, the social organization has been overlooked in all but Harper's analysis of the "fringer" role,[12] and the recent prison studies by Giallombardo, Ward and Kassebaum, and Heffernan.[13] The often-cited books of essays on the prison social organization edited by Cressey and by Cloward contain no materials on the female prison. Moreover, with the exception of the work of the Gluecks,[14] virtually no systematically collected data on the female prisoner exist. Most of the descriptive accounts of women's prisons have been made by former administrators and released inmates rather than by social scientists. Hence the bulk of this literature consists of programmatic items,[15] autobiographical accounts of released prisoners and other works intended to be sensational exposés,[16] historical accounts,[17] and attempts to establish the criminality of women.[18]

In addition, there are several unsystematic investigations and impressionistic reports of institutions for juvenile girls. These are important, however, because they reveal homosexual patterns or the presence of "family" groups; and they provide valuable insights into the social organization of institutions for females as well as data that can be used—very cautiously—for comparative purposes. In 1913 Margaret Otis was the first to describe the important social relationships in one institution for girls as homosexual relations between black and white inmates.[19] Although impressionistic and biased, this is the first paper that suggested that males and females in prison evolve social systems that differ in structural form from those in other places. Ford reports similar conditions in another location fifteen years later.[20] He suggests that such ties occur between inmates who are committed for sexual indiscretions, but he also mentions that individuals who are husbands and wives accept others into their fold as "children." In addition to homosexual relationships among incarcerated juvenile girls, Selling describes an interesting "pseudo family" structure, which he explains as a "nonpathological" adjustment to a correctional institution.[21] Somewhat similar relationships among incarcerated girls in an Eastern state have been described by Toigo.[22] Sidney Kosofsky's and Albert Ellis' content analysis of letters written by the inmates of another institution is significant because of the references that are made in these letters to "family" relationships.[23] In addition, recent questionnaire data obtained by Halleck and Hersko from fifty-seven inmates on the day of their release from the state institution for delinquent girls in Wisconsin indicated that 69 percent were involved in homosexual behavior of one form or another during the period of incarceration.[24] In her study of unwed mothers, Konopka refers briefly to homosexual relationships among the youthful institutionalized girls; she specifically refers to the "butch" and femme" roles as differentiating individuals assuming male and female roles.[25] More than four decades ago Shaw and Myers also reported homosexual and familial relationships between the inmate members of the training school for girls in Illinois.[26]

Evidence that females in other cultures than American society form social relationships defined by kinship ties has been provided by two sources; these data are important because they broaden our base for comparative analysis. Ju-K'ang Tien, in his study of female labor in an industrial setting during the period that China was undergoing rapid social change, points out that the women working in a cotton mill formed "imaginary" kinship groups. One such family grouping, named "Pine Tree Which Lasts Forever," consisted of twelve women who had no common kinship or previous community relationships.[27]

Taylor, in a more recent study of institutionalized delinquents, reports that borstal girls in New Zealand also form relationships similar to those reported previously in American institutions for females.[28] The borstal girls' various relationships with other inmates are subsumed under the collective term *darls*. According to Taylor, they create "artificial kinship groups" with names such as "Hubby, Wifey, Sister, Baby, Daughter, Cousy." All the inmates were involved in darl relationships, but the extent of involvement varied. Taylor's inquiries of the borstal staff indicated that the practice had been operating for at least eighteen years. The social functions of the darls included mutual aid in the form of sharing scarce goods, security from physical attack, emotional security, and "closer physical relationships." Taylor concluded that these relationships were "so binding that some of the girls were quite depressed when they were released before their partners." Moreover, communication by the borstal girls with the school staff after release indicated that they had difficulty in resuming relationships with boys, but Taylor maintains that there was no evidence that the darl relationships led to "permanent homosexuality."[29] According to Taylor, relationships of this type may not be confined to borstal girls; there is "some suggestion" that similar relationships are also formed by the younger and older institutionalized female offenders in New Zealand.

In their study of a California prison, Ward and Kassebaum found that homosexuality is the mode of adaptation to the prison by many women, but they found little evidence of the differentiated types and degree of solidarity reported in prisons for men. These authors conclude that women need more emotional support than male prisoners; the prison experience is more difficult for women than men (a thesis that is difficult to support), creates the need for affection among women, and is responsible for inmate homosexuality. Unfortunately, most of their research is devoted to detailed and repetitious descriptions of homosexual practices, and the authors fail to question how so many dyads could function as relatively autonomous units in the prison community.

A society of dyads could conceivably function as autonomous units if it were possible for each dyad to survive in the prison as a self-sufficient system. But among inmates, like people interacting in group life everywhere, there are needs whose satisfaction requires a broader set of social relationships. Inmates may need certain kinds of labor, protection, information, advice, and affection from other inmates. They also may need scarce goods, which must be obtained from institutional stores, or clothing and other goods, which may or may not be legitimately possessed by other inmates, but access to them requires the cooperation of other inmates. Moreover, inmates are in constant competition with each other for marriage partners because the homosexual marriage makes doing time easier. Without some institutional means to regulate the procurement of marriage partners as well as the social contacts of married inmates with all other inmates, the inmate community would be characterized by a constant "war of all against all."

In Heffernan's study of a women's reformatory in the District of Columbia, the existence of family groups among the incarcerated female prisoners is the most important finding reported.[30] That the original study was not designed to explore more specifically this aspect of the inmates' institutional experience is unfortunate. The study was limited to the felon population (who had longer sentences) because the purpose had been to replicate Wheeler's study.[31] However, it is not clear why the felons (who constituted approximately 50 percent of the entire inmate population) were considered the "core" of the inmate body. That the interview data revealed the existence of relationships defined in terms of kinship bonds would have indicated that the interviewing be broadened to include the sizable group of short-term residents in order to determine what part they played in the family groups; whether they formed isolated kinship links as did the inmates who were confined for longer periods of time; if so, whether they limited their role-playing to certain types of kinship roles because they would soon be released; and the meaning to them of their participation in a family group. The three so-called survival systems—the "square," the "cool," and "the life"—that presumably reflect the felons' differing orientations to the prison experience (the kinship ties are also referred to as a family *system*) clearly are not substantiated by the data; the validity of these data are questionable because of the reliance placed on the staff's assessment of the inmates' participation and the arbitrary assignment of inmates into the "system" categories. Despite these serious limitations, Heffernan's study provides many valuable insights into the inmate world and the social organization of the female prison.

RECENT STUDIES OF THE SOCIAL ORGANIZATION OF THE MALE PRISON. Of the many excellent studies of the male prison, Clemmer's book contains a wealth of material and comments on the prison and remains the classic in the field.[32] The concept most widely associated with Clemmer is that of "prisonization" which posits a steady increase in negative attitudes as inmates become socialized to a negative prison culture—the primary group being of crucial importance in this regard. However, the recent studies of socialization in the male prison by Wheeler,[33] Garabedian,[34] and Glaser[35] call into question the solidary opposition model of inmate culture even within single institutions.

Most of the research following Clemmer's work (including that of Hans Reimer which actually appeared before Clemmer's work), although tending to concentrate on particular aspects of the inmate system, basically views the inmate system as a response to the conditions of prison life. Reimer concludes that there was a common sharing of values by the inmates based on a common condition of conflict, and definite inmate roles centered around that of the "right guy" with a corresponding inmate culture.[36] McCorkle and Korn view the fundamental issue confronting the inmates as one of social rejection and deprivation, and the inmate system emerges as a response to the prison situation.[37] In effect, it makes possible the inmate's rejecting his rejectors rather than himself. The inmate social system is basically exploitative with limited cohesion; social order among the inmates is maintained not through a common definition as McCleery argues, but by the use of power based on violence or the threat of violence.

McCleery's essay examines the relationship between communication and power and shows how the power structure of the administration influences that of the inmate social system; that is, a change in patterns of communication in one system results in a similar change in the other.[38] An inmate code and a system of stratification and degree of solidarity will emerge in the prison under quite different conditions of prison life. Hayner and Ash base the organization of the prison community on a form of economic adaptation devoted to obtaining goods and services denied by the administrators, rather than on the existence of primary groups.[39] Cloward points out that the inmate organization is extremely functional for the maintenance of the system, but at the expense of adherence to formal rules and the reformation of many inmates.[40]

A valuable research is Sykes' analysis of the inmate social system in a maximum security prison.[41] Viewed as a system of roles and functions, the informal social system develops as a response to five major problems involving deprivation. Goffman addresses the same problem, but from the viewpoint of the "total institution."[42] Although he speaks of "mortifications" of imprisonment rather than "deprivations," his approach adheres to the usual structural-functional view of the writers noted above. Irwin and Cressey take issue with this approach, and attempt to arrive at a new synthesis by relating the behavior of inmates to preprison values and attitudes. Roebuck denies the validity of this approach and demonstrates that no clear distinction is made between the subcultures.

Other important observations that tend to support the solidary opposition model of the inmate culture are reported in studies of institutions for delinquent boys by Grosser[43] and Barker and Adams.[44] Analyses suggesting that the inmate social system operates principally to oppose or circumvent the organization's aims include Polsky's comprehensive study of a cottage unit in a private treatment institution,[45] and Rubenfeld's and Stafford's observations of adolescent delinquents living in one cottage of a large training school.[46] Rubenfeld's and Stafford's findings tend to support and confirm those reported by Polsky. Although these institutions vary in size, the values of the inmate system in both the treatment and custodial institutions reflected hostility to the institution's formal goals of rehabilitation to social conformity and alienated the inmates from staff personnel and their values. The foregoing in-depth studies, together with the later study of a state-operated treatment institution by Fisher,[47] are valuable and comprehensive discussions and analyses of the inmate culture among institutionalized delinquent boys.

A more ambitious study designed to overcome the limitations of the "case study" is the comparative study of six institutions by Street, Vinter, and Perrow.[48] This study purports to examine variations in organizational goals systematically. The authors conclude that as the goals of the organizations change under the impact of treatment concepts, inmate orientation and leadership structures alter. However, Fisher's later study of a small treatment-oriented, state-operated correctional institution is at variance with reports claiming that similar institutions are places of effective treatment.

Only a few of the serious limitations of the Street et al. study can be recorded in this context, but others will become apparent or will be suggested herein.[49] Specifically, while the Street et al. study purports to compare six institutions, two of the institutions included in the sample are "open"—that is, they are not "total" institutions. The residents of the open institutions attended the local community schools every day; on school days the boys were gone from the institutions for eight to nine hours and also went home every weekend.

To include these institutions in the study design, a parallel study of the boys' experiences in the community was required, to assess the impact of the community experiences on the inmates and the relationship of these experiences to events inside. Moreover, because the boys in the open institutions only slept there, they should more accurately have been classified as "halfway houses" (although the inmates were actually three-fourths of the way in the community). The function of the staff members at the open institutions was quite different from that of their counterparts at the closed institutions; many functions were shared, or taken over by organizations in the community and by the boys' families and friends during the weekends. This fact alone probably accounts in large measure for the differences in the way routines were organized in the open institutions. The boys were viewed as "normal" youngsters rather than "sick" youngsters in need of various "therapies."

Because the open institutions utilized community facilities, it is not clear why they were placed in the *center* of the "continuum of treatment" rather than at the extreme end. This would mean that one must accept the view that an approach that keeps the youngster in the community and does not disrupt his community and family ties is the most *advanced* "treatment." This concept forces institutional personnel to demonstrate clearly that any other "treatment" will produce a different and more desirable outcome. Moreover, many of the questionnaire items in the Street et al. study did not apply to the boys who lived in the open institutions. The same holds true for the sizable group of inmates classified as "neglected and dependent inmates" (their most serious offense) who should have been eliminated from the analysis.[50] On this basis alone, the research team did not obtain comparable data in the six institutions. Offenses such as auto theft and larceny were classified as "less serious offenses" although they are classified as serious crimes for adults; yet all "sex offenses" committed by the youthful boys—including the vague "sex offense, unspecified"—were classified as "more serious offenses." These differences would be reflected in the number of inmates defined as "serious offenders," making comparison problematic.

These examples are a few of the questions that invalidate the measures used to substantiate differences among these institutions. Even on this elementary level, they indicate clearly that the so-called differences in inmate social structure and leadership patterns that are presumed to differ from one institution to another cannot be said to be substantiated by the data. Indeed, the measurements used to delineate the interpersonal relations among the inmates and leadership patterns are too simplistic to capture the complex interaction patterns that take place in cottage living units. Reliance on questionnaire data alone cannot delineate the character of the informal social system of the inmates nor answer the questions posed in terms of organizational operations; no comparable observation data were obtained that would have afforded an opportunity to investigate areas for which the questionnaires were inadequate. The scanty descriptions of the four closed institutions, however, indicate that they are more alike than unlike even on the basis of the questionnaire data presented. This suggests that the differences among them are probably more indicative of differences in the sheer size of the settings rather than attributable to differences in the organizational goals. We do not know, because the kinds of data that would be required to answer the complex questions involved were not collected. But in view of the scattered anecdotal descriptions provided that detail the discrepant patterns of operation in the treatment and custodial institutions, it is entirely conceivable that if the researchers had spent more than four months to study firsthand the ongoing operation of six correctional institutions, the study might very well have produced findings that would be more in accord with those reported, for example, by Polsky and Fisher.

THE PRINCIPAL OBJECTIVES OF THIS RESEARCH. The findings reported on the adult female prison emphasize the cultural unity that exists between the inner and outer worlds and suggest that we can better understand the prison community by continuing to study the relationship of the external and internal cultures rather than by viewing it as an institution isolated from the larger society. This study is intended to make a further contribution to this orientation by developing the theoretical implications in several institutions for adjudicated delinquent girls that vary in goal emphasis. A comparative analysis of organizations serving delinquent girls is now crucial. I examine both the impact of organizational goals and age statuses on inmate organization. The study is an assessment of the impact of the differential cultural definitions of sex roles upon the informal social organization of the inmates of correctional institutions for court-adjudicated delinquent girls, and of the conditions under which the social system of female inmates is independent of formal organizational arrangements. By isolating the crucial variables of age and organizational goals, we should be able to establish the theoretical connections between the differential cultural definitions ascribed to sex roles in American society and the responses made by males and females of all age levels in the prison setting.

In my earlier study, I found that the structural features of marriage, kinship ties, and family groups in institutions for female offenders are the female counterpart of the informal social system evolved by male prisoners.[51] Based on this, I hypothesize that irrespective of the goals of the formal organization, the structural form of the informal social system evolved by female juvenile offenders will be marriage, kinship, and family groups. Since behavioral expectations with respect to performance in specific social roles are conceptualized in all societies in ways deemed culturally appropriate to the individual's age, we would expect, however, that although the structural features of the social system of juvenile girls will be similar to that of adult female prisoners, the content and behavioral expectations of roles and statuses will vary in ways consistent with the age and maturation level of juveniles.

The broad goals of the research are twofold: (1) to understand the relationship of the external and internal culture by inquiring into the nature and structure of social relationships formed by youthful female offenders; and (2) to learn something about the impact of organizational goals for the direction and focus of the inmate social system.

The significance of this research for the rehabilitation of offenders is evident. The informal social system can be instrumental in encouraging behavior antithetical to the goals of the formal organization, and particularly behavior that is inconsistent with the goals of treatment. Little is known about the nature and structure of informal social systems formed by incarcerated delinquent girls. With rare exception, research efforts have consistently been directed to the problems of male prisoners. This research is intended to help fill the gap. I scrutinized the social life of incarcerated delinquent girls to determine how significant the informal and formal structures of the organization are to the girls. The dynamics of the inmate social role-playing and an inquiry into the processes of acquiring various types of inmate roles also was investigated.

Understanding the nature of such structures and the meaning of their existence in the prison is crucial for treatment to be effective. Generally, it is assumed that the inmate informal social system can be eliminated when the goals of the institution are modified to mitigate the deprivations of imprisonment. This view has obvious implications for treatment. If we reduce the deprivations, inmate society will be more congenial to treatment efforts. However, this assumption may not apply to adolescent inmates. Hence, knowing at what structural level and degree the social system of the female inmates can be permeated is important for influencing the girls not only to accept the goal of treatment but also to cooperate actively with the staff to accomplish the goal.

SCOPE OF THE PROJECT.[52]   The project was designed to examine this problem in three correctional institutions for juvenile girls. A comparative design was utilized to provide a framework for assessing the interrelations and effects of different structural units of each organization, and help to overcome the unresolved problems in generalizing from a single case. While the descriptive results of the study are limited to these particular organizations, the aims of the study were more broadly defined. Building on my work of the adult female prison, the research objective was to examine each institution in depth as a social system while collecting the types of data in each institution that would make possible precise comparisons among the organizations studied. Finally, I compare the empirical findings with relevant literature on male and female prisons to determine common and variable elements, enabling additional understanding or significant questions about these formal organizations. The adolescent status of the youthful inmates must raise questions concerning the structural range of deprivations experienced by this group of inmates as compared with adult inmates. For example, the loss of autonomy and responsibility may be assumed to be deprivational for the adult male or female, but their loss is undoubtedly experienced quite differently by adolescents because their social world in American society differs from that of adults.

The institutions were selected according to the goals of each institution. Correctional facilities differ in the *relative* program emphasis placed on custodial and treatment goals and the characteristic social conditions of deprivation for the inmates. All of the institutions included in the study sample are "closed"; that is, program facilities are provided on the institution grounds. If "open" institutions had been included, the effect of community experiences on inmates would be difficult to assess unless a parallel study of the inmates' community experiences were made. Moreover, the specific institutions included were located in different geographical areas to avoid any cultural bias that might be introduced as a consequence of regional concentrations of particular ethnic populations. An attempt was made to select institutions of different size. This presented a problem because usually there is only one large public institution for girls in each state, and hence there is little actual size variation among institutions for girls. All of the institutions in the sample are state-operated facilities.

Because each institution in the sample was to be studied intensively over a considerable period of time, an effort was made to use rigorous criteria in their selection so that none would be included that did not fit the research requirements. The main criteria used to select the institutions are: (1) Formal published reports and statements of goals and general organizational operation; (2) references to the institution in other published materials and the general reputation of the institution; (3) an interview with the state director or commissioner and, sometimes, other members of his staff, responsible for the institutional program; (4) a visit to the institution prior to the actual field work to insure that the organization met the research requirements for inclusion in the sample; and (5) the presence or absence of treatment personnel and other program facilities. On the basis of this preliminary exploration, the three organizational types that make up the sample were differentiated with respect to the relative goal emphasis placed on custody or treatment as shown below.

Organizational Type Based on Primary Goal Emphasis	Inmate Population	Geographical Location in United States
Custody	205	Northeastern
Intermediate	341	Central
Treatment	159	Western

Juvenile institutions have always been commited to rehabilitation, although *rehabilitation* has been defined differently at various periods. Yet even the institutions that claim to be most "treatment-oriented" must be concerned to some extent with custody. All institutions must resolve the problem of conflicting goals. The distinction between goals lies in the emphasis placed on custodial goals relative to those of treatment and the degree to which they are acclaimed and implemented.

Sociologists must go beyond the official pronouncements of policy. They must distinguish between what is actually going on in an organization and what is said to occur, or what the staff maintains should or might take place, for any future changes that are made in these organizations must be based on present realities. The structure of these organizations is much more complex than the official pronouncements and the reputational claims would have one believe.

The institutions studied not only resemble each other but are similar to all other institutions of this type in that they are characterized by conflicting and competing goals. The institutions are hereafter identified on the basis of their geographical location: Eastern, Central, and Western.

FINDINGS OF THE RESEARCH. Although Eastern, Central, and Western institutions are located in different parts of the nation, opened their doors at different points in time, and differ in size and the auspices under which they operate, the organizational problems faced by institutional officials are similar, as are the solutions provided. Moreover, notwithstanding the differences in treatment strategies and philosophies, the informal culture evolved by the girls at all three schools is similar in structure. This suggests that the inmates in each institution faced the same problems while incarcerated.

Transplanted to the institutions, the adolescent girls find themselves many miles from the communities where their families and friends live. In the impersonal world of the institution, they desire to be accepted and to interact in the context of primary social relationships.

The courtship, marriage, and kinship relationships established by the adolescent inmates represent an attempt to provide a solution to the personal and social deprivations by duplicating the external world. The similarity of the informal social system evolved by the youthful female inmates to that established by the adult female offenders is remarkable. That similar social roles do not emerge in institutions for adult and adolescent male offenders provides evidence that attests powerfully to the hypothesis that the inmate culture is influenced by the differential participation of males and females in the external culture. It is the system of roles and statuses that is imported into the prison setting, not merely the values and attitudes of the individuals who enter the prison world. The culture that emerges within the institutional structure may be seen to incorporate and reflect the total external social structure.

This study provides further evidence that the culture that forms within the prison setting cannot be understood in terms of the structural–functional account which typically views the emergence of the inmate system as a response to the deprivations of imprisonment. Clearly, the deprivations of incarceration may provide necessary conditions for the emergence of an inmate social system, but they are not in themselves sufficient to account for the structural form of the systems. General features of American society with respect to the cultural definitions and content of male and female roles are brought into the prison setting, and they determine the direction and focus of the inmate cultural system. These general features are those concerned with the orientation of life goals for males and females, cultural definitions of passivity and aggression, acceptability of public expression of affection displayed toward a member of the same sex, and perception of the same sex with respect to what I call the popular culture—the stereotype of women as untrustworthy and the self-orientation of the female because of her orientation to the marriage market.

The family group in the female prison is singularly suited to meet the inmates' internalized cultural expectations of the female role; it serves the social, psychological, and physiological needs of the adolescent offenders. Together, the prison homosexual marriage alliance and the larger kinship network provide structures wherein the female inmate's needs may find fulfillment and expression during the period of incarceration.

CHAPTER TWO

Historical Background
and Institutional Settings

EASTERN SCHOOL FOR GIRLS. The Eastern school for girls is located a few miles outside the town of Coleton in the Waterford River Valley. At its founding in 1887, it was operated as a House of Refuge. In 1904 the institution was reorganized as the State Training School for Girls, a title that was still used when the study was in progress, although the term *training* had been officially deleted.

By 1908 the inmate population had grown to 228 girls—approximately the present population size—and the school had a staff of sixty-five, including thirteen teachers. The present staff is more than twice as large due mainly to an expanded school program. Until recently the cottage staff lived in the inmate residence units; hence the number of staff now required to give round-the-clock coverage also is greater.

Girls between the ages of twelve and sixteen from throughout the state are placed or committed to Eastern by family court action. Most of the inmates are "placed" as persons in need of supervision. Commitment to the school as a juvenile delinquent is reserved for the individual who performs an act that, if done by an adult, would be processed as a crime. During the period of the study, twenty-two inmates (11 percent of the

17

population) had been committed as juvenile delinquents. Girls who are adjudicated juvenile delinquents are committed for a period of three years; those in need of supervision are placed for eighteen months with the option that the institution may request an extension for a subsequent twelve-month period. At the expiration of the first extension period the institution may petition the court for another twelve-month extension period. No placement may be continued beyond the inmate's twentieth birthday without her consent, and in no case beyond her twenty-first birthday.

Although placement is more than a flat three-year commitment, the department of social services which operates the state training schools and related facilities has developed the attitude that care of the committed child is a continuum that begins at the point of commitment and is completed only when the individual is discharged from parole supervision. Institutionalization is viewed as only one part of the continuum.

No distinction is made at Eastern as to how placements and juvenile delinquents are managed; in fact, the term *juvenile delinquent* is used to refer to the entire inmate population. (Herein, the term *juvenile delinquent* is used to facilitate the presentation of materials.) The average stay of the inmates at Eastern is ten months.

The institution's external facade is that of a private boarding school for girls. Its many acres of spacious lawns and wooded areas isolate it on all sides from the townspeople. The low stone walls and iron grille fences that enclose most of the grounds also contribute to the noninstitutional appearance of the school; a sizable area where the river serves as a natural barrier has no fences at all. Both entrances have no physical barriers, but the exit which leads more directly to the local town has a manned gatehouse. The other exit is approached by a long winding road, and any pedestrian taking this route would be conspicuous.

Twelve brick cottages border three quadrangles and house the student population in single rooms. Previously, as many as seventeen cottages were in use with an average population of approximately 400 inmates. Recently, however, several cottages were razed, necessitating a decrease in the inmate population. At the time of the study, the daily population averaged slightly more than 200 inmates.

Although several cottages are less than fifteen years old and the auditorium and gymnasium were built recently, many buildings at Eastern were in existence in 1904. With the exception of one freshly painted cottage that was a showcase for visitors, the cottages were badly in need of repair. A few repairs were made in some cottages during the time I was there, but the future of most units remained in doubt due to a serious lack of funds. The walls in the common rooms and the individual bedrooms had peeling paint, cracked plaster, and gaping holes.

Although Eastern no longer has a disciplinary cottage, six bare cells were built in one wing of the hospital shortly after the security cottage was eliminated. These security cells are used for runaways and for inmates who break other institution rules. But the small number of security cells do not tell the whole story: Any room in a cottage may be converted to a stripped cell at any time. Sometimes when the hospital cells were filled, a cottage room would be stripped of all furniture, the window removed, and the inmate confined until the situation was resolved to the staff's satisfaction. A maximum security annex had been built four years prior to the study (formerly it had also been under the administrative supervision of Eastern's superintendent), and inmates who presented "major problems" were transferred to this institution. Located a few miles from Eastern, it was designed to accommodate the "needs" of the inmates who present "control" problems or who have "serious emotional problems" at Eastern and at the smaller facility for girls in this state. Annex units of this type are common in several states, and they are in every sense disciplinary cottages "away from home." Held as a threat to any inmate who resists outward conformity to institutional rules, these units provide the same function as would a maximum security cottage located on the grounds. In addition, its location elsewhere makes it possible to present a public image of the institution that is less than the whole truth, if not altogether false.

At Eastern the cottages are staffed by children's supervisors (formerly called "housemothers") who are called "Ma" by the inmates; the supervisor's surname is also added. Each cottage forms a self-sufficient unit in which all meals are prepared and served by inmates working under the supervision of the cottage supervisor whose tour of duty is the kitchen.

On the first floor of each two-story cottage is a kitchen, dining room, recreation room with television, and laundry where the inmates wash and iron personal clothing. Each inmate has her own room; a few are located on the main floor, but most of the bedrooms are on the second floor. The inmates are not allowed to congregate in the hall at any time and must sit in the recreation room unless they are confined to their rooms.

Each cottage has an attached porch, but the inmates may not venture there without permission, nor may they walk freely about the grounds. The staff specifies the route to be taken when going from one part of the institution to another. A cottage group may go unescorted to the school building but a staff member is posted nearby to observe them. At all other functions, cottage groups are escorted by staff supervisors. Campus

movement by individual girls, however, is controlled by passes issued to
the inmates by the staff. An inmate is not allowed to talk to inmates who
do not live in her cottage; this restriction on communication is related to
the informal social system of the inmates.

The school operates a laundry for the cottage linens and personal linen
for some of the administrative staff. The laundry for several other state
facilities also is processed by the Eastern inmates. At any time, approximately ten to fifteen inmates work at the laundry without pay; the work
is classified as vocational training, although the laundry equipment is
altogether obsolete. Only a few cottages are equipped with washing
machines, hence most of the inmates launder their clothing by hand.

Although Eastern does not have a central food-service kitchen, the
hospital has a small kitchen where meals are prepared for patients. This
facility also provides low-cost meals for a few members of the staff.

Over the many years of Eastern's existence, there have been both male
and female superintendents; at the present time the school is administered by a male. A Board of Visitors, appointed by the governor of the
state, is charged with reporting the conditions of the school. The six
Board members—three of whom must be women—are from different parts
of the state, but only one is from the metropolis from which almost all of
the inmates are sent. No Board members are individuals of the same
racial or ethnic background of the inmates, the vast majority of whom are
black or Puerto Rican. Although the Board meets at the school every
month, its function remains unclear. Reports submitted to the Board for
meeting use are stereotyped in content. The reports of the Board are not
released to the public and, as far as I could determine, the Board had
been inactive in pressing for improvements at Eastern school.

CENTRAL SCHOOL FOR GIRLS.   Central school is the oldest of the
three schools included in the study. Located in a village adjacent to the
Markat River in the central part of the United States, the institution is
surrounded on all sides by farms. The nearest town is approximately ten
miles from the school, and one of the major cities in the state is twenty-
five miles away.

The original purpose of Central school as stated by the state legislature
a century ago was for the "instruction, employment, and reformation of
exposed, helpless, evil-disposed, and vicious girls." At the time, the age
limit was set from seven to fifteen years to accommodate children of dependent status. Consistent with the definition of the children who were
admitted then, the school included in its name the terms reform and industrial. These labels, used throughout the nation to name schools for

juveniles, reflected the prevailing ideology of the purposes of these institutions. Although the trend today is for more "neutral" names for institutions, the operation of schools for youthful offenders is, nonetheless, still premised to a large extent upon the same ideology.

Changing philosophies are reflected in changes in the admission requirements as well as in the names of institutions; both gradually unfold as one examines historically the operation of the century-old Central institution—and to a lesser degree of Eastern and Western which were established more recently. In 1878, for example, a change in the law of Central state omitted the terms *exposed* and *helpless* but added *incorrigible* to the list of behaviors which provided justification for the commitment of adolescents. Also, the admission age was restricted to individuals over nine years and under fifteen years. (The age range was not changed again for another thirty-five years, at which time the commitment age was raised to ten years with an upper limit of eighteen.) Moreover, the name of the institution was changed to exclude the term *reform*—a reflection of the increased focus on the training aspects of incarceration—but the expectation that the inmates were to be *reformed* remained as a primary goal, as it does to this day. When admission regulations were again changed so that girls who were "dependent" or "neglected" could not be committed, the institution's name was changed again; the change paralleled the development of other agencies in the community which now cared for dependent and neglected children.

Like many other schools of this type throughout the nation, Central school originally was organized and administered by the political party in office. The superintendent was appointed by a board of trustees—a board which had been appointed by the governor and empowered with the overall supervision of the school. The practice of having political appointees head the school continued until just before World War I when the top administrative post was placed under civil service.

Until the early 1930s, a man and his wife were customarily in charge of the school. Even when the position of superintendent was abolished in 1911 and the top administrative office was that of matron, it was customary for both husband and wife to be in charge, the woman holding the position of chief matron and the man that of steward of the grounds. Only after the early 1930s was Central in complete charge of a woman. The institution has been under the supervision of a male superintendent since 1955 when the present administrator was appointed.

Jurisdictional transfers from the department of public welfare to the department of mental hygiene and corrections were the result of expanding community services. These changes had important consequences for the type of offender admitted to Central as well as the goals to be accomplished during the period of institutionalization. By 1941, the school accepted no female under the age of twelve years, and only those possessing "normal mental and physical capacity for intellectual and industrial training."

In 1963 Central came under the jurisdiction of a youth commission established by law as a special state department to assume responsibility for the entire state juvenile program. All of the state's facilities for delinquent youth, as well as community service programs, were placed under the commission's control. Consistent with the new emphasis on treatment and rehabilitation, the name of the school underwent a more radical change two years later, so that it was indistinguishable from that of an ordinary private boarding school for girls. However, the training function of the school still remained as an integral part of the school's program. The new label was conceived primarily as one means of reducing the stigma attached to incarceration—a mark of discredit for the individual that remains despite the rhetoric of the juvenile court.

All the adolescent girls who are incarcerated at Central are committed by the courts to the youth commission as juvenile delinquents, and most of them are processed through the diagnostic center located twenty-five miles from the school.[1] Inmates are committed to Central from all counties of the state, and their ages range from twelve to eighteen at the time of court commitment. Because the school operates on the basis of open intake, Central is overcrowded. The concept of open intake, however, is only partially true: At Central (as at Eastern and Western) pressure to admit inmates means that some institutionalized inmates will be released sooner. However, a minimum stay of five months for each inmate at Central is set by law. Mandatory stays were not explicitly set forth for the Eastern and Western institutions, although committing county authorities expected that inmates were not to be released before they had *experienced* a certain period of institutionalization; these expectations were honored by the Eastern and Western administrators.[2] The average length of stay for the inmates at Central school is eight to ten months.

The physical plant of Central consists of ninety acres of gently rolling lawns and wooded areas with more than forty buildings. The original buildings were destroyed by fire soon after the school opened, and were replaced with the buildings in use today. The construction of the cottages spans from 1873 to 1961; hence, the condition of the living units varies considerably. Some of the older cottages have been refurbished by installing interior wall paneling, and plans were underway to improve all the older cottages.

The brick two-story structures vary in size from fifteen to thirty individual rooms. Most of the cottages were built to create and maintain a homelike appearance and atmosphere. In spite of Central's size, the diversity in scale and the architectural detail of the cottages help to decrease the overall institutional look. However, three recently built one-story stone and brick cottages, although attractive in architectural design, tend to have an institution look precisely because they are not as amenable to homelike touches as are the older cottages.

The thirteen living units housing the inmates are spread out over a wide area. Although the rated capacity of Central is 275 inmates, in 1967 the institution had a daily population as high as 480 inmates. At present, the average daily population is about 350 inmates; therefore, seventy-five inmates have roommates. The degree of overcrowding in one cottage was such that office space had been converted to a small dormitory to accommodate four inmates.

Central was the only school that had a separate cottage where incoming inmates spent two weeks in an orientation program. (Both Eastern and Western had phased out their four-week orientation program shortly before the study began. At Eastern, the inmates went directly to the cottage to which they had been classified prior to their arrival, following a brief examination in the hospital. At Western, the inmates spent two or three days at the hospital before they were assigned to a cottage.)

The cottage staff at Central are referred to as cottage parents, although there were no married couples in any of the cottages. The cottage staff were not addressed as "Ma" by the Central inmates.

In many ways the cottages at Central resemble those at Eastern. Each cottage has a recreation room, called "classroom" at Central, where the inmates watch television, play cards, or do their school homework. However, in the older cottages, the basement also is used for recreation; there the inmates roller-skate, listen to records, and dance. In most cottages, the inmates' rooms are all on the second floor. Each cottage was built to be a self-sufficient unit with a dining room and kitchen. At present, however, all food is prepared in the main kitchen and delivered by truck to the cottages. The school also operates a bakery that supplies the institution's needs for baked goods.

Central differs from Eastern in that it has a maximum security cottage in which some inmates are housed permanently; other inmates are accommodated for varying periods of time, depending upon the seriousness of their misbehavior. Central also differs from both Eastern and Western in that it operates a large cafeteria open from early morning to early evening. (Food served in the cafeteria is prepared in the main kitchen.) This facility serves two purposes: (1) It provides vocational training for the inmates; in fact, one room off the main dining area is operated as a luncheon restaurant to train a few inmates as waitresses, hostesses and cashiers; (2) it not only provides meals to the staff at low cost but also gives them a central place to meet informally throughout the day for coffee breaks, and to some extent it facilitated communication between staff members on all levels. No similar provision was made at Eastern or Western schools; the dining room facilities for the staff at these schools could accommodate only a few individuals. Furthermore, there was no employees' lounge or other designated area at either Eastern or Western where staff members could eat their lunch or meet informally.[3] No physical barriers block the two entrances to Central. Fences enclose the spacious grounds except where the river and wooded areas provide unique natural barriers. The exits to the school lead directly to the main highway, making any inmate as conspicuous as if she were observed cutting across the cornfields—in which case the local residents would call the institution officials.

Staff members and visitors to the school drive their cars directly into the school grounds, parking where space is provided. As is the custom at Eastern, the Central staff members also drive directly to the cottages or other buildings. In this sense, both Eastern and Central are "open" institutions as the official publications state—although the male security staff walk or drive around the grounds from time to time. Thus neither institution is altogether "open," although whether "open" or "closed," none of the inmates at any of the institutions studied took unauthorized leave by way of the official exits, preferring to go over the fence.

In addition to the bakery and cafeteria, Central also operates a large laundry plant on the grounds, where the linen for the cottages and most of the inmates' clothing are laundered. (Facilities for hand laundry also are available on the first floor or in the basement of each cottage.) Central also processes the laundry for several other state institutions, as is the practice at Eastern. None of the inmates at either school are paid for working; all work is justified and organized as part of the vocational training program.

Although the well-groomed lawns of Eastern, Central, and Western schools are impressive, they are conspicuously empty of people. The inmates are kept indoors except to attend a few institutionwide activities such as baseball games sometimes scheduled during the summer. At Eastern, the inmates may sit on the cottage steps or on the screened porch during the summer with the permission of the cottage supervisor. At Central, inmates are confined to the cottages, except for a few inmates in one cottage who have earned special privileges. At both Eastern and Central, the inmates are accompanied by the cottage staff whenever they attend campus functions. There is no system of passes at Central.

WESTERN SCHOOL FOR GIRLS. Western was built thirty years ago, and hence may be placed chronologically after the century-old Central school and Eastern which is approximately sixty-five years old. Western receives youthful offenders who have been adjudicated delinquent and declared wards of the state's department of the youth authority. Opened in 1943, the institution is located in the western part of the nation and is part of a correctional system that boasts the most advanced treatment methods in the country. The school has a rated capacity of 259, but two cottage units were not in use. The average daily population at the time of the study was approximately 150 inmates.

The youth authority in the state is a central administrative body authorized to accept children from the juvenile courts, as well as youthful offenders from the criminal courts who are less than twenty-one years of age at the time of apprehension. The Youth Authority Board, however, is responsible for a variety of functions in connection with commitment to youth authority facilities and release of wards. When it was created by the state legislature in 1941, the Youth Authority Board consisted of three members, but due to the difficulty in handling the caseload, the membership has been increased to seven. Members are appointed by the governor and confirmed by the state senate. The chairman of the board is also director of the youth authority department.

The juvenile courts may use discretion in committing offenders to the youth authority, but once an inmate is committed and accepted by the youth authority, her release is determined solely by the board. Upon commitment to an institution, the inmate remains under the control of the youth authority when released on parole until the individual is officially discharged; the age usually stated on parole papers is twenty-one, although theoretically it may be up to age twenty-three. The average length of stay at Western during the study was ten to twelve months.

When Western was opened in 1943, it had a capacity of 100 beds, and individuals who were eight to fifteen years of age were admitted. As one of the two major correctional facilities for delinquent girls in the state, the school had changed its admission policies about a year prior to the field work at this institution, to accommodate females in the age range of ten to twenty-one. The change in admission policy is based on geographical region rather than the offender's age to facilitate visits from family members. Under the old arrangement, when Western served the entire state and girls who were eight to fifteen years of age were admitted, the distance between the institution and the communities where the inmates' families lived was so great that many of the inmates received no visitors. Although the present arrangement has eased this situation, the problem remains because of the large geographical area from which the inmates are drawn. As a result of the new admission policy, Western had an older inmate population at the time of the study than either Eastern or Central.

Like Eastern and Central, Western operates on the basis of open intake. Administrators in public institutions cannot directly control intake, although some administrators do establish informal contacts with individuals in diagnostic clinics and with individuals in other committing units in the statewide system who may help to relieve intake pressures. While such arrangements can be extremely helpful at crucial times, they are at best always tentative and temporary. However, in one area—parole referrals and release from the institution—each administrator can exert direct control over intake. The following memorandum written by Western's superintendent illustrates the procedure followed there; however, since the same method of handling intake pressures occurred at the other two schools, the memorandum may be read as an example of the intake problems faced and the solutions taken by the administrators of Eastern, Central and Western institutions.

To: Cottage Teams, A, B, C, D, E, F

From: Bertha Whitehead

All teams have been asked to step up parole referrals. Our population is beyond capacity and budgeted capacity. We cannot control intake, but we can assert some control over paroles.

In the past three months your team has referred a total of _____ (the actual numbers were stated) to parole. You will convene immediately and refer _____ (quotas given for each cottage) more to parole for January.

We must bring our population down or we can be in difficulty. Girls referred to institutions may *not* be held in clinics and we *must* take all girls sent to us. Therefore, unless we can cut our present population down, we will have kids sleeping on the floor.

Standards for release must be lowered at this time, and we must recognize that treatment goals may not be met while we are in this population bind.

At the end of November, each cottage will be responsible for five referrals for parole in February.

Hence the idea of open intake—even when discussing public institutions—must be qualified. The implications for treatment are discussed in subsequent chapters.

Until a few years ago, Western operated a large farm which was an integral part of the school. Although it was not completely self-sufficient, the farm provided the school with vegetables, fruits, nuts, grains, hogs, sheep, cattle, and chickens; the vegetables and domestic stock were tended by the inmates with the help of farm workmen. Until they were recently phased out, both Eastern and Central also had operated large farms—a common operation in schools for delinquents. The underlying reasons behind the farming concept in schools for delinquents were: (1) its practical value for the institutions from the standpoint of food; (2) vocational training for some inmates; and (3) its therapeutic value for the inmates—it was widely believed at the time that some delinquent girls "found themselves" by working with animals and crops.

Originally built as a home for the aged, Western was established by utilizing existing structures. The present physical plant consists of a centralized group of residences for the inmates; they are called dormitories, although each inmate has her own room. (Herein they are referred to as cottages.) Recent additions to the physical plant include the centralized administration building, the detention cottage, control center, and the hospital which also serves as the reception unit. In addition, there is a centralized kitchen where all the food is prepared (the food is placed in containers on portable carts and brought to the living units by two inmates from each cottage who have been assigned the task of transporting the food). The cottages have combination kitchen and dining rooms, but meals are prepared in the cottages only in special circumstances.

The school also operates a laundry where all the institution's needs are met and almost all of the inmates' clothing is washed. As is true of Eastern and Central schools, the inmates assigned to work in the laundry at Western are not paid. The laundry "detail" is defined as "work experience," and the Western inmate receives school credit for working as a "laundry trainee;" school credit also is given for other work details. The laundry equipment is considered to be obsolete by the laundry supervisors.

The school is completely enclosed with brick and mortar or security fences. Hence, while Eastern and Central schools were "open" in the sense that there were no physical barriers blocking the exits from the schools, Western's exits were closed.

With their spacious lawns, wooded areas, and informal cottage groupings, Eastern and Central schools have the external appearance of private boarding schools. The same cannot be said of Western school. Concrete buildings, with flat concrete sides and lean-to roofs, grouped close to each other give the school an institution look.

Also present were symbols of security such as windows that can be opened out only a few inches. Inmates did not escape through the windows (as the inmates sometimes did at Eastern and Central), but the ventilation provided by the blocked windows, especially during the warm season, was inadequate for the inmates. Set back a few hundred yards from a major highway, the front of Western institution consists of a series of units linked to one another—the administration offices, detention quarters, control center, and hospital wing—which together serve as a security wall. Everyone must enter through the administration building. No one may drive into the institution grounds where the inmates live; all motor vehicles—those of the staff as well as of visitors—are parked in an area in front of the administration building. To go into the courtyard where the cottage units are located it is necessary to pass the control room in the administration building. The desk inside the control room is placed at an angle so that the seated staff person may glance at an overhead mirror fixed to the wall to observe anyone walking up the ramp leading to the cottages, school classrooms, and other buildings. All common buildings at Western surround the small courtyard. Five residence cottages for the inmates are located on one side. Directly opposite are the school classrooms, auditorium, gymnasium, and outdoor swimming pool. One cottage is set a short distance away from the other cottages; built as a maximum security unit, each room has a toilet and washbasin, and a small yard for the inmates of this cottage is enclosed by a security fence. In addition, each cottage at Western has two security rooms, referred to as "holding rooms" or "thinking rooms" which are immediately available for rule violators; these security rooms are empty except for a bed and toilet.

At both Eastern and Central it is possible for anyone to drive directly into the grounds. Indeed, the staff park their cars behind the cottages where they work. Moreover, the Eastern staff who live in the nearby town often use the local taxi service. When summoned, the taxi drivers drive directly to the cottage named, to pick up staff passengers. At Western, however, the cottage staff check into the control room to pick up their keys and sign out there; other staff members check keys in and out at the control room but sign out at the switchboard in the administration building.

An important task of the control center staff is to monitor the sound level in the cottages and other buildings. Equipment of this type is not used at Eastern or Central, although security staff periodically check the grounds and buildings.

At Eastern and Central the presence of the male security force is unobtrusive. By contrast, the security office at Western directly faces all the cottage units; two walls are of glass so that the male security staff can view the inmates' movements from the cottages to all parts of the institution; this office is manned on a twenty-four hour basis. The security staff are charged with the responsibility of keeping the inmates at "eyeball level" at all times. I observed security officers using binoculars to identify inmates who were walking less than forty feet away.

Western has a Citizen's Advisory Committee, but its function is not so broad as that established for Eastern's Board of Visitors. The Citizen's Advisory Committee, made up of residents who live in the county in which Western was located, met monthly except during the summer months. According to Western's administrative head, the function of the Committee consists mainly of obtaining and providing Christmas gifts for the inmates. The comments that were made previously in connection with Eastern's Board of Visitors are applicable to the Citizen's Advisory Committee—that is, such groups are ineffective due to the fact that they are not citizens who truly represent the interests of the incarcerated inmates.

SUMMARY. The three institutions are not only located in different regions of the nation, but the operation of each dates back to a different point in time. Central was founded in the middle of the nineteenth century; Eastern traces its history to the turn of the century; and Western had been in operation less than thirty years at the time of the study. The institutions also differ in the size of the resident inmate population.

But the schools differ in another important respect—namely, in terms of the central administrative body under whose auspices they function and from whom the administrative heads must take their direction. Each of the schools is part of a larger system, and this has important consequences for the organization of the school and the treatment strategies that may be put into operation (although each administrator may exercise, within circumscribed limits, some discretion in the allocation of resources).

Despite these differences, the problems and the ways in which they are resolved are similar in each institution. Furthermore, although the treatment strategies and philosophies differ in each school, the structural elements of the schools exhibit notable similarities. This is the case not only for the formal organization, but for the inmate culture as well.

Social Background Characteristics
of the Inmate Population

AGE AND LENGTH OF TIME SPENT IN INSTITUTION. Girls who range in age from ten to seventeen are admitted at Eastern; at Central, they range in age from twelve to eighteen; at Western they are from ten to twenty-one years of age. Adolescents beyond age eighteen are not admitted to Eastern and Central, although at Central their incarceration may be continued beyond this age. (See Table 3.1.)

At the time of commitment, the age range of the Eastern inmates actually was eleven to sixteen years, but at Central the age range was from twelve to eighteen. The inmates at Western were older—from thirteen to twenty-one years of age (Western may accept inmates ages ten to twenty-one, and during previous years inmates who were eleven and twelve years old had been committed to Western school).

The average age of the inmates at Eastern at the time of the study was fifteen, slightly older than fifteen at Central, and sixteen at Western. (The age distribution of the inmates during the time of the study is shown in Table 6, Appendix B.)

The institutions have little direct control over accepting inmates within the legal commitment age range. However, all the institutions do control

Table 3.1   Commitment Age Distribution of the Inmate Population

Age (years)	Eastern		Central		Western	
	Number	%	Number	%	Number	%
11	1	0.5	—	—	—	—
12	12	5.8	2	0.6	—	—
13	43	21.0	18	5.3	5	3.1
14	63	30.7	52	15.2	18	11.3
15	69	33.7	108	31.7	39	24.5
16	17	8.3	108	31.7	42	26.4
17	—	—	49	14.4	33	20.8
18 or more	—	—	4	1.2	22	13.8
Total	205	100.0	341	100.1	159	99.9

admissions to some extent by not releasing inmates. This practice is a temporary solution and works only when bed space is limited; it has important consequences for the inmates, however, in that it can keep them at the institution a few extra months. It also has consequences for other agencies; for example, it may contribute to a "pile-up" of inmates in diagnostic and detention facilities, thus contributing to their overcrowded conditions.

The reverse process also occurs. When the detention and diagnostic centers are overcrowded, pressure is brought to bear upon the administrators of the correctional schools to admit inmates. For the incarcerated inmates, this state of affairs may have important consequences: The administrative officials may find it necessary to thin the ranks of the current inmate population earlier than would otherwise be the case.

The length of time that an inmate spends in an institution depends upon the policies of the institution regarding the optimum time required to bring about the desired change in the direction of conformity to societal norms and the existence of foster homes in the outside community—the lack of which may increase an inmate's stay appreciably, as inmates are kept at the institution until a foster home is located. In the case of a few inmates, this period of time was as long as a year. Table 3.2 indicates the length of time spent in each institution by the inmates at the time they completed the questionnaire.

Two categories of commitment were used at Eastern: Persons in need

Table 3.2   Length of Time Inmates Institutionalized to Date

Length of Time (months)	Eastern		Central		Western	
	Number	%	Number	%	Number	%
Less than 3	42	20.5	174	51.0	56	35.2
3–6	53	25.8	98	28.7	50	31.4
6–9	46	22.4	49	14.4	31	19.5
9–12	25	12.2	15	4.4	15	9.4
12 or more	39	19.0	5	1.5	7	4.4
Total	205	99.9	341	100.0	159	99.9

of supervision (PINS) and juvenile delinquents. Although 89 percent of the inmates were defined as persons in need of supervision when they were committed, they were not handled differently from those committed as juvenile delinquents; moreover, both terms were used to refer to the inmate population.

Ninety-one percent of the Eastern inmates were fifteen years of age or less when they were committed, and because they were committed as persons in need of supervision, they tended to remain in the institution longer than the inmates of Central and Western institutions.

But considerable discretion is given to the institutional administrators of all the schools regarding the actual length of an inmate's commitment. In only a few instances was the period of commitment specifically stated; they included five cases for Eastern and one case for Western school. Apart from these distinctions, all the inmates were committed for periods of eighteen months or more.

RACE AND RELIGION.   The racial distribution of the inmates varies from one institution to another, and in large measure it reflects the institution's geographical location, juvenile court procedures, and existing institutional facilities in the states. Table 3.3 summarizes the racial distribution for the inmate populations of the three schools studied.

In all the institutions, staff tended to lump together as "nonwhite" the inmates of Mexican or Puerto Rican background. In this study, Indians, Japanese-Americans and Chinese-Americans were coded as Mongoloid, and those of Puerto Rican and Mexican background as white.

Table 3.3   Racial Composition of the Inmates

Race	Eastern Number	Eastern %	Central Number	Central %	Western Number	Western %
White	73	35.6	197	57.8	114	71.7
Black	128	62.4	142	41.6	41	25.8
Mongoloid	4	2.0	2	0.6	4	2.5
Total	205	100.0	341	100.0	159	100.0

Some differences in racial and ethnic composition are a consequence of geographical location. Eastern, for example, draws almost its entire population from one metropolis that has a large Puerto Rican and black population. There were more inmates at Eastern who were of Puerto Rican ancestry than the other two institutions; and Eastern was the only institution where the blacks outnumbered the whites. At Western, there were more inmates whose social origins were of Mexican and Spanish ancestry than at Eastern and Central. However, at Central these distinctions were relatively unimportant because inmates of Puerto Rican and Mexican ethnic background were not present in the same numbers as at Eastern and Western. Eastern's racial composition was more predominantly black (62.4 percent), with 35.6 percent of the inmates white. The pattern at Western is just the reverse, with 71.7 percent white and 25.8 percent black. At Central the racial balance is somewhat more evenly distributed, with 57.8 percent white and 41.6 percent black.

State training schools are unique in that they are the only public schools that make provision on their organizational payrolls for full-time chaplains. Local church facilities are never used by any of the schools; Eastern boasts a separate chapel building, although a large Catholic church and several Protestant churches were located less than a mile away. Central and Western are more physically isolated from the nearby community than is Eastern. All the schools employed full-time Catholic and Protestant chaplains. (At Eastern, the salary of the chaplains was more than that of the social workers and teachers.) Yet their role in institutions for delinquents continues to be problematic. Their presence may be viewed as a carry-over from the days when it was held that erring citizens, whatever their age, were to be "saved." Church services are compulsory for the inmates at Eastern, Central, and Western. At Western, a "religion course" was incorporated into the academic school curriculum, and all the inmates had to attend classes scheduled for this course every Friday.

Table 3.4 shows the religion in which the inmates were reared.

Table 3.4   Religion in Which Inmates Were Reared

Religion	Eastern		Central		Western	
	Number	%	Number	%	Number	%
Protestant	131	63.9	296	86.8	106	66.7
Catholic	71	34.6	45	13.2	53	33.3
Jewish	2	1.0	—	—	—	—
None	1	0.5	—	—	—	—
Total	205	100.0	341	100.0	159	100.0

EDUCATION AND INTELLIGENCE. The actual educational grade level completed by the inmates prior to their current commitment is shown in Table 3.5.

Table 3.5   Educational Grade Completed by the Inmates Prior to Commitment

Highest Grade Completed	Eastern		Central		Western	
	Number	%	Number	%	Number	%
Completed 1–4 years	—	—	1	.3	—	—
Completed 5–7 years	74	36.1	73	21.4	24	15.1
Completed elementary school	70	34.2	107	31.4	45	28.3
Completed 9th grade	42	20.5	106	31.1	40	25.2
Completed 10–11 years	19	9.3	54	15.8	44	27.7
Completed high school	—	—	—	—	6	3.8
Total	205	100.1	341	100.0	159	100.1

The institutional case files in all the schools were found to be incomplete or ambiguous with regard to certain types of information. I found this to be particularly true in the case of recidivists for whom information was rarely brought up to date. The administration may not have thought it to be worth the trouble, especially since little of this information really made much difference as far as planning an inmate's institutional program is concerned.

At Eastern, 22.9 percent of the inmates had not been tested for IQ level, either before or after their commitment. The Eastern institutional academic program was geared through the tenth grade; Central and Western institutions provided for a full high school curriculum. At Eastern, and to some extent at Central and Western, very little was made of the accuracy or inaccuracy of IQ scores. The IQ breakdown for the schools sampled appears in Table 3.6.

Table 3.6   IQ Score Breakdown of Inmate Population

IQ Score	Eastern Number	%	Central Number	%	Western Number	%
120–140	1	0.5	12	3.5	3	1.9
111–119	5	2.4	16	4.7	14	8.8
91–110	41	20.0	150	44.0	65	40.9
81–90	44	21.5	83	24.3	50	31.4
71–80	55	26.8	64	18.8	21	13.2
70 or below	12	5.8	15	4.4	4	2.5
Unknown	47	22.9	1	0.3	2	1.3
Total	205	99.9	341	100.0	159	100.0

All IQ information must be interpreted with considerable caution. The official files in all the schools indicated not only that different tests were used to measure IQ, but that the information available sometimes was several years old. There were instances where two test scores appeared in the file, sometimes indicating a very wide spread between IQ scores. For these cases, the score that the institutional officials designated to be the inmate's IQ was taken, although its accuracy could not be verified.

MARITAL STATUS AND NUMBER OF CHILDREN. I attempted to obtain information of the marital status of the inmates and the number of children born to them. Only 3.6 percent of the inmates had at any time been legally married (two of the Central inmates were legally separated before incarceration). Although only nine of the adolescents had been legally married, seventy-nine inmates—approximately 11 percent—had borne children. (Some of these children were put up for adoption, and others were being cared for by the inmate's mother or other relatives.) (See Table 3.7.)

Table 3.7   Number of Children Reported for the Inmate Population (Case Files)

Number of Children	Eastern		Central		Western	
	Number	%	Number	%	Number	%
None	186	90.7	298	87.4	142	89.3
One	18	8.8	38	11.1	14	8.8
Two	1	0.5	5	1.5	2	1.3
Three or more	—	—	—	—	1	0.6
Total	205	100.0	341	100.0	159	100.0

There is little difference among the inmates in all three institutions; of those with children, the majority have one child, but nine inmates have had two or more children.

Multiple offenses were listed as a rationale for commitment for the inmates of all the institutions, and premarital sex figured prominently. If the latter did not appear on the court petition itself, it often appeared in other, more detailed court reports. Table 3.8 reports the history of premarital sex experience recorded in the case files as a prominent part of the juvenile's problems.

Table 3.8   Premarital Sex of Juveniles

Premarital Sex	Eastern		Central		Western	
	Number	%	Number	%	Number	%
Yes	54	26.3	220	64.5	73	45.9
No	151	73.7	121	35.5	86	54.1
Total	205	100.0	341	100.0	159	100.0

Less than one-third of the inmates at Eastern had a record of pre-marital sex, as compared with 64.5 percent of the Central inmates and 45.9 percent of the Western inmates. Some differences are due to the way in which the information is compiled by the social agencies and the stress that is placed on some forms of behavior. Also, the age differences may be a factor in some instances.

It is not unusual for "sexual promiscuity" to appear on the court records as the rationale to refer the adolescent "for her own protection." However, sexual promiscuity was not cited often as the primary reason for commitment; prostitution, promiscuity, or pregnancy were listed as the offenses that led to referral and commitment for only nineteen inmates. Nevertheless, sexual promiscuity appeared on the records of forty-one inmates as a second offense and was listed as a third offense for an additional forty inmates. Only a few inmates were committed for prostitution.

DRUG AND ALCOHOL USE. The recorded history of narcotic use of the Eastern, Central, and Western inmates is shown in Table 3.9. Considerable caution should be exercised in interpreting these data because of the record keeping of the social agencies supplying information to the courts as well as the diligence with which some probation officers and case workers may or may not obtain information. Also, the question must be raised whether any of the youngsters were "pressured" into making a statement that they had used specific drugs when in fact they had not, and whether drugs had been used in the past or more recently.

Table 3.9   History of Narcotic Use or Other Noxious Agents

Most Serious Drug Used	Eastern Number	Eastern %	Central Number	Central %	Western Number	Western %
Heroin	6	2.9	1	0.3	7	4.4
Barbiturates	2	1.0	3	0.9	39	24.5
LSD	—	—	4	1.2	15	9.4
Marijuana	16	7.8	16	4.7	35	22.0
Glue for sniffing	6	2.9	4	1.2	2	1.3
Other	2	1.0	2	0.6	—	—
None	173	84.4	311	91.2	61	38.4
Total	205	100.0	341	100.1	159	100.0

Table 3.9 indicates that 84.4 percent of the Eastern inmates and 91.2 percent of the Central inmates had not used drugs compared with only 38.4 percent of the Western inmates who had not used drugs. Most of the inmates in all the schools were drawn from metropolitan areas; many of the Western inmates were drawn from a geographical area with a reputation of providing a haven for youthful drug users. Certainly there were more inmates at Western who identified themselves as "addicts"; however, the figures at Eastern and Central are probably underrepresented. Some inmates flatly deny to the authorities that they have used drugs, but the talk in the cottages often centers around the use of drugs. However, some inmates may claim to have used drugs when speaking to other inmates in order to be accepted into the inmate culture. The population at Western also includes many more older inmates.

The alcohol usage differences among the institutions are much less dramatic than were the data for drug use; 23 percent of the Eastern inmates, 17 percent of the Central inmates, and 32 percent of the Western inmates have a history of alcohol use.

Some differences clearly are a function of the official forms used to compile information on each individual. If a space is allotted for certain types of information, the question concerning the existence thereof at least will be raised a good part of the time. At Central, the question of the inmate's alcohol use was not asked directly. Any references to alcohol use usually appeared in connection with the offense record of the inmate. The Eastern and Western inmates usually were not questioned about alcohol use until they were in detention. At Western, however, the emphasis was on drug use, and alcohol use was more apt to be made part of the record when it was related to the behavior that led to the court's action.

As inaccurate as these data must be, they are of interest for the very reason that they *are* made part of the written record.

RESIDENTIAL BACKGROUND. It is important to know whether the inmates are from large metropolitan and other urban areas in order to assess accurately the kinds of environmental factors to which they must adjust when they are returned to the community.

In Table 3.10 accurate information is presented of each inmate's residential background.

The vast majority of the inmates are from large metropolitan areas: 86.8 percent of the inmates at Eastern, 79.5 percent of the inmates at Central, and 73 percent of the inmates at Western. The implications of these tabulations are discussed in Chapter 4 where comparisons are made with the social origins of the staff.

Table 3.10   Residential Background of the Inmates

Place of Residence	Eastern		Central		Western	
	Number	%	Number	%	Number	%
Rural (farm)	4	2.0	11	3.2	—	—
Village (up to 2500 population)	3	1.5	11	3.2	11	6.9
Town (2500 to 5000 population)	1	0.5	6	1.8	4	2.5
Town (5000 to 30,000 population)	19	9.3	42	12.3	28	17.6
City (30,000 to 100,000 population)	12	5.8	57	16.7	47	29.6
Metropolis (over 100,000 population)	166	81.0	214	62.8	69	43.4
Total	205	100.1	341	100.0	159	100.0

INMATE OFFENSES, RECIDIVISM, AND COURT HISTORY. Adolescent females are often incarcerated for multiple offenses. Usually two offenses are listed, and sometimes three, as the justification to refer an inmate to the court.[1]

The listing of offenses that appears in Table 3.11 is based upon the first offense listed on the court petition or other legal document used to incarcerate the individual. Second or third offenses were tabulated separately, and are reported in Tables 2 and 3, Appendix B.

By far the greatest number of inmates are incarcerated for school truancy, incorrigibility, and running away from home. Two categories—running away from home, and incorrigibility at home—account for the offenses of 57.1 percent of the Eastern inmates, 59 percent of the Central inmates, and 39.6 percent of the Western inmates. At Western, 16.4 percent of the inmates were referred for incorrigibility in, and/or running away from, a child-care institution.

School truancy and incorrigibility in school are offenses that include fairly large numbers of the Eastern and Central inmates.[2] Running away from home, incorrigibility in school and at home, or habitual truancy appear as the first offense cited for 72.3 percent of the Eastern inmates, 71.6 percent of the Central inmates, and 42.1 percent of the Western inmates. The same offenses were listed as second offenses for 44.4 percent of the Eastern inmates, 61.9 percent of the Central inmates, and 22.7 percent of the Western inmates.

Table 3.11 Primary Reason for Referral to Court

Type of Offense	Eastern		Central		Western	
	Number	%	Number	%	Number	%
Homicide	—	—	1	0.3	1	0.6
Assault or threat to assault	6	2.9	4	1.2	10	6.3
Robbery	2	1.0	1	0.3	3	1.9
Burglary (break and entry)	2	1.0	2	0.6	5	3.1
Car theft	2	1.0	9	2.6	3	1.9
Theft (other) or posession of stolen goods	11	5.4	13	3.8	6	3.8
Arson	—	—	2	0.6	—	—
Vandalism	3	1.5	1	0.3	—	—
Check forgery	—	—	3	0.9	2	1.3
Driving without a license	—	—	1	0.3	2	1.3
Drugs	—	—	—	—	8	5.0
Habitual truancy	27	13.2	32	9.4	3	1.9
Running away from home	83	40.5	125	36.7	42	26.4
Incorrigible in school	4	2.0	11	3.2	1	0.6
Incorrigible at home	34	16.6	76	22.3	21	13.2
Violation of probation/ parole	7	3.4	13	3.8	9	5.7
Drinking and intoxication	2	1.0	5	1.5	1	0.6
Prostitution	—	—	4	1.2	3	1.9
Promiscuity and pregnancy	3	1.5	15	4.4	1	0.6
Association with undesirable companions	3	1.5	2	0.6	2	1.3
Incorribible in and/or running away from child-care institution	13	6.3	19	5.6	26	16.4
Suicide attempt(s)	—	—	1	0.3	2	1.3
Miscellaneous delinquencies	3	1.5	1	0.3	8	5.0
Total	205	100.3	341	100.2	159	100.1

Moreover, these same offenses appear frequently enough as third offenses to indicate that these are the major reasons most of the adolescent girls have been removed from the community and committed to institutions many miles from their families and friends.

The court's rationale for institutional commitment is couched in the rhetoric of rehabilitation and treatment. The formal documents imply reassuringly that the decision is the most appropriate means to meet the needs of the individual. However, when a child is committed by the court to an institution there is usually an expectation—and indeed, understanding—on the part of law enforcement agencies that the child is to remain in the institution for a certain length of time, ostensibly to "protect the community," although the implications of such expectations are clearly incompatible with the concept of "treatment." Theoretically, some individuals could be "treated" in a single day, one month, or three months. Yet administrators complain that they must keep the inmates for a longer period of time because there are individuals in different counties who "get upset" when the inmates are released before a five- or six-month period has elapsed. Some communities go so far as to refuse to accept a child after she has been institutionalized and, presumably, rehabilitated and treated.

Differences in the statistics also reflect the institutional facilities available to accept inmates who are committed for certain offenses. For example, Central had one cottage unit to accommodate adolescents who were committed for pregnancy; hence the larger number of inmates committed to Central for pregnancy and promiscuity. Eastern and Western did not keep any inmate who was pregnant; the Eastern inmate was immediately transferred to other community facilities, and the Western inmate was transferred during the seventh month of pregnancy.

In addition, although drug use appears on many of the inmates' records, very few of them were institutionalized specifically for drug abuse. There was no drug program at Eastern and Central, and inmates who were drug addicts were not committed to these schools. For some of the older Western inmates, however, the drug culture was an integral part of their lives; many of them demanded drug therapy to be rehabilitated. In their view, this was the purpose of institutionalization, although there was no drug program at Western. Shortly before I left, one staff member tried to get a program underway for a handful of inmates, aided by a few individuals from the community. However well-intentioned this effort, the isolated location of the institution would preclude the possibility that community resources could be effectively mobilized and sustained on a continuing basis.

The figures in Table 3.12 show how many of the inmates are recidivists of Eastern, Central, and Western institutions.

Table 3.12　Number of Previous Commitments to the Present Institution

Number of Commitments	Eastern		Central		Western	
	Number	%	Number	%	Number	%
None	168	82.0	246	72.1	113	71.1
One	32	15.6	80	23.5	36	22.6
Two	5	2.4	13	3.8	8	5.0
Three or more	—	—	2	0.6	2	1.3
Total	205	100.0	341	100.0	159	100.0

Eighteen percent of the Eastern inmates, 27.9 percent of the Central inmates and 28.9 percent of the Western inmates have been incarcerated one or more times in these facilities prior to their present commitment. There is little difference between Central and Western schools regarding the number of recidivists, whereas the figure is lower for Eastern. This difference is due in part to the lower age of the Eastern inmates as a group. However, it is also due in part to the fact that Eastern school does not often accept inmates for placement more than twice, hence other facilities are used for such inmates. In this connection, detention facilities are used for some inmates for fairly long periods of time—three to six months is not unusual. In effect, the use of these community diagnostic and detention facilities for fairly long-term confinement serves to broaden the function of these facilities as quasi-correctional institutions; this applies equally for the diagnostic and other detention facilities of Central and Western states.

Some of the inmates in all of the institutions studied have a history of placement in other public and private institutions for children. Table 3.13 shows that 13.6 percent of the Eastern inmates, 41.3 percent of the Central inmates, and 50.9 percent of the Western inmates have been institutionalized previously.

Many of the Eastern, Central, and Western inmates also have been incarcerated in detention facilities, juvenile halls, and diagnostic center facilities awaiting court disposition (or bed space in an institution) for considerable lengths of time—sometimes as long as six months and in a

Table 3.13   Placement in Private and Public Institutions
(Prior to Current Commitment)

Number of Place- ments	Eastern		Central		Western	
	Number	%	Number	%	Number	%
None	177	86.3	200	58.6	78	49.1
One	27	13.1	99	29.0	48	30.2
Two	1	0.5	29	8.5	22	13.8
Three to four	—	—	11	3.2	11	6.9
Five or more	—	—	2	0.6	—	—
Total	205	99.9	341	99.9	159	100.0

Table 3.14   Placement in Detention Facilities
Awaiting Disposition of the Court[a]

Number of Times	Eastern		Central		Western	
	Number	%	Number	%	Number	%
None	45	22.0	7	2.0	—	—
One	61	29.8	183	53.7	3	1.9
Two	51	24.9	124	36.4	30	18.9
Three to four	44	21.5	27	7.9	56	35.2
Five or more	4	2.0	—	—	70	44.0
Total	205	100.2	341	100.0	159	100.0

[a] Each detention two weeks or more.

few cases for as long as one year. This information is set forth in Table 3.14.

When a child was removed from her home and remanded or confined to a facility such as a youth house juvenile center, state diagnostic and treatment center, detention or juvenile hall, or other similar facility for delinquents pending court disposition of the case, and confined therein continuously for a period of two weeks, the confinement was tabulated as one. It was rare that the Western and Central inmates were confined for less than thirty days prior to institutional commitment or release to the community—depending upon the disposition of the court. This was also usually the case for the adolescent girls at Eastern; however, the period of confinement in that state occasionally was for a period of three weeks or less.

The Eastern inmates told me that anyone remanded to the youth house juvenile center learns about the informal social system in less than two weeks; in fact, the informal social system in this facility (as well as other detention facilities) is similar to that which exists at Eastern institution. Some inmates form kinship ties in the youth house juvenile center that they continue to acknowledge when they are committed to Eastern. In short, when an adolescent is remanded to detention centers of this type for two weeks or more, the experience for the individual can hardly be said to be neutral—that is, it *does* make a difference that she was remanded there at all. Certainly, the inmate is knowledgeable about the informal social system (if not an active participant) when she arrives at the institution.

Inmates who were confined to detention facilities for two weeks or less were not included in the data presented in Table 3.14. It was not unusual for the adolescent girls to be picked up and placed in these detention facilities for a few days and then released. Hence the data in Table 3.14 actually underestimates the precise number of times that the adolescent girls have been picked up and confined in these facilities.[3]

Unless one includes all detentions as a reference point in discussing recidivism, one is left with a grossly misleading picture of the experiences of the adolescent girls in these various institutional facilities, as well as the work of the juvenile court which must process all referrals. The female adolescent inmates have a fairly broad background as far as a history of recidivism is concerned. The data on total recidivism are shown in Table 3.15.

The vast majority of the inmates have had two or more confinements in institutional facilities apart from the one in which they are presently confined. Again, data are probably underestimated and should be used with caution. Also, the fact that Eastern inmates who are committed from some counties may spend only a few days in one or two jails—or none at all—before they are brought to Eastern accounts in large part for the 16.1 percent of the Eastern inmates shown to have no history of former recidivism.

Only when we have knowledge of the number of times that an adolescent has been confined in long-term and short-term confinement facili-

CHARACTERISTICS OF THE INMATE POPULATION

Table 3.15 Total Recidivism: Present Institution, Other Public and
Private Institutions, and Detention Awaiting Court Disposition

Number of Times	Eastern		Central		Western	
	Number	%	Number	%	Number	%
None	33	16.1	1	0.3	—	—
One	51	24.9	106	31.1	1	0.6
Two	54	26.3	92	27.0	21	13.2
Three to four	59	28.8	117	34.3	47	29.6
Five or more	8	3.9	25	7.3	90	56.6
Total	205	100.0	341	100.0	159	100.0

ties can we begin to understand and refine the meaning of recidivism for the inmates, as well as the implications for the juvenile court in processing the same cases over and over again.

Most of the inmates have had many contacts with the courts, and many have been committed to institutions for varying periods of time prior to their current commitment. The total of this experience for a few of the inmates may add up to several years. (The latter does not include the time that inmates have spent in short-term facilities awaiting the disposition of the court, which may add up to as long as a year for some inmates.)

All contacts with the court do not, however, result in commitment to institutions. Some inmates are placed on probation and others are placed in foster homes.[4] The information concerning probation and foster home placements for the inmates of all three institutions is shown in Table 3.16.

What is particularly striking about the court history of the adolescent inmates of Eastern, Central, and Western schools is the fact that they have made so many court appearances. Obviously, probation is not used often for adolescent females. Furthermore, when probation is used, it tends to be used on a one-shot basis; continued appearances before the authorities are disposed of in other ways—a few individuals are placed in foster homes, but more frequently institutionalization is used. At Eastern, 37.6 percent of the inmates have been placed on probation once, but only 7.3 percent have been placed on probation two or more times; 54.6 per-

Table 3.16   Court History of Inmates:
Probation and Foster Home Placement

	Placed on Probation						Placed in Foster Home					
	Eastern		Central		Western		Eastern		Central		Western	
Number of Placements	Num-ber	%	Num-ber	%	Num-ber	%	Num-ber	%	Num-ber	%	Num-ber	%
None	113	55.1	140	41.1	17	10.7	197	96.1	259	76.0	60	37.7
One	77	37.6	186	54.6	94	59.1	7	3.4	53	15.5	34	21.4
Two	14	6.8	15	4.4	34	21.4	1	0.5	14	4.1	28	17.6
Three to four	1	0.5	—	—	14	8.8	—	—	11	3.2	23	14.5
Five or more	—	—	—	—	—	—	—	—	4	1.2	14	8.8
Total	205	100.0	341	100.1	159	100.0	205	100.0	341	100.0	159	100.0

cent of the Central inmates have been placed on probation once compared with 4.4 percent of the inmates who have been placed on probation twice. Essentially the same pattern emerges for the inmates of Western institution with 59.1 percent of the inmates placed on probation once as compared with 30.2 percent placed on probation two or more times. Undoubtedly the factors that underlie these differences are complex, and any comparisons made must of necessity remain tentative.

The differences may be attributed in some instances to the lack of probation personnel to supervise the inmates in the community. This factor still does not explain satisfactorily why commitment is used so often—especially when we consider the nature of the offenses for which the vast majority of the adolescent females have been institutionalized. The probation data for the Western inmates are pertinent because the philosophy of treatment in Western state presumably places considerable emphasis on the use of community resources for delinquent children rather than institutionalization; the counties are given a financial subsidy for each delinquent it "treats" in the community as opposed to institutional commitment. Thus, the larger proportion of Western inmates who have been placed on probation more than once is hardly striking. Moreover, there is a greater tendency in Western state to dispose of a case by foster home placement—both before and after institutionalization—than is the case in Eastern and Central states. However, none of the committing and ancillary agencies in these states attempt seriously to work within the structure of the family unit itself, preferring instead to remove the adolescent from her home.

Comparing the number of probation placements with the data of total recidivism—the institution where presently confined, other public and private institutions, and detentions in the short-term facilities—it is clear that the removal of adolescents from the community is the rule rather than the exception.

The inmates are referred for court review by law enforcement officers, the school, welfare and social agencies, and other sources; but by far the most frequent sources of referral are the inmate's parents or other relatives. Often the parents contact the authorities when a child stays away from home or is truant from school. The child is picked up and more often than not is taken to detention facilities rather than brought directly home. The source of referral for the inmates' present commitment is set forth in Table 3.17.

Table 3.17   Source of Referral to Juvenile Authorities for Inmates' Present Commitment

Source of Referral	Eastern		Central		Western	
	Number	%	Number	%	Number	%
Probation Officer	6	2.9	18	5.3	9	5.7
Law enforcement officer	18	8.8	47	13.8	35	22.0
Parent or relatives	132	64.4	180	52.8	38	23.9
Welfare or social agency	24	11.7	54	15.8	30	18.9
Individual	16	7.8	16	4.7	28	17.6
School	9	4.4	21	6.2	2	1.3
Other source	—	—	5	1.5	17	10.7
Total	205	100.0	341	100.1	159	100.1

Because the Western inmates as a group are older, many of their offenses are such that referral is often made by a law enforcement officer; yet 23.9 percent were referred by parents and relatives. Also, 14.5 percent of the Western inmates were living with foster parents; any referrals that were made by foster parents are included in the residual "other" category.

FAMILY BACKGROUND OF THE INMATES.   Each inmate's case file was examined to obtain data on the characteristics of the inmate's natural family to enable the construction of a "family profile"of the institutionalized delinquents.

Any attempt to construct a picture of the inmate's social origins from the case files leaves much to be desired, however. These data are limited because of the serious inconsistencies in the information compiled by the courts and other agencies. Yet the fact that these gaps exist is important because it directs attention to the factors that are given priority in the treatment process.

MARITAL STATUS OF PARENTS.   The marital status of the inmates' natural parents is shown in Table 3.18.

Table 3.18   Marital Status of the Inmates' Parents Prior to Commitment

Marital Status	Eastern		Central		Western	
	Number	%	Number	%	Number	%
Married (living together)	49	23.9	95	27.9	34	21.4
Married (not living together)	9	4.4	26	7.6	12	7.6
Divorced	19	9.3	103	30.2	65	40.9
Legally separated	36	17.6	10	2.9	3	1.9
Father deserted	2	1.0	8	2.4	4	2.5
Mother deserted	2	1.0	1	0.3	2	1.3
Father dead	11	5.4	25	7.3	11	6.9
Mother dead	6	2.9	7	2.0	7	4.4
Unmarried	68	33.1	60	17.6	20	12.6
Other	3	1.5	6	1.8	1	0.6
Total	205	100.1	341	100.0	159	100.1

Few of the inmates' natural parents whether married or unmarried, are living in the same household. Only 23.9 percent of the parents of the Eastern inmates are married and living in the same household; 27.9 percent of the Central inmates' parents are married and living together; and slightly fewer, 21.4 percent, of the Western inmates' parents are married and living together.

A sizable number of the inmates' parents have been divorced—40.9 percent of the Western inmates' parents, 30.2 percent of the Central inmates' parents, and 9.3 percent of the Eastern inmates' parents. Although fewer of the Eastern inmates' parents are divorced, 17.6 percent of their parents are legally separated rather than divorced, thus this difference may well reflect religious considerations. A larger proportion of the Eastern inmates' parents are unmarried—33.1 percent compared with 17.6 percent of the Central inmates' parents and 12.6 percent of the Western inmates' parents. Some of the divorced parents have remarried, thus altering the living arrangements of the children. Table 3.19 presents data indicating the last living arrangement of the inmates prior to institutional commitment.

Table 3.19   Living Arrangement of the Inmates Immediately Prior to Present Institutionalization

Living Arrangement	Eastern		Central		Western	
	Number	%	Number	%	Number	%
Both natural parents	45	22.0	89	26.1	34	21.4
Mother and stepfather	15	7.3	40	11.7	31	19.5
Father and stepmother	11	5.4	11	3.2	10	6.3
Mother only	90	43.9	105	30.8	41	25.8
Father only	6	2.9	6	1.8	7	4.4
Grandparents or other relatives	14	6.8	39	11.4	4	2.5
Foster parents	10	4.9	18	5.3	23	14.5
Child care institution	10	4.9	25	7.3	4	2.5
Friends	3	1.5	1	0.3	1	0.6
Other	1	0.5	7	2.0	4	2.5
Total	205	100.1	341	99.9	159	100.0

When the parents were married and living together, the child was usually living at home. Many of the parents, however, were divorced or had never married, and this is reflected in the living arrangement of the inmates. Some of the inmates were living with relatives prior to commitment, although the greatest number were living with their mothers.

Forty-four percent of the Eastern inmates were living in the mother's household (more than one-third of their parents had never married) compared with 30.8 percent of the Central inmates and 25.8 percent of the Western inmates. Only a few of the inmates were living with the paternal parent prior to commitment, and in these cases it was usually because the adolescent's mother had died.

FAMILY SIZE. Most of the Eastern, Central, and Western inmates come from large families; however, individual families range in size from one child to as many as seventeen children. (See Table 3.20.)

Table 3.20   Number of Children in Inmate's Family[a]

Number of Children	Eastern		Central		Western	
	Number	%	Number	%	Number	%
One	13	6.3	14	4.1	5	3.1
Two	22	10.7	25	7.3	12	7.6
Three	26	12.7	45	13.2	33	20.8
Four	20	9.8	68	19.9	29	18.2
Five	44	21.5	50	14.7	17	10.7
Six or more	80	39.0	139	40.8	63	39.6
Total	205	100.0	341	100.0	159	100.0

[a] Figures include inmate.

More than 50 percent of the Eastern, Central, and Western inmates come from families of five or more children. Only 29.7 percent of the Eastern inmates, 24.6 percent of the Central inmates, and 31.5 percent of the Western inmates are from homes with three or fewer children.

EMPLOYMENT STATUS AND FAMILY INCOME. To provide a more complete picture of the inmates' home situations, I investigated the sources of family income and the employment pattern of the parents. Relative to the data on income, I also tabulated the educational background of the inmates' parents. (See Table 3.21.)

This information is totally lacking in many cases, especially for the parents of the Eastern and Western inmates. In a few instances the information was sought but was unavailable, as when the whereabouts of the

Table 3.21 *Educational Attainment of Inmates' Parents*

	Father						Mother					
	Eastern		Central		Western		Eastern		Central		Western	
Highest Grade Completed	Num-ber	%	Num-ber	%	Num-ber	%	Num-ber	%	Num-ber	%	Num-ber	%
Never attended school	2	1.0	3	0.9	—	—	2	1.0	—	—	—	—
1–4 years	6	2.9	14	4.1	3	1.9	7	3.4	3	0.9	2	1.3
5–7 years	18	8.8	45	13.2	5	3.1	28	13.7	38	11.1	4	2.5
Elementary school	12	5.8	48	14.1	2	1.3	21	10.2	60	17.6	7	4.4
9–11 years	28	13.7	89	26.1	9	5.7	55	26.8	116	34.0	17	10.7
High school graduate	13	6.3	31	9.1	12	7.6	17	8.3	60	17.6	9	5.7
1–3 years college	2	1.0	7	2.0	2	1.3	5	2.4	2	0.6	7	4.4
College graduate	1	0.5	1	0.3	4	2.5	—	—	1	0.3	1	0.6
Graduate or pro-fessional school	1	0.5	1	0.3	—	—	1	0.5	—	—	—	—
Not recorded or unknown	122	59.5	102	29.9	122	76.7	69	33.7	61	17.9	112	70.4
Total	205	100.0	341	100.0	159	100.1	205	100.0	341	100.0	159	100.0

mother or the father was unknown; more often, however, it was because the information was simply not made part of the social history. In Western state only two of the committing counties to Western institution had space for educational level on the standardized forms used to record the social history; such information is not considered relevant to the adolescent's problems. "Treatment" is focused on the individual, quite apart from the larger context of the home and community situation.

Of the three institutions, Central had more complete information on the inmates' family and home situations, but there were some differences among the committing counties: the agencies in rural areas with more limited staffs tended to prepare sketchy reports.

Only a few of the parents have completed high school, and a handful have had college training. We would expect, therefore, that few of the inmates' parents would be employed in positions other than unskilled and routine labor. Data based on the occupation of the head of the household (usually the father, but in some cases the mother or another member of the household) are shown in Table 3.22:

Most of the heads of households are working in blue collar occupations: 51.2 percent of the Eastern inmates' fathers (or other individual as household head) were working in jobs classified as blue collar; at Central, 63.6 percent, and at Western, 55.4 percent. A sizable proportion of the individuals who were designated as heads of households were not in the labor force—35.1 percent for Eastern, 29.3 percent for Central and 24.5 percent for Western. The latter figures exclude the household heads who were temporarily unemployed and were actively seeking work. Table 3.23 shows the current employment status of each juvenile's mother and father.

CARNEGIE LIBRARY
LIVINGSTONE COLLEGE
SALISBURY, N. C. 28144

Table 3.22   Occupational Category of Father or Other Household Head

Occupational Category	Eastern		Central		Western	
	Number	%	Number	%	Number	%
White collar	17	8.3	16	4.7	17	10.7
Blue collar	105	51.2	217	63.6	88	55.4
Not in labor force	72	35.1	100	29.3	39	24.5
No information recorded or unknown	11	5.4	8	2.3	15	9.4
Total	205	100.0	341	99.9	159	100.0

Table 3.23   Employment Status of Inmate's Parents

	Father						Mother					
	Eastern		Central		Western		Eastern		Central		Western	
Employment Status	Number	%	Number	%	Number	%	Number	%	Number	%	Number	%
Full time	80	39.0	159	46.6	71	44.6	51	24.9	71	20.8	28	17.6
Part time, seasonal, intermittent	11	5.4	37	10.8	4	2.5	19	9.3	44	12.9	24	15.1
Disabled, and/or retired	5	2.4	11	3.2	8	5.0	—	—	1	0.3	1	0.6
Unemployed	24	11.7	5	1.5	7	4.4	112	54.6	191	56.0	75	47.2
Other	12	5.8	45	13.2	15	9.4	9	4.4	15	4.4	11	6.9
Not recorded or unknown	73	35.6	84	24.6	54	34.0	14	6.8	19	5.6	20	12.6
Total	205	99.9	341	99.9	159	99.9	205	100.0	341	100.0	159	100.0

Again, employment status was not provided for a large number of cases: 35.6 percent for Eastern, 24.6 percent for Central, and 34 percent for Western.

Twelve percent of the Eastern inmates' fathers were unemployed; and only 39 percent of the Eastern inmates' fathers were working full time compared with 46.6 percent of the Central inmates' fathers and 44.6 percent of the Western inmates' fathers.

Approximately one-third of the mothers of the institutionalized juveniles in all three schools are working either full time or part time. Most of the institutionalized inmates are from large families, and most of the mothers remain at home to care for them. However, even with young children at home, some mothers were working either part time or full

CARNEGIE LIBRARY
LIVINGSTONE CO
SALISBURY, N. C.

time during the day or night to alleviate the family's serious financial plight. The lack of day-care facilities available makes the situation particularly burdensome for many of the older girls.

Despite the unstable employment pattern, the main source of income for 46.8 percent of the families of the Eastern inmates was solely from earnings; this is also the case for 61.6 percent of the families of the Central inmates, and for 52.2 percent of the families of the Western inmates. (See Table 3.24.)

Table 3.24   Source of Family Income

	Eastern		Central		Western	
Income Source	Number	%	Number	%	Number	%
Earnings	96	46.8	210	61.6	83	52.2
Public assistance only	67	32.7	89	26.1	42	26.4
Earnings and public assistance	37	18.0	34	10.0	25	15.7
Not recorded	5	2.4	8	2.4	9	5.7
Total	205	99.9	341	100.1	159	100.0

One-third of the Eastern families derived their income solely from public assistance programs, as did approximately one-fourth of the Central and Western families. Other families had income from both earnings and public assistance; a few families who were receiving some income from social security are included under public assistance.

FAMILY STRUCTURE. Data have been provided of the marital status of the inmates' parents, family size, educational level of parents, source of family income, as well as the employment pattern of the principal wage earner. While these data are important and useful, they do not give us the complete picture of the home situation. It is also important to know something of the social climate in the home and the quality of the interaction among the family members to make possible a description of the family structure as stable or unstable.

Very few of the families could be described as stable with no serious problems within the family. The problems cited in the case files were multiple and cumulative. Only 8.3 percent of the Eastern inmates' home situations could be described as stable with no problems. The corresponding figure is 3.8 percent for the home situation of the Central inmates and 7.6 percent for the Western inmates. The consistently negative descriptions of the families permitted no choice but to code almost all of them as unstable; the possibility of using an intermediate code such as "usually stable" proved to be of no use.

Many of the problems attributed to the family centered on or were related to the unemployment or underemployment of the household head and an income inadequate to supply the family's basic needs. Yet in the case files there was no consideration of upgrading job opportunities and family income level, remedial educational and vocational training for the parents and other family members, family counseling, or engaging in other explorations to upgrade the quality of life within the family structure. Nor was there any attempt to make the educational system accountable even when the adolescent's offense is truancy. The case reports are written in such a way that whatever the so-called "offense" for which the adolescent is committed, responsibility is placed squarely on the adolescent girl. This system provides both the rationale and justification for the removal of the adolescent from the community to institutions for "treatment." Physically removing the adolescent from the community "in the juvenile's interest" is stated in case reports in vague terms, as, for example, "her own protection," "to protect the child"; or occasionally it is given a twofold purpose: "to protect the child and the community." But *why* this is so, and *how* this is to be accomplished is never spelled out.

In examining the case file reports which become the official record for the institutional staff's use and were the source of the data presented above, one is struck by the sheer volume of material that has been compiled for each inmate. At the same time one is left with the distinct conclusion that most of it is very stereotyped in content. Moreover, the reports describing the inmate and the family situation are not arranged in any logical order, and the information is often scanty and out of date. The most basic information on the inmate's family must be searched out of the various "clinic" and other reports and the pieces fitted together. Although the material contained in the social history is sometimes the outcome of a brief visit by a caseworker to the inmate's home, it may be based solely on secondary sources—the impressions of individuals presumed to have had contact with the inmate or her family without any independent verification. Glaring contradictions and discrepancies are to be found in reports within the same case file, and the conflicting conclusions of specialists are left unresolved in the summaries.

CHAPTER FOUR

Characteristics of the Staff

Most studies of institutionalized persons are concentrated on the social characteristics of the inmates, but references to the social characteristics of the staff with whom the inmates interact are nonexistent or sketchy and speculative. We know very little about the background of the staff and even less about how the staff differs, if at all, from the parents of the inmates. Are staff similar to the inmates who have been committed to their care for "treatment and rehabilitation"? In what crucial ways do they differ? To what extent can the staff identify with and understand the life style and needs of the inmates who are almost all drawn from urban communities?

The following data were reported by the staff members who filled out questionnaires during the last phase of the study in each institution. The individuals have sustained contact with the inmates; they include all cottage personnel, nursing staff, social workers, academic and vocational teachers, and supervisors of work areas. Clerical workers and top administrative staff were not included.

AGE, RACE, and RELIGION. The age range of the staff at Eastern and Central is from twenty to over sixty-five years; at Western no staff member was older than sixty-four years. The Eastern staff members

Table 4.1   Current Age of the Staff

	Eastern		Central		Western	
Age (years)	Number	%	Number	%	Number	%
20–24	7	4.8	27	17.1	5	5.3
25–29	11	7.5	11	7.0	12	12.8
30–34	12	8.2	13	8.2	11	11.7
35–39	16	10.9	19	12.0	11	11.7
40–44	16	10.9	24	15.2	15	16.0
45–49	25	17.0	16	10.1	15	16.0
50–54	26	17.7	17	10.8	13	13.8
55–59	23	15.6	22	13.9	5	5.3
60–64	9	6.1	8	5.1	7	7.4
65 and over	1	0.7	1	0.6	—	—
No response	1	0.7	—	—	—	—
Total	147	100.1	158	100.0	94	100.0

tended to be older than those employed at Central or Western. The complete distribution appears in Table 4.1.

Only 31.4 percent of the Eastern staff are less than forty years of age, while 44.3 percent of Central's staff and 41.5 percent of Western's staff are less than forty years of age. The median age was 47.3 for the Eastern staff, 41.9 for the Central staff, and 42.7 for the Western staff.

The racial composition of the staff contrasts sharply with the racial composition of the inmates. At Eastern, 65.3 percent of the staff members are white; at Central 67.7 percent of the staff, and at Western 85.1 percent of the staff are white. Three of the blacks at Western were concen-

Table 4.2   Racial Composition of the Staff

	Eastern		Central		Western	
Race	Number	%	Number	%	Number	%
White	96	65.3	107	67.7	80	85.1
Black	51	34.7	51	32.3	9	9.6
Mongoloid	—	—	—	—	5	5.3
Total	147	100.0	158	100.0	94	100.0

trated in the academic school where it was difficult to recruit competent staff; two of the three black teachers were males. But at Eastern 62 percent of the inmates are black; 42 percent of the Central inmates are black; and 26 percent of the Western inmates are black. (Inmates of Puerto Rican and Mexican background were included within the white category; more of these group members were committed to Eastern and Western.) (See Table 4.2.)

The majority of the staff are of the Protestant faith; namely, 69 percent at Eastern, 86 percent at Central, and 66 percent at Western. The complete distribution is shown in Table 4.3.

Table 4.3 Religion in Which Staff Reared

Religion	Eastern		Central		Western	
	Number	%	Number	%	Number	%
Protestant	101	68.7	136	86.1	62	66.0
Roman Catholic	43	29.2	18	11.4	20	21.3
Jewish	1	0.7	3	1.9	1	1.1
Greek Orthodox	2	1.4	1	0.6	3	3.2
None	—	—	—	—	8	8.5
Total	147	100.0	158	100.0	94	100.1

SEX, MARITAL STATUS, AND FAMILY SIZE.   Most of the staff members in all three institutions are females. None had cottage parents—that is, a man *and* a woman assigned to each cottage—although a man *or* a woman may work a tour of duty. (At Central the cottage supervisors were referred to as cottage parents.) (See Table 4.4.)

Table 4.4 Sex of the Staff

Sex	Eastern		Central		Western	
	Number	%	Number	%	Number	%
Female	123	83.7	143	90.5	71	75.5
Male	24	16.3	15	9.5	23	24.5
Total	147	100.0	158	100.0	94	100.0

The administrators of all the schools recently have made a concerted effort to add more male staff members in order to provide a "male image" inside; the administrators assume that the presence of male staff will "normalize" the institutional situation and thus function to inhibit the formation of homosexual alliances and family groups among the inmates. (However, as we shall see later, the presence of male staff members is not a factor in this regard.)

Most of the staff members are married: 60.5 percent of the Eastern staff, 62.7 percent of the Central staff, and 50 percent of the Western staff. (See Table 4.5.)

Table 4.5   Marital Status of the Staff

	Eastern		Central		Western	
Marital Status	Number	%	Number	%	Number	%
Single, never married	20	13.6	23	14.6	19	20.2
Married	89	60.5	99	62.7	47	50.0
Divorced	9	6.1	18	11.4	22	23.4
Separated	16	10.9	2	1.3	3	3.2
Widow	13	8.8	16	10.1	3	3.2
Total	147	99.9	158	100.1	94	100.0

More widows are employed at Eastern and Central than at Western, which has more single and divorced employees. The divorced and single group at Western account for 43.6 percent of the entire staff, as contrasted with 19.7 percent at Eastern and 26 percent at Central. No age limit was placed on the hiring of staff personnel at Eastern and Central, but at Western an upper age limit of forty-five for youth counselors has recently been imposed; hence, the cottage staff at Western tended to be younger.

Approximately one-third of the staff of Eastern, Central, and Western schools have no children. (See Table 4.6.)

Although the family size of individual staff members varies, in general their families tend to be smaller than those of the inmates' parents. The majority of the staff have three children or fewer. Only 16.3 percent of the Eastern staff have families consisting of four or more children; for the Central staff the figure is 18.4 percent, and for the Western staff it is 13.8 percent.

Table 4.6   Number of Children

Number of Children	Eastern		Central		Western	
	Number	%	Number	%	Number	%
None	44	29.9	51	32.3	29	30.8
One	22	15.0	29	18.4	14	14.9
Two	28	19.0	29	18.4	19	20.2
Three	29	19.7	20	12.7	19	20.2
Four or more	24	16.3	29	18.4	13	13.8
Total	147	99.9	158	100.2	94	99.9

RURAL–URBAN ORIGINS. Although the inmates are for the most from major metropolitan areas, the staff of Eastern, Central, and Western institutions have been brought up on farms or very small towns. (See Table 4.7.)

Most of the Eastern inmates are drawn from a single metropolitan area that is approximately 125 miles from Eastern, but only 6.8 percent of the Eastern staff grew up in a similar urban environment. Similarly, only 15.2

Table 4.7   Residence During Childhood Years

Place of Residence	Eastern		Central		Western	
	Number	%	Number	%	Number	%
Farm or open country	40	27.2	41	26.0	23	24.5
Village (up to about 2500 population)	20	13.6	17	10.8	4	4.3
Town (2500 to 5000 population)	12	8.2	16	10.1	15	16.0
Town (5000 to 30,000 population)	40	27.2	35	22.2	17	18.1
City (30,000 to 100,000 population)	24	16.3	25	15.8	20	21.3
Metropolis (over 100,000 population)	5	3.4	14	8.9	8	8.5
Metropolis (over 500,000 population)	5	3.4	10	6.3	7	7.4
No response	1	0.7	—	—	—	—
Total	147	100.0	158	100.1	94	100.1

percent of the Central staff and 15.9 percent of the Western staff maintained that they spent their childhood in cities of more than 100,000 population. In contrast, 86.8 percent of the Eastern inmates, 79.5 percent of the Central inmates, and 73 percent of the Western inmates are from major metropolitan cities.

Sizable numbers of the institutionalized populations are black, Puerto Rican, or Mexican-American; the inmates who do not fall into these racial and ethnic groups may almost all be categorized as "disadvantaged poor." The majority of the staff, however, are white and have lived all or most of their lives in rural or small town communities. The slum areas and deprived conditions of the inmates' home situation are foreign to their experiences. Furthermore, they have had little or no training that would equip them to understand and respond to the needs of urban minority groups. Since all of the institutions are isolated from the urban communities, most staff members will continue to be recruited mainly from the rural and small town communities surrounding the institutions.

EDUCATION AND OCCUPATIONAL STATUS. While we have noted few differences in community origin among the staff members of our three schools, there are important differences in educational attainment. The highest educational level of the staff members of Eastern, Central, and Western institutions is shown in Table 4.8.

To some extent the staff's educational differences that emerge among the institutions are a function of the geographical location, salary scale, and other job opportunities in the local community. But these differences also reflect institutional policies regarding educational requirements. Although Eastern's superintendent thought it desirable that cottage personnel have at least a high school education, the geographical location made it difficult to recruit and hire individuals who were high school graduates; an eighth grade education had been established at Eastern as a minimum requirement for cottage staff. High school graduates were preferred at Central, but standards were lowered occasionally to meet institutional needs. At the time of the study, all but fourteen of Central's cottage staff and four work detail supervisors had completed high school; the vocational staff instructors had at least a high school education, but none had a college degree. At Western, the educational requirements for the cottage counselors recently had been changed; a high school education was a minimum requirement, but individuals with some college training received preference.

More staff members at Western were college graduates and holders of

Table 4.8   Educational Level of the Staff

Highest Grade Completed	Eastern		Central		Western	
	Number	%	Number	%	Number	%
Some grade school	2	1.4	—	—	—	—
Completed grade school	15	10.2	—	—	2	2.1
Some high school	41	27.9	18	11.4	—	—
High school graduate (or passed high school equivalency test)	37	25.2	69	43.7	27	28.7
Completed 1 year college	5	3.4	11	7.0	9	9.6
Completed 2 years college	7	4.8	14	8.9	23	24.5
College graduate	12	8.2	28	17.7	12	12.8
Some graduate school	14	9.5	7	4.4	5	5.3
Graduate or professional degree beyond the bachelor's	8	5.4	5	3.2	12	12.8
Nurse's training	6	4.1	6	3.8	4	4.3
Total	147	100.1	158	100.1	94	100.1

graduate degrees; 30.9 percent of the Western staff had completed college, compared with 23.1 percent of the Eastern staff and 25.3 percent of the Central staff. Moreover, 34.1 percent of the Western staff had some college training, compared with 15.9 percent of the staff at Central and 8.2 percent of the Eastern staff.

At Western, those with more education were not necessarily those who were in positions of highest authority in cottage management.

The institutions appear to be very similar in the distribution of staff positions, suggesting uniformity of the organizational framework of these institutions. These data are shown in Table 4.9.

The emphasis in treatment services may differ from one institution to another in crucial ways as resources are deployed to conform to organizational needs. The differences in staff positions among the three schools and their implications are discussed in Chapters 5, 6, and 7.

Western has fewer recreation employees and fewer vocational teachers but more supervisors of work details than either of the other schools. Because almost all the inmates attend school, there are fewer cottage staff at Central.

The data of the staffs' service record are shown in Table 4.10.

Table 4.9   Occupational Position Presently Held by the Staff

Position	Eastern		Central		Western	
	Number	%	Number	%	Number	%
Cottage children's supervisor, cottage parent, or youth counselor	84	57.1	86	54.4	54	57.4
Supervisor on work detail	14	9.5	15	9.5	11	11.7
Social worker, case worker, or therapist	11	7.5	11	7.0	6	6.4
Academic teacher	20	13.6	22	13.9	13	13.8
Vocational teacher	5	3.4	9	5.7	3	3.2
Clinic staff	8	5.4	8	5.1	5	5.3
Recreation staff	5	3.4	7	4.4	2	2.1
Total	147	99.9	158	100.0	94	99.9

Table 4.10   Total Length of Time Staff Employed in the Institution

Total Time Employed	Eastern		Central		Western	
	Number	%	Number	%	Number	%
Less than 6 months	13	8.8	22	13.9	10	10.6
6 months to 1 year	7	4.8	17	10.8	4	4.3
1–2 years	9	6.1	22	13.9	14	14.9
2–5 years	28	19.0	31	19.6	19	20.2
5–10 years	45	30.6	31	19.6	25	26.6
10–15 years	33	22.4	29	18.4	17	18.1
15–20 years	5	3.4	5	3.2	4	4.3
20 years or more	6	4.1	1	0.6	1	1.1
No response	1	0.7	—	—	—	—
Total	147	99.9	158	100.0	94	100.1

More employees at Eastern have worked for ten years or more—30 percent of the Eastern staff as compared with 22.2 percent of Central's staff and 23.5 percent of Western's staff. Fewer of the Eastern staff have been employed less than two years.

Data concerning the type of job held by the staff members prior to their current employment are presented in Table 4.11.

Table 4.11   Type of Job Held Prior to Present Employment

Regular Job	Eastern		Central		Western	
	Number	*%*	*Number*	*%*	*Number*	*%*
"Yes, I had the same job in another institution."	4	2.7	7	4.4	3	3.2
"Yes, I had a similar job in another institution."	9	6.1	6	3.8	18	19.2
"Yes, I had another job in the correctional field."	4	2.7	5	3.2	5	5.3
"Yes, I had another job but not related to correctional work (another job in some other type organization or business)."	104	70.8	94	59.5	49	52.1
"No, I had no other regular job."	25	17.0	46	29.1	19	20.2
No response	1	0.7	—	—	—	—
Total	147	100.0	158	100.0	94	100.0

The vast majority of the employees of all three institutions have worked previously, but only a few have held jobs that are the same as or similar to their present jobs. At Western school, 19.2 percent of the staff maintain that they have worked in similar jobs; however, in Western state, no distinction is made between correctional institutional workers and mental hygiene aides in terms of civil service classification, and some of the Western cottage counselors worked previously in mental hospitals or institutions for retarded children as ward aides.

The Organization of Treatment Services:

Eastern

During the past few years, individual and group treatment strategies have been steadily gaining adherents in institutions for delinquent offenders. However, these methods are usually introduced piecemeal into the existing programs, so the traditional services remain relatively unchanged. New programs often involve only a few members of the inmate population and of the staff. The degree to which the treatment goal is implemented may vary from one month to the next as programs are curtailed or forgotten temporarily to meet organizational "crisis" situations such as budget cuts, increased population pressures, runaways or instances of other rule violations, and a lack of qualified staff.

Unfortunately, the vague descriptions of programs and resources that fill the pages of official brochures mislead rather than provide the reader with an understanding of the actual operation of these facilities; they remain relatively unchanged from one year to the next even when program changes have been made. Prepared for general public consumption, these documents convey the impression that the goals ascribed to the institution are being met; no discussion whatsoever is made of the problems of integrating the various functions. The fact that no figures are given in these documents concerning the number of inmates who are recidivists tells us a great deal.

TRADITIONAL AND "SPECIAL" TREATMENT PROGRAMS. All institutions for juvenile delinquents are expected to keep their inmates in safe custody in order to protect society; they are also expected to bring about desirable change so that upon release to the community the inmates will not engage in forms of social behavior that would lead to incarceration. In general, institutions for juvenile delinquents are expected to offer balanced programs consisting of academic and vocational training, recreation, and work programs related to and coordinated with institutional maintenance needs. Moreover, they are expected to provide services such as medical and dental care, social work and other clinical services, and religious services and spiritual guidance for the inmates. These services are sometimes referred to as the *"traditional"* or the *"routine"* program. Within this framework, however, institutions may be differentiated on the basis of the particular type of treatment strategy by which the administrative head identifies the institutional program. Thus, for example, an administrator may state that the institution's treatment program consists of "individual therapy," "group therapy," "community counseling," "school" or "vocational training," "behavior therapy," "point system"; or it may be a combination of the foregoing as well as other treatment strategies.

The services provided at the schools sampled include the traditional program, but within this general framework, Eastern, Central, and Western differ in the relative emphasis given to a single treatment method that presumably has institutionwide significance. Thus, Eastern's administrative head maintained that the "cottage community meetings" were the most important aspect of the program; at Central, "the primary focus of the program is held to be through a strong educational and vocational training emphasis," and at Western, the claim was made that the "entire institution is geared to treatment." The main thrust of Western's program emphasized the "therapists" who were to provide "individual counseling" for each inmate. In addition, the "team approach" is a poorly integrated structural unit in all three schools.

The administrative heads of the three institutions adhered to the principles of rehabilitation and treatment. However, each also acknowledged the importance of custody and explained that it was necessary to fit the maintenance requirements into the program because there was no staff to perform these tasks. The work to be performed in connection with maintenance needs went under the guise of "training."

ADMINISTRATIVE DIVISION OF ORGANIZATIONAL FUNCTIONS. While the overall responsibility to carry out Eastern's organizational goals rests with the superintendent, major organizational functions were delegated by him to three assistant superintendents who were responsible for administration, business management, and program; the director of the academic school, however, was under the jurisdiction of the superintendent. Eastern's administrator kept informed on matters concerning the school's operation through formally scheduled meetings with his administrative staff and other top-ranking personnel as well as through informal contacts.

Specific responsibility for the execution of certain tasks is shifted for the sake of organizational efficiency. For example, when the director of student life resigned to accept a position in a private children's school, the administrative responsibility for recreation, health, and dental services was delegated to the assistant superintendent for administration. This change was made primarily to ease the work load for the individuals who had been promoted to the student life department. (This assistant superintendent also coordinated the religion program.)

The other major functional area at Eastern was the division of student life. This unit also included "cottage service" (the principal children's supervisors) which was responsible for internal security. Administrative responsibility for the division of student life was delegated to the assistant superintendent of program, but the specific duties for both units were carried out by his two assistants. Intake, review, and release procedures were handled by one assistant, and the cottage service functions by another assistant. All of the cottage service staff, including the director, had risen from the ranks of cottage supervisor. The director of cottage service screened the applicants for cottage personnel, but final review and hiring were left to the assistant superintendent.

The division of student life included a part-time psychologist who was available for testing two evenings a week. There was no full-time psychiatrist, but psychiatric services could be obtained locally when needed. Almost all of the inmates were processed through a youth house juvenile center in a major metropolis where such tests usually were made and incorporated into the case files that accompany the inmates when they arrive by bus. Inmates from small counties were driven to Eastern by the county sheriff; the case histories were mailed by the court, but it was sometimes necessary for the institution to write requesting this information.

Although each staff member plays an important part, the social world of the inmates is in a very real sense played out in the cottage living units, and although trained and untrained "clinical" staff may be present, the cottage supervisors have the most continuous and sustained contact with the inmates. They are present when the inmates rise, remain throughout the entire day, and lock the inmates in their rooms when they go to bed. (At Eastern, however, the inmates' doors are unlocked shortly thereafter except in the case of the inmates who are on *locked status* for disciplinary purposes.) The senior supervisor is responsible for the entire cottage; one of the cottage supervisors is assigned to and remains in the kitchen, but all cottage staff have the same general responsibility as far as the inmates are concerned.

Even when the social workers are "decentralized" to the cottage units, as they were at Eastern before I left, a concomitant change in the working hours of the social workers does not take place. Social workers work Monday through Friday during the hours when all but a handful of inmates are either working at assigned jobs or attending classes in school. Unlike the social workers and other administrative personnel, the cottage supervisors work round-the-clock, and they also work during the weekend. Moreover, the special events scheduled for the inmates attract neither clinical staff nor administrative personnel; the cottage supervisors are in attendance.

The inmates use the prefix "Ma" before the cottage supervisor's last name; however, they use a formal mode of address for the social workers and other institutional staff.

INSTITUTION GOALS AND IMPLEMENTED TRADITIONAL PROGRAM. The broad goal of the department of social services which operates Eastern State's system of training schools is to "help children with problems." More specifically, the department maintains:

> Every phase of institution planning is geared to this philosophy: ". . . to provide a healthy environment in which rebellious adolescents can grow in physical and emotional stature with the counsel of those who understand the fears and needs of youth.". . . It is fully appreciated that a stay at one of the training schools might well be the last chance to rehabilitate a youngster on the way to becoming a confirmed criminal. Thus, the programs at the schools are planned to provide the leadership, authority, stability, treatment, and individual attention necessary to prepare a boy or girl for proper readjustment in his or her community.

To accomplish these multiple goals, each institution must include in its program the traditional services: academic and vocational training, organized recreation, work programs, medical and dental care, clinical services, and religious services. Beyond this, however, each administrator is free to develop programs he feels best meet the needs of the resident population. (This is only partially true, inasmuch as budget requests for new programs must be approved in the central office, and control over new programs may be exercised.)

Eastern's rationale of training as one of the means by which inmates learn socially acceptable behavior was set forth by the superintendent in a recent notice wherein the cottage staff's responsibilities were outlined:

Girls come to the training school for a period of training because they have not been able to get along at home or in the community. Everything that happens at the school is part of this effort at training—housekeeping duties are only important insofar as they provide girls with the necessities of life and with experience which will be useful in redirecting their interests and energies. Living in a cottage and performing the duties assigned to her, a girl has the experience of living with others and of performing tasks at a scheduled time and a given way. All of this gives the girl the opportunity to live in accordance with certain well defined limits. This is important because for most of the girls their limits have never been adequately defined. The counselor [cottage staff] has much to contribute to the girls by way of precept and example. The very fact of knowing an honest moral person who can be affectionate and for whom a girl can feel affection is in itself important to many girls who have never before had this opportunity. . . . Each counselor bears a large responsibility for providing leadership to the girls and for recognizing the importance of her role in the supervision and training of the girls in socially acceptable behavior, and in the orderly performance of the many duties involved in daily living.

Like the prison programs for adult women, academic and vocational programs for female juvenile delinquents also stress the traditional roles of wife, mother, and homemaker. An important part of the academic school curriculum at Eastern consisted of the following "vocational education" courses: home care, home nursing, cooking, problems of family living, and sewing. In the "welcome" pamphlet for the new inmates, the vocational program of the school was described in this way: "Girls have assignments to train them in vocational areas such as cooks, waitresses, nurses' aides, salechecks, office positions, and other skills." In addition to the "vocational skills" that the inmates presumably acquired, it was also maintained that working "helped" the inmates in some way. The staff accepted the procedure of work assignments as the only means whereby the maintenance work of the institution would be done—short of hiring more staff, which was an unlikely prospect.

The vocational school curriculum also included a beauty culture course which was offered to the "more mature and stable" inmates. The course fulfilled all requirements toward the state license, but the period of time most inmates remained at Eastern was not long enough; to complete the course, a very few inmates were kept longer than was actually required. The beauty culture students functioned as beauticians for the entire inmate population because all the inmates were required to have their hair done in beauty culture. They were not allowed to cut their own hair because the staff did not want them to have men's haircuts. In addition, the blacks at Eastern were not allowed to wear their hair in a full Afro, although a modified Afro that met the staff standard of "good taste" had been approved for a few girls. Pressing irons (mechanical devices used to straighten hair) were not allowed in the cottages, and it was necessary for the black inmates to go to the beauty shop for this type of service.

Salesclerk training was available to a few inmates who were assigned to the Saturday "canteen" in the storehouse; office runner-type positions were available in the dental clinic and the school office for two or three inmates. The nurses performed only clinical tasks, and the entire hospital building was designated as a vocational area. At least seven inmates were assigned to the hospital kitchen, and many more inmates were assigned the routine housekeeping and janitorial tasks. In fact, the maintenance of the other institution buildings was designated as a vocational area. Included among the latter was the teachers' cottage. The cottage living units are sizable buildings and require a great deal of upkeep. Several inmates in each cottage are assigned to do the major cleaning, but each inmate has a cottage work assignment such as straightening up the recreation room. Each cottage inmate group also was responsible for the general cleaning of certain parts of the institution at designated times. The staff supervised the inmates at work, but they did not share in it. The work assignments that were held by the Eastern inmates are summarized in Table 5.1.

All of the "vocational assignments" were fitted into the maintenance needs of the institution. There were no janitors at Eastern; the inmates did all the cleaning in the academic school, chapel, and administration and other buildings. To accomplish this, many of the inmates went to school only in the morning or the afternoon and worked the rest of the time.

Clearly, the inmates' academic education was not of primary concern. The fact that the inmates had to work so many hours doing "vocational" work would put most of them at a serious disadvantage when they returned to their own community schools. The existing situation particularly handicaps the inmates who are already academically retarded, perhaps functioning to close off altogether the possibility that they will ever work in the positions to which they aspire. No facilities were provided

Table 5.1   Work Assignments

Work Assignment	Number	%
Cook	49	23.9
Beauty parlor	18	8.8
Clothing room	1	.5
Storehouse	4	2.0
Administration building cleaning	15	7.3
Cleaning in other buildings, including cottage cleaning	94	45.8
Hospital kitchen	7	3.4
Dental and school office assistant	3	1.5
Laundry	10	4.9
No work assignment	2	1.0
No information	2	1.0
Total	205	100.1

where the inmates could study. The library was available to each inmate only once a week during the school day. There were no desks in the inmates' rooms, and the dining room tables were not put to this purpose.

In addition, because of its location Eastern had considerable difficulty in obtaining qualified teachers. However, the hiring of trained and qualified staff may rest on many considerations; this is apparent in the excerpt of a memo written in 1964 by the administrative head to the incoming superintendent.

Miss Margaret Norwood, Vocational Supervisor (Homemaking) failed the examination three times for this position. On July 29th, she had to be removed from the position back to her permanent item of Teacher. She will be taking the examination again in the Fall. There was only one person on the list so that I rejected it. In terms of the responsibility here, no change was made in Miss Norwood's position. She is listed by us as Assistant Director of Education and continues in this function. She is a terrific worker and is vitally important to the operation of the School's program at this time.

Even with its present teaching staff, other factors prevented the school from utilizing all of the staff's time for educational purposes. Inmates are prohibited from talking to other inmates when they meet anywhere on the institution grounds because of the staff's fear that the inmates will establish homosexual relationships. This concern took precedence over all other matters, and even had an impact on the teachers' work routine. Teachers were assigned to act as hall monitors in the school building; the teacher's task in this role was to sit behind the desk located near the bathroom to ensure that only one inmate at a time went into the bathroom after showing her pass to the hall monitor.

Unlike Central and Western, Eastern's academic school offered instruction only through the tenth grade. Because some girls have low reading levels when they arrive, classroom groups at Eastern were based on reading achievement rather than the traditional grades. Courses in key punch operation, office practice, and typing also were part of the school curriculum. Although the school is accredited by the state department of education, accreditation does not necessarily mean that the resources of the school are adequate or that they are as good as or superior to the schools in the local community or the schools in the community to which the inmates will one day return. The teachers generally felt that their resources were inferior to the schools in the local community.[1] Moreover, although Eastern's school library was extremely limited, none of the inmates had access to the library facilities in the local community. The inmates had only limited access to their own school library; once a week during the regular school hours two classroom groups went to the library for forty-five minutes at designated periods. Although the inmates protested that this library schedule was rigid and not conducive to stimulating creativity and interest in their school work, the schedule remained unchanged to ensure administrative convenience. Also, the librarian (a former teacher at Eastern) tended to adopt a proprietary view toward the book collection, at times demanding to know why the inmate wished to check out a book.

The hospital was staffed by the nurses and a part-time physician. Serious illnesses and emergencies were referred to the hospital in the nearby community, but infirmary and outpatient medical care was provided in Eastern's hospital. A dentist was located in the hospital unit. The nurses also had to assume responsibility for the inmates who were in the disciplinary cells located in one wing of the hospital.[2]

Most schools for juveniles have highly developed recreation programs to fill in the "idle time" when inmates are not in school or working. Extracurricular activities of this type tend to have limited budgets, but they require trained staff. Hence their inclusion into the program is often a fortuitous event. When staff is available, the activities are introduced; but if the staff member terminates her employment, the activities may not be part of the program for a year or more, although they will very likely still be listed as part of the institution's program. At Eastern, all activities that were not directly part of the academic or vocational program (such as dramatics, photography, modern dancing, ceramics, and other arts and crafts) were not part of the academic school program, but rather were classified as part of the recreation program. These activities were all conducted in the basement of one of the cottage units, and the makeshift space attested to the low priority given to them.

Because the academic summer school program included only a few of the inmates (the school director and most of the teachers did not work during the summer), a number of college students were hired as recreation workers to help fill in the inmates' increased leisure time. Calisthenics were an important part of the summer recreational program, as were the ball games between the cottages. Each cottage group spent one week at a camp away from the institution grounds. Weekly movies shown in the auditorium and monthly exchange dances with several schools for adjudicated male delinquents were an important part of the recreation program. However, these dances usually involved two cottage groups, hence only once or twice during her entire stay would it be possible for an inmate to participate in them.

COMMUNITY THERAPY AND COTTAGE ADMINISTRATIVE STRUCTURE.   If some part of the inmate's day must be devoted to the institution's maintenance needs, clearly the inmate's interests are compromised, however else this state of affairs may be phrased officially. Yet dramatic changes have been made at Eastern, particularly in the organization of the cottage staff's work. Until shortly before the present administrator assumed office, Eastern staff brought their children to work and the inmates functioned as babysitters for them. The memorandum below, dated October 23, 1957 and addressed to "all cottages," indicates Eastern's policy.

> We are aware that a number of staff members have children who occasionally come to work with them. There are no objections to this practice provided it is not carried to extremes.

> This is to remind all staff members that family members are not to participate regularly in cottage activities unless prior approval for same has been given by Cottage Service. Each of us has a responsibility to the girls under care. Therefore, it makes it increasingly difficult to do a good job in the treatment of the children when we have our own at work and are responsible for them during our tour of duty.

Clear with your housefather or housemother first on the matter of bringing your child to work, and he or she in turn will refer this to the cottage supervisor for final clearance and approval.

Not until May 11, 1964 when the acting superintendent raised the subject "children on the job" did the practice cease:

It has come to my attention that people are bringing children on the job. (Some are their own and some are relatives.) You are employed to give the girls in the Institution 8 hours of your service. This cannot be divided with your family. Bringing children to the job is not acceptable for the following reasons:

1. You cannot give adequate service to the girls when part of your time is shared in looking after these children.
2. We are not covered related to accidents which may occur.
3. You are exposing your children to the possibility of serious harm in many ways by such presence.
4. The girls on campus cannot be expected to take care of these children even if you pay them because they have a full program for the day.

The meaning of the above memoranda is important not only for the organization of the staff's work in relation to the inmates, but also in terms of the staff's perception of the inmates as normal rather than abnormal or "sick" individuals. It appears that the staff had no qualms that interaction would "contaminate" their own children.

Shortly after assuming office, the present administrator introduced several programs designed to involve both the inmates and the staff. The aim from the beginning was to create an institutional structure to promote a change in the inmates' attitudes that would identify them as conforming members of society. In the total structure of institutional change, the inmate culture was given a central place: Eastern's administrator viewed the inmates' informal social system as a powerful force that obstructs the staff's attempts to rehabilitate the inmates. He did not believe that the informal culture could be eliminated, but he maintained that it could be utilized as a positive force for rehabilitation. The treatment process was conceived as a joint enterprise between the staff and the inmates. His expectations are partially spelled out in the following exchange with the members of the Superintendent's Council[3] on November 17, 1965.

SUPERINTENDENT.   To catch up a little bit on what is going on, it seems that the major problems that we have—any time we look into the difficulties that we have, we find at the bottom of it the *racket*.[4] Can any of you give me an example of when the racket has been good to you and has done the girls any good? Is it a helpful thing?

COTTAGE REPRESENTATIVE.   When the girls are put away—they have problems at home—and when they're in their rooms they cry. But when they're in the racket, they have something else to think about and not home. For some girls it is helpful.

SUPERINTENDENT.   The only reason you come to an institution is to help yourself, and when you leave here you say, "The institution didn't help me any." It seems to me what the racket does is cause some problems which really hurt some girls. Right now we have a group of girls who call themselves the Gay Bishops. This group is made up of girls from Cottage 5 and 7. These girls have some problems over the racket with girls from cottage 9 who call themselves the Valdez, as well as the racket within their own cottage.

Now let me tell you how much good this has done so far: Margaret Robson and Rhoda Saginaw were transferred to the Annex [maximum security facility] last night. It didn't help them any. . . . This makes me very angry because I see what kids are doing to each other. If you want this kind of program where you can help yourselves, have some responsibility and make some decision as to what is going to happen to you, then we need your cooperation, and without your cooperation we cannot have that kind of program. This makes me feel bad because we are not doing the job we are supposed to be doing. It seems to me that you ought to think about this. If most of you want a good program, we can have it. If you don't, we can't have it. It is no fun being in an institution. It is not pleasant. When this sort of thing crops up, when you have too many privileges and you can't take the responsibility that goes with it, we don't have the time to do the things we want to do. You have to help each other—you have to assume some responsibility. Does this make sense to you or not? Are there any questions about this?

COTTAGE REPRESENTATIVE.   It makes sense, but how can we help each other?

SUPERINTENDENT.   I want to see how many of you feel you have helped girls since you are here. How many of you have had another girl come to you and give you some good advice? It seems to me that this is one thing you can do. I know you listen to each other, you trust each other. When you have a cottage really involved in the racket, something is wrong. There is something wrong, or you don't belong in this institution. I think you have to start making decisions for yourselves—what you want—what kind of life you want for yourselves. Do you want to wind up in an institution for the rest of your life?

It seems to me that when something like this happens, nothing good comes out of it. It prevents you from doing something right. You're here in this institution and you are going to be here for a period of time and you have to decide what you are going to do for yourselves. The choice is yours. I cannot make you do anything. I can lock you up, and if things get worse, I can send you off campus. That is all I can do. So far there have been four girls sent to the Annex because of this business. What I am saying is if enough of you kids want a decent program, you can have a good program, a program that is not only good for you, but for the kids to come after you. The decision is yours. I have been just as honest with you as I can be. What I would like to see—I happen to have a lot of faith in you kids—I want to see you go back to your cottage and see what you can do. You are a respected person and the leader in your cottage. Some of the kids will listen to you.

COTTAGE REPRESENTATIVE.   When you say you want us to go back and talk to the girls about this, regardless of what you say to them, what they want to be they are going to be anyway. If you're going to be something, you are going to do it.

SUPERINTENDENT.   It seems to me that we have to give people as many chances as we can. If you think there is no reason for changing, you will not change. Most kids don't want to try because they think they can't.

COTTAGE REPRESENTATIVE.   If you really want to change, you don't have to come up here to change. You can change anytime. You don't have to be sent away. If they wanted to change, they could have changed when they were home.

SUPERINTENDENT.   Why do you think they sent you up here? I think you are right that you have to recognize that this institution has two functions. One of them is giving a person a chance to make some kind of change. The other function an institution has—and this is the reason why taxpayers support us—is because it is to keep you from making a nuisance of yourselves, and to get you off the streets. Some kids have done things they should be locked up for. The most important function is to give you a chance to make some kind of change, but the other function is to keep you here for a period of time.

The decisions you make right now are very important. It helps you decide what you are and what you are going to be, or where you are going to be five years from now. I know some kids have the feeling that you do what you want to do now and tomorrow will take care of itself.

COTTAGE REPRESENTATIVE. I know there are some girls on campus, some of the *hard daddys* and they want to get out of the racket, but they're afraid to get out because the kids will call them sissies.

SUPERINTENDENT. If enough kids help them to stay out, they will stay out. People usually do what is expected of them. That is why you can be helpful. Sometimes that is hard to see, but I believe it; if I did not believe it, it would be easier to march you kids around the institution and watch you all the time.

The major program innovation was the practice of conducting daily "cottage community meetings"; this structural feature differentiated Eastern's program from that of Central and Western. The cottage community meeting was the framework for *community therapy*; it was assumed that an inmate's participation in this process would help her to develop internalized individual and social controls. The cottage meetings were considered to be the most important part of Eastern's program; other changes might be made in the daily routine, but the cottage meetings were to take place from 4:00 to 5:00 each afternoon, Monday through Friday. The purpose of the meetings was stated to staff and inmates alike as the place for "girls to discuss their problems and to help each other." Attendance at the meetings was compulsory for the inmates and all staff members who were in the cottage at the prescribed time. Due to the work shifts, however, it was possible for only two of the six cottage staff members to attend regularly; the others attended when they worked as relief staff.

Although the rationale behind the community meeting structure as an effective treatment vehicle ostensibly was the impact of the peer group on an adolescent's behavior, other factors were also acknowledged as important; they encompassed the "kinds" of inmates who were admitted, the length of the incarceration period, and the belief that the structural features of the inmate culture ruled out a treatment approach that placed emphasis on the relationship between therapist and client.

In the documents which were circulated to the administrative staff, Eastern's administrator expressed his views of delinquency in this way:

> [T]he basic problem of the delinquent is one of adherence to a deviant value system and, as a consequence, the central task of institutional treatment is to achieve stable changes in the offender's values and attitudes. Though there may be emotional disturbances associated with his behavior, the delinquent is committed to an institution because he has failed to adhere to the prevailing "norms" of the larger society. Personality problems must be dealt with whenever they obstruct necessary changes, but the central problem of institutional treatment remains one of devising a treatment approach which will bring about strongest adherence to conventional values.

One of the perplexing problems in institutional administration is how to reduce the conflict between the custodial and the clinical staff. The role to be played by the clinical staff in making disciplinary decisions is crucial. To minimize the conflict, Eastern's administrator broadened the social workers' role in cottage affairs by delegating the authority for cottage administration to them. In restructuring legitimate lines of authority, the senior cottage supervisor was established as the mediating link between the social worker and the cottage staff and inmates. The social workers' task had several separate but interrelated dimensions: (1) They were expected to make decisions concerning disciplinary matters, and this knowledge—together with other training received by them—was to be used to help the untrained cottage staff deal more effectively with the inmates; (2) it was anticipated that this role change would result in more efficient processing of treatment plans for the inmates, as the social workers could now supervise more directly the progress reports prepared by the cottage staff; and (3) the social workers would gain an intimate knowledge of the inmates as they functioned in the cottage social structure.

The staff who had received social work training held administrative posts; each was "responsible" for a number of cottages in the quadrangles—especially staff training—but they did not work directly in the cottages. "Training" was sporadic and coincided with the resolution of crises, either those between staff members or situations involving the inmates; as a rule such "training" would be confined to a single cottage.

To form one administrative unit, the social workers were moved from their office in the administration building to separate offices in the cottages. The "decentralization" of the social workers was not completed at one time; rather, it emerged gradually as more social workers were added to the staff, but even after two years the process had not been fully completed. Although the social workers were officially decentralized to the cottage units in 1967, it was actually not until the latter part of 1968 that enough social workers had been hired to "cover" most of the cottages. At Eastern (and this is probably true of correctional facilities that are administered by a statewide department that controls correctional policy), staff positions for new programs must be requested, justified, and approved. In such statewide correctional systems, an administrator is not free to hire staff whenever he chooses, however desirable this might appear to be for program development and implementation. Hence the time span between program planning, central office approval, and staff recruitment may be a very lengthy process.

When the study began, there were three cottage social workers, one of whom had been employed at Eastern for approximately nine months and the others for two years. In addition, three cottage service staff (principal children's supervisors) also functioned as cottage social workers. Their major responsibility, however, was cottage service, and their work as social workers was mainly confined to the preparation of reports for inmate reviews (these written during odd moments while performing their normal duties) and the handling of disciplinary disputes. Two of the principal children's supervisors were high school graduates, and the other had completed two years of college; although one of them had worked less than two years, the others had been at Eastern more than ten years, and were familiar with the cottage routine as they had worked as cottage supervisors. None of the principal children's supervisors functioned as community group leaders; in fact, they rarely attended the meetings due to the fact that their presence was required in the cottage service office. By the time the study ended, five more individuals had been hired to function as cottage social workers. They had worked less than six months when the study ended. Except for the cottage service staff, all the cottage social workers were college graduates who had majored in one of the social sciences, but none had been trained in social work methods. When speaking of the Eastern social workers in the remainder of this report, we refer to the eleven staff members discussed above.

The new arrangement certainly facilitated contact between the cottage staff and the social workers; however, inasmuch as the completion of the inmates' progress reports more often than not was contingent upon cottage conditions—and especially the behavior of the inmates—they continued to be hastily assembled and submitted late.

The social workers' understanding of the inmates' behavior in the cottage units was increased only to a limited degree, however, because a concomitant change in their working hours did not occur. There was little correspondence between the hours that the inmates were in the cottages and the working day of the social workers. The social workers did not remain in the cottages during the inmates' lunch period. A work schedule from 2:00 to 10:00 p.m. would have been more efficient. Theoretically, more contact between the cottage staff and the social workers was possible regarding cottage affairs, in general, and disciplinary matters, in particular; nevertheless, the cottage staff continued to exercise discretion in making most decisions or they were made in consultation with cottage service due to the different work schedules of the cottage supervisors and the social workers. Also, the cottage social workers were not trained; and since the administrative staff who were charged with in-service training did not take the initiative, the cottage social workers tended to rely upon the senior cottage supervisors for direction in many matters.

The presence of the social workers had minimal impact on "community therapy." After community cottage meetings had been held daily in each cottage for several years, Eastern's administrator conceded that they had fallen short of accomplishing their "therapeutic" objective. The meeting time was taken up with a discussion of institutional events, such as shortages of cottage supplies, recreational events, and the violation of or changes in the institutional rules. More often than not, the topic for discussion was the inmates' participation in the informal social system. Most of the staff had lost their enthusiasm for the cottage meetings, and they would have preferred, as did the inmates, that the meetings be discontinued. Nevertheless, the superintendent insisted that the cottage staff continue to meet daily with the inmates explaining that in the long run—with more staff training—the community meetings would be effective. Not surprisingly, staff meetings tended to revolve about crisis situations. The main point of such meetings was the resolution of a particular problem, but it was hoped that training elements would be introduced into the discussion.

Why was the anticipated outcome of the community meetings difficult to achieve, even on the most basic level of obtaining the inmates' cooperation? First, the inmates disliked discussing their families before the entire cottage group, as they considered such information to be personal. In their view, to do so would indicate disloyalty to their parents and other family members. To be sure, the staff emphasized that everything discussed in the community meetings was confidential and was not to be related to anyone outside the cottage. Nevertheless, each inmate had concrete evidence that clearly indicated otherwise. Without a moment's hesitation, she could recall the experiences of particular inmates who had "discussed problems" in community meetings only to discover several days later, "It was all thrown up in my face!" not only by the inmates but by the staff. Many of the inmates also felt that their problems at home were external to the institution—that is, the problems existed in the community, and a discussion of them *inside* appeared to be irrelevant. As put by the inmates: "Everything will be the same when we go back." This is not to say that the inmates at any of the three institutions ruled out the possibility that adults, either in the institution or in the community, could help them; rather, they made sharp distinctions about what it was that they could or could not do. Third, the inmates did not accept the theory that every inmate in the cottage was capable of helping them; they maintained that when they needed advice on certain kinds of situations, their friends could be trusted to function in this capacity. Fourth, the normative structure of the informal social system of the inmates ruled out the kind of behavior that the therapeutic society demanded. Some inmates took advantage of the opportunity provided by the community therapy meetings to "get back" at an inmate who had not conformed to the expectations of the inmate culture. It was common knowledge that an inmate's cottage "family" would come to her defense if anyone "brought up" her behavior. Finally, the meetings—with the long lapses of time between "problems"—were boring to the inmates regardless of who conducted them. The social workers, however, could be expected to persist undaunted until 5:00, whereas the cottage supervisors would sometimes terminate the meeting early in order to get on with the business of the final preparations for the evening meal. (The kitchen girls were always excused early.)

The community group leaders spent much time going from one inmate to another, asking "Who has a problem they'd like to discuss?" This procedure was often exasperating to the inmates. As one inmate put it: "He [social worker] don't seem to understand that I go many days without a problem!"

Taking into account all these factors, Eastern's administrator introduced an intensified training program for the staff approximately four years after assuming office.[5] As Eastern's administrator explained, "Now I'm on this last kick. The heck with the girls, and let's see what we can do with the staff. To get them to talk to one another."

The specific techniques used in the staff training sessions were T-groups and sensitivity training. Eastern's superintendent was familiar with the literature on organizational development and the use of T-groups for organizational development. In fact, he had attended a month's session at the Bethel, Maine, training program, and he had recently made arrangements for thirty-eight members of the more senior staff to participate in groups at an off-campus site. Many members of Eastern's staff felt that this type of training was an infringement because their "private feelings" were their "own business," and they did not think it was necessary to "bare your soul in order to do your job." A few individuals who had a social science background questioned the entire procedure as one which "tore people down but did nothing to build them back up." One social worker refused to participate altogether on the grounds that he could not see the relationship of this training to the problems he faced every day in the cottages in his job of rehabilitating incarcerated juvenile delinquents.

The Organization of Treatment Services:

Central

The following statement expresses the philosophy and goals set for Central by the state youth commission which administers the statewide facilities for delinquents.

> [Central school] has been established to offer the adjudicated female youth social, educational and vocational opportunities in order to prepare her for a successful return to community life. The primary focus of the program is through a strong educational and vocational training emphasis.
>
> The purpose of the institution is to furnish a controlled environment in as nearly a homelike atmosphere as possible.
>
> . . . In order to assist the girls in accepting the responsibility that they may face when returning to the community, it is the function of [Central] to give them opportunities to develop positive attitudes, goals, and a more positive self-image. This is accomplished through opportunities to develop stable relationships with significant adult figures, counseling in various forms, and through structured educational, recreational, and vocational programs geared to meet the individual needs of each girl.

The state youth commission's goals were stated broadly, and it was incumbent upon all the institutional administrators to manage each facility in such a way that the commission's mandate was put into operational terms. The broad goals set forth by the commission have been restated and interpreted by Central's administrative head as follows:

> The primary purpose of [Central] is to *motivate, educate* and *rehabilitate* all girls committed so that they might hopefully return to the community as contributing rather than consuming members of society. One of the major objectives is to establish or perhaps modify the values of life and a positive living pattern through the many day-to-day experiences each student confronts. To accomplish this, we rely heavily on milieu therapy. Our major program area is in academic and vocational training.

> Two of the greatest obstacles in carrying out our objectives are the lack of motivation of the girls with whom we work, and the apathy of the general public. However, it should be remembered that we are dealing with girls that are insecure, lack love and understanding and have deep-rooted emotional problems, unhealthy environmental situations, exhibit antisocial behavior, and lack mores that are acceptable to society. These children have been before the courts. . . . To change these patterns of life we offer programs in three basic areas: academic, vocational and group living. . . . Our programs are geared to the needs and interest of teen-aged girls. . . . In many cases, the girls are receiving for the first time opportunities in life which they have been deprived because of environment or other circumstances. We offer motivation and stimulation in positive living.

> All corrective actions necessary to accomplish this objective are prescribed for the individual girl consistent with the treatment objective of the school and individual plan of treatment for the girl.

To understand Central's operation, it is necessary only to mention briefly the range of services provided, which are similar to those provided at Eastern. To implement the goals of the institution, the focus of Central's operation was placed on the academic and vocational training offered to the students. More than ninety-five percent of the inmates participated in the academic and vocational program. The inmates who did not participate in the academic and vocational program were placed in the "on the job training" program; the inmates in the latter program were overage for their grade level placement and they had no plans to return to school upon release.

ADMINISTRATIVE DIVISIONS AND IMPLEMENTED PROGRAMS.
The organizational framework of Central school was sharply divided into two main divisions: direct services and indirect services. The functional responsibility for the operation of these divisions was delegated by Cen-

tral's administrator to two deputy superintendents. The division of indirect services at Central handled the aspects of organizational administration that related specifically to the institution's fiscal matters, including plant maintenance, plant security, and personnel record keeping; all of the subdivision tasks were delegated to key staff members in the departments charged with specific functions. Our concern in this chapter is solely with the direct services division; this unit coordinated the institutions' program for the inmates.

Unlike the situation at Eastern where the academic school principal reported to the superintendent, lines of authority at Central were drawn so that all departments came under the jurisdiction of the deputy superintendent for direct services; the delegation of specific functions, however, was broad and each department head had considerable autonomy. Like Eastern, the traditional program at Central included academic and vocational training, recreation, work programs, medical and dental care, social work, other clinical services, and religious and spiritual guidance. In addition, two cottages had what were referred to as "special programs," but these programs were not highly developed. The program in one cottage was designated as "peer group interaction"; and the program in the "opportunity cottage" presumably gave the inmate residents more opportunity for responsibility such as deciding how much time they should study; and to a limited degree, the inmates in the opportunity cottage had more freedom of movement on campus than did the rest of the inmate population. The program in the peer group therapy cottage consisted of meetings with the inmates who participated in guided group interaction. The meetings, however, were sporadic, and more often than not they coincided with rule violations by cottage members.

Until quite recently, cottage assignments were based on certain characteristics ascribed to the inmates. One cottage had been designated for the "more emotionally disturbed" inmates, another for the "more aggressive girls," and a third for the "lower intellectual level girls." Cottage assignments were made on the basis of age. However, because Central accepts court adjudicated delinquents from every county in the state, the crucial factor is the available bed space. Only in a superficial sense, therefore, could the cottage populations be differentiated on the basis of the foregoing classifications. At present, with the exception of the two cottages mentioned, the cottage programs are identical, notwithstanding the characteristics that may be ascribed to the inmates. During the time of the study, the only differentiation concerned the pregnant inmates who were housed in one cottage near the hospital. Formerly, pregnant inmates were dispersed throughout all the cottages.

Central differed from Eastern in that one housing unit was an orientation cottage. All the inmates, with the exception of the recidivists who are brought directly to the maximum security unit, spend two weeks in the orientation unit before they are assigned to cottages. At all three schools, inmates were released to balance the number of inmates who were admitted. However, since the program at Central was educationally oriented, this procedure posed more of a problem than it did at Eastern and Western. Central's educational focus forced the staff to confront specific criteria in assessing an inmate's readiness for release, especially when the inmate's education was to be continued in the community or the inmate was to obtain a job. Under these conditions, an inmate's release cannot be as easily justified as when a more general "treatment" model is pursued. A vague "treatment" model makes possible a more elastic approach; in fact, release itself may be interpreted as treatment. While inmates at Central were sometimes released sooner than they otherwise would be, this usually occurred when the population at the institution soared, or there was a "backup" at the diagnostic center.

The only other residential facility for female delinquents in Central state is a maximum security unit with a room capacity for 150 inmates. It had been in operation about seven months before the study began. Inmates from Central are transferred to this facility for severe infractions of institutional rules. This unit is held out as a threat to the Central inmates and functions in the same way as Eastern's maximum security annex. However, the disciplinary cottage at Central was utilized for all but the most severe and persistent violators. The inmates whose behavior was consistently troublesome or who ran away were first transferred to the disciplinary cottage for a period of time; transfer to the off-campus facility might be made later.

Central had a full-time physician on its hospital staff, and unlike Eastern, all the nursing staff at Central were registered nurses. A special program for pregnant inmates had been established by the hospital staff. A nurse's aide program was in the planning stage, and the few inmates who were assigned to this program functioned as housekeeping aides; no school credit was given for this hospital work.

Central had earned a reputation as "one of the most progressive training schools in the country." Of the three institutions studied, it had the most developed academic school. The program was geared to duplicate at least (and it was the school principal's aim eventually to exceed) the educational resources of the community schools. Its library had an extensive book collection; in no small measure, this was due to the fact that Central had to meet the standards set by the state department of education for the public schools, and these standards included expending a specified sum (based on student enrollment) during the year for additional library resources. Teachers at Central were allowed to teach only in the area in which they were certified; this situation contrasted sharply with Eastern where no such standards existed and only seventy-five percent of the teachers were certified. A member of Central State's departmen of education visited the school annually to evaluate the institution's program in terms of teacher certification, student recordkeeping, building maintenance, facilities and equipment, and courses of study. Thus, Central staff members were more conscious of their accountability to an outside agency than would otherwise have been the case if only annual written reports had been required.

By contrast, Eastern's library had few books and most of the recent acquisitions had been made possible through a Federal grant. Western's academic school did not have a library; a few books were housed in a small room in the school complex. The inmates could check them out, but the volumes were not arranged in order, nor was space provided for the inmates to sit. Another important difference between Central and the other schools that underscores Central's educational focus was the greater accessibility of the library to the inmates. The Central inmates could go to the library every day and could use the library facilities in the evening (and sometimes on Saturday) when their cottage group was scheduled.

Central's year-round academic and vocational curriculum was organized to provide instruction in grades seven through twelve for approximately four hundred inmates. The graduation were held in January, June, and August in an effort to coordinate the school program to the needs of the inmates; the school is accredited in both academic and vocational areas. Accreditation does not necessarily mean that the program is adequate (the academic school departments of all three institutions were accredited); however, the school program offered at Central was much more extensive than that provided at Eastern or Western. In the senior high school tract (a general education tract) enough courses had been added to the curriculum by the Central education department to prepare individuals who wished to enter college; and some of the Central inmates did make plans to enter college upon graduation and release. Central was the only school that taught a foreign language. Central inmates could participate in a wide variety of clubs associated with the academic school such as the history, French, drama, art, science, and library clubs, as well as other organized school activities.

In the adult prison, inmates are expected to earn part of their keep by contributing their labor in a wide variety of tasks. As to incarcerated delinquent children, the entire question concerning work has always been an ambiguous issue. Given the "treatment" thrust of the juvenile court—and the fact that no specific guidelines have been set down for the institutions to follow—there is a tendency for institutions serving adjudicated delinquents to rationalize inmate labor by couching the maintenance tasks in the language of "vocational training" or "therapeutic training" to a degree that is not to be found in the adult prison. The so-called vocational programs are often treated as extensions to the academic school, as was the case at Central and Eastern.

Central's administrative head was interested in relating the inmates' work experience and job skills to jobs that they could obtain upon release. To this end, in 1966 ten teachers were added to the trades and industry educational department ostensibly to expand the vocational program. However, even with more staff such a goal can be implemented only to a limited extent unless community resources are tapped. The Central inmates could earn school credits by "enrolling" in "vocational areas" such as bakery, laundry, needle trades, cosmetology, and housekeeping aide services. With the exception of cosmetology, these vocational areas are related to the maintenance needs of the institution. The specific work assignments of the Central inmates appear in Table 6.1.

The department of education at Central (unlike that of Eastern and Western schools) had established specific criteria to aid the staff in mak-

Table 6.1   Work Assignments

Work Assignment	Number	%
Cafeteria	26	7.6
Cosmetology	9	2 6
Needle trades	7	2.0
Bakery	11	3.2
Housekeeping aides	12	3.5
Greenhouse	7	2.0
Office: clerical and runners	5	1.5
Nurse assistant	5	1.5
Laundry	31	9.1
Truck delivery	3	0.9
No work assignment	225	66.0
Total	341	99.9

ing decisions to enroll individuals in vocational areas. The criteria include: (1) the existence of a similar program in the community, thus making it possible for the inmate to complete the program in the community and graduate; (2) the determination that an inmate must work when released; (3) the existence of job opportunities in the training area; (4) an inmate's inability to function in an accredited academic or trades and industry program; (5) the presence of academic retardation to such a degree that the inmate cannot function in an academic setting, even though she is still of school age (in this case vocational training was "to be considered therapeutic rather than job oriented"). Individuals who were older than sixteen years of age and academically retarded were to go to school for one-half day and spend one-half day in a "therapeutic training area."

To what extent were these criteria actually taken into account in planning an individual's program? Table 6.1 shows that sixty-eight inmates were assigned to work in the laundry, cafeteria, and the bakery. The operational functions of these departments had high priority, and the school counseling department was notified immediately when shortages existed. This was also true in varying degrees of the other departments, but "short help" could not be tolerated in the laundry, cafeteria, or bakery even for a brief period of time. In addition, some inmates were assigned as housekeeping aides, nurse assistants or aides, greenhouse workers, and truck delivery assistants to help in transporting food from the cafeteria and bakery to the cottages. Due to the confidential nature of the case files, inmates could not be placed into office jobs, but several inmates were placed in clerical and runner positions.

Although an attempt was made at Central to give the maintenance tasks a measure of respectability by coordinating vocational theory with the specific work tasks, in only a superficial sense was this possible. First, the equipment used in the bakery and laundry was outdated; second, most of the tasks performed by the inmates could be learned on the job in a few hours. The fact that the inmates were kept working for many weeks in the same assignment attests unequivocally to the priority given the institution's maintenance needs. Finally, all of these jobs have doubtful transferability to the community. None of the institutions studied had on record any information whatsoever in this regard, as they had made no inquiries about the job market in the communities to which the inmates would return. Nor had the field staffs attached to the schools provided the institutions with this information. All public statements to the contrary, the inmates who must seek work before release are left almost entirely to their own resources. Central school differed from Eastern and Western, however, in that two school counselors were part of the education department staff. Due to the efforts of a recently hired counselor, a beginning had been made to provide the inmates with informational literature concerning requirements for certain community jobs, how to apply for them, and particularly the role of the state employment department.

Central's cafeteria was organized in such a way that the inmates learned waitress and hostess work, and these skills possibly could be put to use in the community. The same may be said for the *work knowledge* gained in the cosmetology, typing, shorthand, and other business related courses.

The criteria established for vocational placement presupposes that the inmates who are admitted will possess the "right" characteristics, thereby making it possible to channel predictable numbers of inmates to specific vocational areas. Incoming inmates do not always meet the established criteria; hence the inmates' vocational training must be fitted to the institution's maintenance tasks. This state of affairs posed a conflict for Central's school department. The task imposed upon it to supply the vocational areas with inmate labor meant compromising the school department's professed educational goals for each student. Once a commitment is made to an educational goal based on traditional principles and standards, the structure itself imposes unique limits that leaves little room for compromise, for to change the basic principles is to emerge with a structure that is fashioned of adjusted means and ends—an adaptation that is ever-changing but falls short of adherence to stated principles. This is what happened at Central, and is the situation faced by other institutions with similar problems.

Unlike Eastern and Western schools, every inmate at Central was not assigned a work task. Table 6.1 shows that 66 percent of the inmates had no work assignment. Central had the largest physical plant of the three schools studied. Theoretically, all the inmates could have been assigned work tasks—even if they were of the "make work" variety—but Central's program emphasis encouraged conformity to the educational goal to a much greater extent than was the case at Eastern or Western where academic education played a secondary role. Central was the only institution that employed a male janitor who cleaned the school department. In addition, a few inmates from one of the state's facilities for delinquent boys helped with trash collection and general maintenance. Although some of the Central inmates engaged in general clean-up around the cottage areas and in building maintenance, this was kept to a minimum compared with Eastern and Western institutions.

Nevertheless, all the institutions studied found it necessary to exploit inmate labor. Staff are not recruited to perform the general maintenance tasks in institutions for delinquents; in this regard they differ from public schools in the community. None of the organization tables for Eastern, Central and Western provided for such staff positions. Adjudicated delinquent girls are expected to function in these work roles at the same time that they are to be "rehabilitated" and "treated."

THE ROLE OF THE SOCIAL SERVICE STAFF. Central differed importantly from Eastern in the organization of the social service and cottage staffs. Each social worker at Central had an office in the administration building. The social workers at Central had more prestige and power than did their counterparts at Eastern or Western. All the top-ranking administrative staff at Central had been trained in social work; the superintendent and the deputy superintendent had advanced degrees in social work. As a group, the social workers at Central were more highly educated than their counterparts at Eastern and Western. The director of the social service staff, his assistant, and three of the workers had Master degrees in social work; the other social workers were college graduates with a social science background; several had attended graduate school.

Central also differed from Eastern and Western in terms of the greater stability of the social service department. Four social workers had worked between two and ten years, and the remaining four social workers had been employed at Central less than one year—only one of whom had been employed less than six months. Each social worker's caseload consisted of one cottage; the workers with Master degrees in social work supervised the caseloads of the other social workers.

Unlike Eastern and Western, the department of social services held weekly meetings to discuss mutual problems in connection with the cottages, the relationship of the institution to the diagnostic unit, and their problems with the field staff who completed the release arrangements when an inmate's name was placed on the alert list by her social worker. Eastern had similar arrangements with a field staff, but at Central each social worker worked more closely with the field worker who was assigned to her own cottage; the field workers made bi-monthly visits. In addition to these internal and external management problems, part of the meeting time was utilized by the director of social services for training. New trends and theories in the field were discussed in terms of their possible applicability for rehabilitating delinquent girls. Central's administrative staff members were familiar with treatment procedures currently in vogue and they compared them to their own operation with a view to improving services. The weekly meetings of the cottage life administrators, however, were not attended by the social workers, but all cottage staff meetings that were scheduled by a social worker—especially those planned for training—required the cottage administrator's attendance. All department heads were present at the deputy superintendent's regular meetings, during which time policy matters concerning the program were formulated and discussed; although the academic school principal was present at these meetings, the teachers were not assigned to cottage teams.[1] The staff psychologist attended the social service meetings occasionally, but contact between the social service staff and the psychologist was limited to the testing of inmates. There was no psychiatrist at Central; the program was geared to the academic school and inmates with psychiatric disorders were not admitted.

The social workers' casework functions in connection with the progress reviews—to be made every two months—brought them into contact with all other departments. When a change in another department's program was made or a program area was added, the supervisor of the program was invited to the social workers' meeting to discuss the issues. In addition, it was incumbent upon the social workers to notify the academic school counselors when an inmate was to be referred to parole, as the school transcript was to be mailed to the community school on the day of the inmate's release to ensure continuity of the inmate's education.

Another important way in which Central differed from Eastern was in the relationship of the cottage life department to the social service staff. The cottage life department had its own director and three assistant directors, but was under the administrative jurisdiction of the deputy superintendent of direct services who was in charge of all program activities. (Although cooperative arrangements existed between the social service and cottage life departments as far as cottage program is concerned, each department had its own secretarial and clerical staff.)

At Central, the cottage teams included the cottage youth leaders (called housemothers at Central) and the cottage administrators of the cottage life department. Each cottage administrator had an office in the administration building; but the administrators spent some time each day in the cottages discussing management and discipline problems with the cottage housemothers. The senior housemother and the rest of the cottage staff were supervised directly by the cottage administrators; however, the social workers were responsible for the overall cottage program. The cottage administrators were charged with institutional security and control, as well as the cottage administration of the clinical program and other cottage activities. The recreation program was supervised by the director of the cottage life program. Social workers served as advisers and consultants at all times.

Decisions concerning discipline were in some cases made jointly with the cottage social workers, but the incident reports were made out by the cottage administrators and cottage staff. Officially, major disciplinary actions were to be made by a cottage adjustment committee consisting of a deputy director of the cottage life department and the cottage social worker, but sometimes the social worker was bypassed. When there was disagreement between the cottage social worker and the cottage administrator as to the appropriate action indicated in a given situation, the social worker's decision took precedence. Perhaps it was for this reason that the social worker was not always notified or consulted in matters of discipline—although the fact that the social workers worked only during the day certainly was an important consideration. Although the cottage administrators worked the same hours as did the social workers, the cottage life department had deputy directors on duty twenty-four hours a day. None of the social workers or cottage administrators worked during the weekend or on holidays. Consequently, the same situation existed at Central as at Eastern, the cottage staff had the most sustained and continuing contact with the inmates.

Central was the only school studied where corporal punishment ("swats") was officially allowed, to be administered when other disciplinary actions had not produced the desired conformity. In 1968 a discussion of the use of corporal punishment revealed that the social service staff and most of the administrators actually favored abolishing it, but the cottage staff and a few of the cottage administrators attested to its effectiveness when "all else had failed"; hence corporal punishment continued to be used "with restraint." Written reports were sent to the superintendent, deputy superintendent, and the directors of social service and cottage life when corporal punishment was used.

The recreation division had a permanent staff that was larger than similar units at Eastern and Western, but all recreational activities at Central were channeled through the cottage life department. Lines of supervision leading directly to the cottage life staff decreased the possibility of developing an organizational structure uncoordinated with other institutional activities; since the recreation department was forced to compete with the many year-round academic school activities for the inmates' time and allegiance, the channeling of recreational activities through the cottage life department meant that competing events could be adjusted. Unlike Eastern and Western, one hour was set aside as a study hour in the cottage dining room after the evening meal. The inmates could also study in their rooms; but as was the case at Eastern and Western, the overhead lighting was inadequate. The fact that there were no electrical outlets in the inmates' rooms ruled out the use of table lamps.[2] Structured recreational activities were more varied at Central than they were at either Eastern or Western. The school had a swimming pool in the gym, a miniature golf course, weekly movies, occasional coeducational dances with inmates from the nearby boys' institutions, a variety of arts and crafts activities, baseball games, roller-skating, and the academic school's "little theatre" group. A camp also was operated on the grounds during the summer. Although Central provided more on-campus activities, the three institutions studied were similar in that few off-campus activities were planned for the inmates.

ADMINISTRATIVE PROBLEMS OF PROGRAM IMPLEMENTATION. There was no cottagewide system of group therapy meetings at Central. However, the social workers were free to develop "special" programs in their cottages, and a few social workers sometimes organized "small groups." Departures from the usual routine tended to follow disruptions in the cottages, and "group therapy"—to include a few inmates—sometimes would be introduced; when the cottage reached a stage of equilibrium, the groups would be discontinued.

At Central, "special programs" were identified in two cottages but these programs were not fully implemented—a situation that is certainly not uncommon in institutions. One reason is that cottage populations do not remain stable; the introduction of new inmates and the release of other inmates inevitably disrupts the stability and continuity of cottage programs. But perhaps a more compelling reason is that such programs depend upon the program head for their continued operation. Typically, the individuals who head such programs have more formal education, and there is the most rapid staff turnover among them. It seems that as soon as an innovative cottage program begins to "get off the ground," the crucial staff members associated with its operation terminate their employment. When the program head leaves the institution, the entire cottage routine may revert to that of an earlier period, or it may limp along as a "special" program with staff who are ill-equipped to carry it out. Also, daily work pressures, vacations, and training meetings may result in the suspension of a special program's goals for short periods of time. Such actions give the cottage staff the impression that these programs are justifiable only under certain conditions, and may provide the rationale for suspensions of programs that are unrelated to these reasons.

The social workers at Central occupied themselves with casework functions to a greater degree than did the social workers at Eastern and Western. Much of their time was spent in assembling materials from all the departments for the bimonthly progress reports. Each social worker was expected to schedule at least two formal meetings each month with the inmates in their caseload. The inmates who received the most attention, however, were those who became involved in disciplinary actions. The working day of the Central social workers posed special problems as the inmates were engaged in school activities during the day. The social workers did visit the cottages, but these contacts tended to be structured about meetings and other specific issues of a formal nature.

Notwithstanding the specialized training of Central's social service staff, the progress reports that they prepared were as superficial as those prepared at Eastern and Western. The same material (often from the court history summary) was either repeated verbatim or reworded slightly in subsequent reviews, even though its historical relevance was open to question. The social service staff had difficulty coordinating their efforts with the field staff workers who were to function as the linkages between the institution and the inmate's family and the community, and upon whom the institutional workers were dependent for current information. The field staff's bimonthly visits to the institution were confined to two days of each week. All the field workers were expected to adhere to the established time table. Changes in the schedule would conflict with the regularly scheduled staff meetings at Central. Changes could be made, but not without difficulty; for a field worker to visit Central at a different time, the regional director had to obtain prior approval from either Central's deputy superintendent or the chief social worker. In short, the procedure established often was inconvenient for the social workers and the field staff alike. As a consequence, many progress reports were completed with little or no information of the inmate's current home situation, or the court history summary continued to be used.

Although these shortcomings in organizational operation were discussed in staff meetings as deficiencies to be corrected in order to provide better "service" to the inmates, the overriding concern of Central's top-ranking staff was to bring about fundamental and radical changes in the institution's operating procedures. Central's department heads were more critical of their program—and the position taken by the parent organization—than were the staffs at Eastern and Western. They thought of and described themselves as institutional workers with *expertise*, and hence believed that they were placed in a unique position to determine Central's future role and the kinds of services to be provided. As early as a year before the study began, the deputy superintendent's department head's meetings had been taken up with a discussion of their traditional services, and each department's separate goals projected over a five-year period. Many months later, these discussions formed the substance of a "position paper" that was submitted—after review and approval by the superintendent—to the state youth commission. By taking a "where we stand" position, the Central staff thought that the youth commission would be pressed to spell out its future plans for Central specifically, and for corrections in the entire state generally. Many of the staff—although by no means all—agreed with the view taken by a Protestant minister who played an active part in all institutional affairs. In a report entitled: "A Look into the Future," he commented as follows:

With deep appreciation for the many positive changes that have taken place, there is at the same time a feeling that the pendulum has swung too far in the direction of formal, academic training as the chief function of training schools under the [State] Youth Commission.

This seems to arise out of our desire to impose middle-class standards on youngsters to whom such standards are completely foreign. We try to train these children as though they were our own. In one sense that is commendable, but they are *not* our children and the vast majority of them will never live in the manner which we desire for our own children. These children were born in the inner city. There they will live out their lives and most of them will die in those same surroundings. These are the cold hard facts of life which we seem to grasp only vaguely.

In this field, one grows familiar (and often a little weary) with the bulky, psychological evaluations which become a part of the case history and diagnosis of our children. To what purpose is this lengthy and costly study? In most cases it has, at best, only a slight relationship to any remedial program which will be instituted within the training schools.

We need a wholly new and practical kind of evaluation based on the actual life situation of the child. . . . These children remain with us only a brief time. That time is all too brief to be wasted on efforts which are not clearly related to their actual functioning in their own community.

The question raised by the Central staff—and to which they were seeking definitive answers—concerned the use to which the institution would be put in the future, and the extent to which the commission's resources would be allocated to community-based facilities. Although the administrative staff at Central believed that a "need" for a "place" like Central would always exist, they advocated strict intake control in order that Central could concentrate on target populations. Convinced as they were that future commitments increasingly would be "hard core children" such as drug users, hippies, political prisoners, and civil rights activists, they urged that no child be committed to the youth commission unless his or her behavior was such that if committed by an adult it would constitute a legal offense.

Yet the administrative staff's philosophy and the goals to be pursued (which advocated a humanistic approach consistent with social work practice) were as vague in concept and design as the formulations of which they were so critical. Apart from simply stating that certain institutional departments should be expanded, or that new programs should be introduced, no reasons were given why existing procedures should be changed or eliminated, nor were the required new methods spelled out. Nor could they explain why they had been unable to implement the treatment procedures advocated by recognized authorities, with which the administrative staff members were familiar. This last is all the more surprising because the Central staff had—short of demanding nonexistent funds—virtually a free hand to make program changes within the institutional structure, although some limitations existed in terms of external relations with and the demands of the administrative bodies of the youth commission.

CHAPTER SEVEN

The Organization of Treatment Services:

Western

Unlike Eastern and Central, Western institution is administered by a youth authority, whose Board has been delegated the authority to commit individuals to institutions and to authorize institutional release; hence the Western inmates meet with the Board before parole. The three institutions studied were characterized by a certain uniformity of format and nomenclature in record keeping that was typical of each statewide correctional system, but Western's institutional program resembled the existing programs in the authority's other institutions. This was directly related to the program uniformity that was imposed by the parent organization. At Eastern and Central, the administrative heads had more autonomy in the internal operation of their institutions, and they had considerable freedom to implement treatment programs and models of their own choosing. By contrast, the situation at Western was more restricted. Programs and treatment models were often planned by the youth authority staff and implemented by the institutional superintendents. Sometimes a new program would be tried in one institution, and other institutional administrators would "wait to see" before implementing a similar program in their own institution. For example, Western's superintendent continued the practice of mail censorship (although the inmates complained) because noncensorship of mail had been "tried for a while" in an institution for males, but problems with contraband had been experienced. The "wait to see" stand had other important consequences: Even though a restructuring of organizational functions to cottage teams had already been made, the authority for decision making had not been delegated to the treatment teams.

In fact, the structural changes observed during my study were begun almost a decade earlier. The major innovation was the structural reorganization along the lines of an integrated team approach, patterned after the mental health concept of a therapeutic community. In its developed state, this conceptual framework means a fundamental change in organizational structure; the "specialists" who normally have only formal ties to each other and to institution department units are combined into integrated treatment teams. Ideally, a cottage team approach combines all the direct service disciplines so that divisions between custodial and professional distinctions are nonexistent. To be effective, authority for decision making must be shifted from the institution classification committee—consisting of an individual from all the traditional service areas—to the practitioner level of the team. With a fully operational integrated team structure, the traditional institution classification committee is functionally obsolete. This was not the outcome at Western, however, because authority for high-level decision making had not been delegated by the superintendent to the cottage teams. Thus in only the most superficial sense was a team approach operative in each of Western's living units. Rather, a "cottage team" structure had been superimposed on the existing custodial framework. Because the existing custodial hierarchy and other administrative groupings remained functionally intact, important decisions concerning institutional operation continued to be made from the basic viewpoint of custody.

In short, although it was declared publicly that cottage teams had been established as the important functional unit, the institution operated essentially according to the traditional organization framework of discrete departments as outlined on the formal organizational chart.

INSTITUTION GOALS AND IMPLEMENTED TRADITIONAL PROGRAMS. The mission of the department of the youth authority as defined in the youth authority Act of Western state is

> . . . to protect society more effectively by substituting for retributive punishment methods of training and treatment directed toward the correction and rehabilitation of young persons found guilty of public offenses.

The broad program goals for institutions serving juvenile delinquents in Western state are set forth in an official document as follows:

> Treatment efforts of the youth authority are directed toward care, custody and rehabilitation of young offenders. Individualized treatment is stressed. Varied institutional and parole programs have been developed, and the department has been credited with national leadership in new treatment approaches.
>
> Each child committed to the youth authority is first sent to a reception center and clinic for a complete diagnostic study in his case. Through this study to determine the causes of delinquency, the most effective rehabilitative approaches and techniques can be included in the individual's program. Assignment can then be made by the youth authority Board to one of the many different programs. . . . Youths are sometimes placed in institutions operated by the State department of corrections.

The institutional brochure prepared for public distribution by Western's superintendent stated that "the entire institution is geared to treatment." Despite this pronouncement, I observed that Western's much talked about treatment program had not been fully implemented.

Like Eastern and Central, the overall responsibility to carry out Western's organizational goals had been delegated to a single administrative head. The administrative structure of Western, however, was drawn sharply along the lines of three major departments: (1) a department of business services supervised by a business manager; (2) the custodial department headed by the head group supervisor; and (3) a department responsible for clinical and casework services called the *psychiatric treatment unit*. But whatever programs were incorporated into the organizational structure, it was assumed that the traditional services would continue to be provided, including academic and vocational training, organized recreation, work programs, medical and dental care, clinical services, and religious services.

No attempt had been made at Western to coordinate the treatment and custodial departments under the supervisory control of one administrative head. (As Eastern and Central moved in the direction of increased treatment, this administrative structure had been developed by the superintendents of these institutions.) Western's superintendent exercised direct supervisory control over all the major departments, although an intermediate but extremely limited stratum of supervisory control—regarding the head group supervisor and the supervisor of academic instruction—

had been delegated to the assistant superintendent. In the handling of most institutional matters, Western's superintendent contacted the department heads directly, thus maintaining tight administrative control from above.[1]

The cottage organization that was present at Eastern and Central was also observed at Western. Western's cottage staff consisted of the group supervisors, and a senior group supervisor was functionally responsible for the overall cottage operation. However, the custodial hierarchy officially extended from the cottage group supervisors to the assistant head group supervisors. The head group supervisors were at the top of the chain of authority as far as inmate discipline was concerned; moreover, they exercised supervisory jurisdiction of the cottage group supervisors and evaluated their job performance. This structure of control had important implications for the subsequent cottage team units. Meanwhile, the custodial orientation was reflected in several organizational structures. The traditional "classification" department (still housed in the administration building) had been retained as a functional unit, although the classification section as such was functionally obsolete due to (1) the reorganization of the cottage units; and (2) the fact that classification and diagnostic services were provided in the authority's reception centers prior to institutional commitment.

The basic custodial orientation of Western school was also reflected in other features of its organizational structure. For example, the laundry, housekeeping, and food service departments—production areas which utilized inmate labor for their continued operation—were all placed under the jurisdiction of the business manager.[2] Similar functional areas at Eastern and Central had been incorporated into the vocational departments of the academic schools; indeed, at Central—and to a more limited extent at Eastern—inmates who were enrolled in vocational areas of this type participated in related classroom instruction. At Western, however, the inmates' participation in the production areas was necessary because there were no staff to perform these tasks. The work assignments were described to the Western inmates by a classification counselor rather than by a cottage team. The academic school merely received the names of the inmates who had been assigned to specific jobs in order to give the inmates school credit for "enrolling" in a production area.

The rhetoric of "training" and the possible applications of this training to future work roles was made by Western's administrator. In the memorandum reproduced below, the broad rationale for the inmates' participation in various work assignments is set forth.

August 26, 1969

To: All Cottages

Subject: Ward Work Assignments

Work assignments in the institution are of necessity production-oriented, and need to be regarded in this light for staffing is based on this premise. Therefore, when a girl does not report for an assignment, production at the institution suffers.

Girls are selected for assignments based on the girl's own request, but she is expected to stay on the assignment for a period of time [three months] in order to derive benefits from that assignment. She receives school credit. She learns new skills and work habits which may be helpful to future employment, and she has an opportunity to interact with another adult with whom she will very closely work.

Therefore, assignments are not to be taken lightly, and attendance should be maintained as part and parcel of the girl's growth toward responsibility. Medical reasons, documented by our medical department, should be the one valid reason for not attending a work assignment. On occasion there may be a documented reason, such as an unexpected visit from her family and so forth. However, reluctance or a feeling of indolence should not be sufficient for a supervisor on a cottage to excuse a girl from her work assignment. Her volunteering for an assignment other than her regular one should not be an excuse to get out of a regular assignment.

In other words, if a girl has signed up for an assignment she has the responsibility to carry through. If for any compelling reason a girl wishes to change her assignment she should first talk with her work supervisor, and then with Mrs. Thompson [academic school supervisor]. Mrs. Thompson can then check with the work supervisor for her recommendation.

If a regular assigned girl is not to report to her assignment because of a medical excuse or visitors, other girls on the cottage should be rotated into the assignment for that shift.

Bertha Whitehead
Superintendent

The subject of inmate labor had never been challenged by Western's cottage staff. As is true of all correctional schools, inmate labor at Western was taken for granted. Table 7.1 indicates clearly that the work tasks to which the Western inmates have been assigned are fitted into the maintenance needs of the institution.

Table 7.1   Work Assignments

Work Assignment	Number	%
Central kitchen and cottage kitchen (includes cart girls)	68	42.8
Housekeeping (buildings other than cottages)	15	9.4
Cottage housekeeping workers	31	19.5
Laundry	9	5.7
Clothing room	1	0.6
Nurse, dental, teacher's, and ward aides	7	4.4
State hospital aides	6	3.8
No work assignment	22	13.8
Total	159	100.0

The administrative heads of all three institutions faced similar operational problems in connection with maintenance. The differences among them regarding the number of inmates assigned to specific tasks are due mainly to the size of the physical plant and differences in organizational structure. For example, since Western did not operate a canteen or commissary, there were no salesclerks. (The Western inmates who wished to purchase certain items—they could spend $3.00 of their own funds every two weeks—presented a shopping list to a staff member who did the shopping at a small store near the school.) All the inmates at Western were expected to work, and soon after their arrival they were assigned to specific work tasks.[3] Most of the inmates are assigned to work in the laundry, central kitchen, housekeeping, and cottage kitchen, with a few inmates holding the more specialized jobs such as nurse, dental, and teacher aides. When an inmate "signed up" for a work assignment, she bound herself to a *contract* for a period of three months. During this time, an inmate could not change her work assignments. If an inmate is assigned to work in the kitchen, she performs the same task for the entire three months—if assigned to clean vegetables, for example, she cleans vegetables for three months. Moreover, an inmate was kept working beyond the three-month period if a replacement was not available—especially if she worked in the main kitchen. The Eastern and Central inmates could change their work assignments under some circumstances, although work tasks were rotated once a month.

Table 7.1 shows that six inmates were working as state hospital aides; these inmates worked in a nearby hospital for mentally retarded children five days a week—four hours each day—and they were paid fifty cents an hour. Only six inmates were participating in the program at the time that the inmates completed the questionnaire, although a total of twelve inmates could be accommodated. The hospital aide training was made possible through a federal grant.

Because most institutions are located far from the resources of urban communities, work programs and other community linkages are not only extremely difficult to arrange and sustain, but also, the major expenditures of such programs are allocated to administrative costs. At Western, most of the program's funds were allocated to staff salaries: It was necessary for two youth counselors to accompany the inmates to the hospital site and supervise them while they worked there. One staff member had been diverted from the academic school to devote all her time to the administration of this program; secretarial staff also added to the total cost.

Although it was maintained that the subject matter of Western's academic school ranged from remedial work through high school in order to accommodate the inmates' needs, it was in fact extremely limited compared to the curriculum of Eastern and Central. Fewer courses were offered at Western, and there was less emphasis on classroom instruction; programmed workbooks were used without any discussion by the teachers. There was no library at Western. Federal funds had made possible an arrangement whereby the public library located ten miles away operated a bookmobile one day a week at Western. None of the inmates were transported to the community public library, nor was such an arrangement explored when the plans for bookmobile service were made. The inmates could check out two books every two weeks.

Vocational programs did not exist at Western. The cosmetology course at Western was not certified because the necessary space, equipment, and instruction did not meet the standards set by the state licensing department. Large numbers of inmates attended classes in cooking and family living. A course in arts and crafts was part of the academic school's curriculum. Although a course in typing was offered at Western, there were none in office practice, shorthand, office machines, and related business subjects—all of which were standard courses at Central and at Eastern. Many of the Western inmates—especially the older ones—expressed a keen interest in such subjects, as possibly providing skills for future employment. There was no educational program for the Western inmates who had already completed high school, nor was it possible for them to attend schools outside the institution. School clubs in connection with course work and other academic school activities were nonexistent.

Because of the severe restrictions placed on campus movement, the recreation program at Western was more limited than at Eastern and Central. Most of the recreational activities provided (such as swimming in the outdoor pool) were part of the academic school's physical education classes. Evening recreation (usually in the school gymnasium) was infrequent and involved very few inmates. Unless an inmate's "off-campus privilege" had been approved, her movement on campus during the evening was altogether prohibited. In general, movement "after dark" was kept to a minimum for all the inmates, and most activities at Western were held during the day. Movies were shown every two weeks on Saturday afternoon; dances with incarcerated delinquent boys were still considered to be in the "experimental" stage, and were held very infrequently. In short, there were few structured recreational activities at Western.

Clearly, education played a secondary role at Western. In the classroom, the participants were constantly being interrupted by the ringing of the telephone. Most of the calls were to notify the teacher that a student's presence was required elsewhere. The inmates were called from classes for a wide variety of reasons—small group counseling, individual counseling with the inmate's "therapist," other procedural matters in connection with casework functions, cottage progress review sessions, substitute help in work areas—especially in the main kitchen,[4] to obtain and return library books, to obtain the services of the nurse or dentist, and for many other matters.

The hospital staff with its physican, dentist, and nursing staff (the latter were registered nurses) were altogether isolated from general campus affairs. To some degree, the charge could also be leveled at Eastern and Central. However, at Eastern and Central, an attempt was made to coordinate the hospital staff's functions with vocational training, and representatives from all hospital service departments participated in all top-level staff meetings. By contrast, Western's hospital staff members were restricted to performing outpatient services and caring for an occasional bed patient in the hospital wing and the new arrivals who were hospitalized for a day or two before being assigned to a cottage. The fact that a youth supervisor is detailed to the hospital is indicative of Western's custodial emphasis, although the official statements are couched in the language of treatment.

THE "PSYCHIATRIC STAFF" AND COTTAGE TEAM STRUCTURE.

Clinical services at Western were provided by the "psychiatric staff" consisting of a supervising social worker, six therapists (sometimes referred to as social workers),[5] a psychiatrist, and the psychiatric treatment unit supervisor. Western was the only institution with a full-time psychiatrist, although the treatment unit supervisor maintained that "little use" was made of the psychiatrist except as an occasional "consultant" to the staff. At Western, tranquilizers as a form of social control were used more often than they were at Eastern and Central; and the cottage staff (especially in the maximum security unit) often requested the psychiatrist's help in handling their "disturbed" inmates.

Despite the presence of a separate psychiatric treatment unit building, Western was similar to Eastern and Central in that only very recently had "social work coverage" been extended to all the cottages. The tenure of the therapists ranged from less than six months for some of them to fifteen years for one individual; three therapists had worked approximately two years. All were college graduates, but their educational background varied; four had received social work training, one had majored in English, and another in psychology. The supervisor of the unit had received some graduate training in psychology. Until very recently, the therapists each had a caseload of two cottages, and their major responsibility had consisted of casework functions. Like the social workers at Eastern and Central, Western's clinical staff worked only during the day; their work week was not adjusted to provide services at times convenient to the inmates. Nor had the effort to reorganize the Western staff into integrated teams been accompanied by a change in the hours and days worked by the professional staff. In all three institutions, the cottage staff had the most continuous and sustained contact with the inmates.

All staff members at Western were not included in the cottage team structure: the cottage teams included the cottage group counselors, a therapist, and one or two representatives from the teaching staff. Western was the only school to assign teachers to cottage teams—although all the teachers were not members of teams. Officially, two or three teachers were members of each team: usually only one teacher on each team attended the daily community counseling meetings, and sometimes there were none at all. The teachers did not participate in the small group meetings. Decision making was to be shared by the team members, hence absenteeism posed special problems. The staff's solution to absenteeism was to redefine the team structure as made up of the "team members who are present." When one considers the work schedule of the therapists and the teachers, it becomes apparent that the "team" sometimes consisted of one cottage youth counselor.

Unlike the situation at Eastern and Central, the social workers at Western were merely members of a team. When the cottage youth counselors' title was changed from that of *supervisor* to *counselor,*[6] their duties were broadened to include the writing of progress and Board reports. The social workers supervised only the "clinical aspects" of the youth counselor's work, such as the preparation of case reports. All other aspects of the counselor's role were evaluated by the assistant head group supervisors, which indicates the emphasis placed on the custodial aspects of the youth counselor's role.

In theory, each team was under the jurisdiction of a team *coordinator;* the individuals so named were the head group supervisor, an assistant head group supervisor, a classification counselor, the training officer, and the treatment unit supervisor. The "team coordinators," however, continued to function in their traditional work roles as if the teams had not been formally instituted. The team coordinators did not attend the group therapy meetings and, indeed, rarely went to the cottages.

Authority for decision making was still concentrated at the top of the administrative hierarchy; the cottage teams dealt only with superficial matters. The team structure had been superimposed on the existing organizational framework, but the traditional lines of authority remained intact. The teams' suggestions and "decisions" were reviewed by the classification committee and other administrative groups; the latter were differentiated by name and meeting schedule but they essentially duplicated one another in function and membership. However, if the cottage teams were fully operational in the functional terms claimed for them, the middle management positions—especially the classification counselors and supervisory custodial and treatment unit personnel—would be obsolete. In short, there was wide disparity between the official claims regarding the functions of the treatment teams and their place in the actual operation of the institution.

The social workers were marginal to the hierarchical framework that traced structural authority from the head group supervisor to the assistant head group supervisors and, finally, to the cottage staff. As we would expect, the cottage staff turned for guidance to the custodial supervisory staff—their immediate superiors—rather than to the social workers. The lack of leadership attributable to the cottage teams meant that the institutional program's conservative orientation persisted, and all decisions at the cottage level continued to be made in accordance with custodial principles. This process was facilitated by the fact that the team coordinators were old-line personnel who had worked at the institution for many years[7] and could be expected to implement treatment programs at the cautious pace set by Western's administrator.

A recently hired youth counselor, a college graduate, explains the dilemma from her point of view:

> When I first began to work here I was fresh out of college. You have all these ideas about all the changes you're going to make—to apply all the things you learned in college to rehabilitate. You try to express your views to the rest of the staff—that other ways of doing things might be more effective. But after you're here a while, you become institutionalized. You find out that's not what's wanted. People who have been here a long time are the ones that make the decisions. They're the ones who call the shots. They really don't want change. Things are comfortable the way they are, and you have to conform if you want to stay. All we're doing is getting the girls to adjust to the institution; and they're so adaptable—they'll adapt to anything. It doesn't even make a difference if you have a college education. After a while you change. You do things just like they've always been done here.

When individuals who have special training are dissatisfied with the existing treatment programs, they usually terminate their employment; the staff members who remain perpetuate traditional institutional methods by conforming to the status quo. For this reason, organizations are more likely to exhibit rapid structural change when trained personnel—with unquestioned authority to implement program innovations—are brought into an organization for this purpose, rather than to leave the task of innovative organizational change to old-line personnel.

Western's program differed from that of Eastern and Central institutions in that the treatment model used throughout the cottages combined community group therapy, small group therapy, and individual therapy. In all the counseling activities, the inmates' participation was mandatory. The teachers participated only in the cottage counseling meetings that were held after each school day for thirty minutes. A half-hour following the meeting was to be utilized by the team members in a *critique* of the group discussion. During the critique, the inmates were locked in their rooms.

Both the therapists and the cottage youth counselors had "caseloads"; each caseload converted to a "small group" for which each staff person was to provide individual therapy for the members. Inasmuch as each therapist conducted only one small group therapy session—the large group meetings were conducted by the senior youth counselors—most of the small group leaders were youth counselors. For individual therapy, both the youth counselors and the therapists presented themselves as "therapists" to the inmates.

To "provide" each youth counselor with a small group, cottage populations were divided into five small units; these groups varied in size from a few that listed one inmate member to others that had as many as eight members. The everchanging composition of the small groups created serious problems for group leaders. Because new inmates had to "prove" to the other inmate members that they could be trusted, the equilibrium necessary for significant group participation was rarely achieved, and the topics discussed were often on a superficial level. Moreover, the staff's reaction to the inmates' informal social system was so compelling that the meeting time of both the large and small group meetings often focused on this subject.

Although officially scheduled to meet each week for one hour, many of the small groups met infrequently because of the competing demands on a staff member's time, or simply inertia on the part of the staff. No staff member was responsible for ascertaining that the weekly group and individual counseling requirements were met; nor were substitute arrangements for counseling services made when group leaders went on vacation or were ill. One small group had not had a meeting for three months, although the names of the group members continued to be listed on the weekly roster.

The method of having the inmates of particular groups go to their group leader with their problems fell short of providing individual treatment to the inmates. Some staff members refused altogether to "do things" for inmates who were not in their caseload; furthermore, when an inmate was placed in room confinement, discussion would be postponed until her "therapist" came on duty, although this might be for an entire day or longer. Also, an inmate's mail might be delayed, as the task of censoring an inmate's mail properly was that of the "therapist." In most cases, cooperative arrangements had been worked out—whoever was on duty in the cottage read the mail. But even these informal arrangements were ignored under some circumstances. A staff member explains:

When two staff people have a difference, they'll get back by taking it out on one of your girls. A girl will want her mail and she [staff on duty] won't read it so the girl has to wait a few hours before she gets her mail from home. The therapist is supposed to read a girl's mail, but on our dorm whoever's on the dorm is supposed to read the mail.

One might believe that group counseling was a new treatment method at Western. Actually, group counseling had been introduced on a piecemeal basis almost ten years earlier because group counseling had become common practice in the authority's other institutions. The gradual expansion of group counseling at Western has been uncoordinated and unplanned; nonprofessional staff members are used interchangeably with the professional staff, but there has been little staff training. The methods employed by the staff varied from those who assumed a passive role as group leader to others who tended to be authoritarian and/or didactic. In most cases, group counseling took the form of inmate bull sessions; some group meetings consisted of a question-and-answer period based on institutional matters—especially the informal social system of the inmates; and in a few groups conducted by the trained social workers, the meetings followed the model of informal sessions designed to develop insight into a member's attitudes and behavior. During the teams' critique sessions that followed, the content of the group meetings usually was not discussed; instead the team discussed other institutional matters, engaged in gossip, or went about cottage duties unencumbered by the presence of the inmates. Because of the convenience afforded the staff, the inmates were often kept locked in their rooms beyond the time that had been established for critique.

In addition to the lack of trained staff, a major administrative problem was the obsolescence of the physical plant. The cottages simply had not been designed for activities of a more complex nature than that of confining inmates in their rooms, mass feeding in the dining room, and limited quiet recreational activities in the living room area. Consider the implications of conducting group therapy meetings in this limited space! Some of the small group therapy meetings were held in the combination kitchen-dining room. This arrangement was held to be unsatisfactory by the professional social workers because other inmates wandered into the kitchen when the meetings were in session; and staff members—especially assistant head group supervisors—would use the telephone in the kitchen. The constant ringing of the telephone irritated the group members.

Most of the youth counselors were expected to supervise the entire cottage group while they conducted their small group meetings; hence these meetings were often held in the dayroom so that the youth counselor could at the same time supervise the other inmates who were watching television. The lack of privacy imposed by this arrangement created serious problems on a number of levels for the therapy group. The available space in the psychiatric treatment unit and in the administration building was not used for small group meetings mainly because the movement of the inmates was highly restricted—especially during the evening and weekend when a skeleton staff was on duty.[8]

Locating a suitable meeting place also had to be resolved in the case of individual therapy, together with the task of fitting the process itself into the staff's work schedule. The therapists often used their offices for "individual," but the youth counselors usually "talked" to the inmates who made up their caseload while performing other duties as, for example, when supervising the inmates who worked in the cottage kitchens. It was difficult to perform these functions simultaneously in any case, but the fact that other inmates interrupted the therapy process by contacting the staff member added to the problem. The Western inmates were never called from their work assignments to participate in "group" or "individual," although the inmates were frequently removed from academic school classes for this purpose. The experiences of the two staff members who are quoted below sums it up for Western's cottage staff.

If I didn't keep her in the cottage from school when I first come on duty in the morning, I would never get to talk to her. The morning youth counselor calls girls out of school for individual. They have to if they're going to talk to them—otherwise they won't be on the dorm.

We had a party on the dorm, and there were girls that had to be in the kitchen to do some things, and I had to supervise them. So I took this girl in and said: "I'll have to talk to you in there." There was nothing else I could do. There's no time on the dorm. You do it when you have time—*if you can!* When other things come up on the dorm, or meetings or other activities—you have to forget your group meetings or individual.

Once an inmate is assigned to a youth counselor's caseload by the cottage social worker, she cannot change her therapist; indeed, there was considerable resentment by the staff when another staff member assumed reponsibility for inmates who were not in her caseload. Moreover, the informal social system of the inmates affected all relationships between staff and the inmates. An inmate had only to state that a staff member "can do nothing to help me," point to another whom she perceived to be more successful in the treatment role, and the rejected staff member would very likely imply that the interaction between them should be examined. The following exchange between a youth counselor and an inmate during a group therapy meeting provides an example.

[During the meeting no topic had been brought up for discussion. The group leader was observed whispering to one inmate. The other inmates were carrying on separate conversations. After thirty-five minutes had elapsed, the group leader turned to one of the inmates and began to speak.]

GROUP LEADER. What's wrong?

INMATE. I don't feel I can talk to you. You don't talk to me. All you do is throw us in our room and leave us there, but you never come in to see how you can help. That's why I like Ikeda [staff member]. She really shows concern, and she can talk to me. She comes in and talks. She's the only one that does that—that shows she cares. Here, they just throw you in your room and leave you there.

GROUP LEADER. [Her face was flushed and her eyes brimmed with tears.] I think you should think about your relationship with Ikeda.

INMATE. What do you mean—*relationship*? I've just told you. I feel she understands, and I can talk to her. I feel she really cares about what happens to the girls—about *all* the girls. Not like most people who work in institutions, and I've been in a few, so I know what I'm talking about.

A social worker who was assigned to a cottage other than that of the group leader above brought up the same theme:

The staff have their personal jealousies. If a ward says: "The only one who can help me on this dorm is *so and so!*" it makes the other one jealous. Or she might say: "You can't help me. I can't talk to you; I can only talk to *so and so*." There was a situation on the dorm last week—it almost split the dorm staff in two. It concerned Patricia Kane [youngest staff member] and one girl talking to her. The staff thought it was *too close!* She [the ward] didn't talk to anyone else on the dorm—the other staff. Staff deeply resent it when other staff talk to the wards in their caseload. And the wards are aware of this.

THE "SPECIAL" TREATMENT STRATEGIES. Although many members of Western's staff and all the inmates had been involved in group and individual therapy for almost a decade, these treatment methods had not been evaluated by either the Western staff or the youth authority's central office staff. Nevertheless, these methods were being augmented by other treatment methods that recently had been implemented elsewhere in the authority's institutions. Although the programs were not yet fully operational, "special treatment programs" based on I-level (interpersonal maturity level) classifications officially identified two living units at Western; and a "special" program in another cottage was referred to as the "behavior modification system program."[9] Although all the inmates' I-level was to be determined at the diagnostic and reception center, and the *type* incorporated in the "clinic" reports, the center failed to provide I-level classifications for all the inmates. Even so, Western's administrator often cited as an "accomplishment" the fact that inmates were assigned to two living units on the basis of two I-level classifications, namely, I_4Nx and I_4Na.[10] But an examination of the official records indicated that the reception clinic had not provided I-level classifications for fully 38.4 percent of Western's inmate population. Moreover, in the cottage reserved for "Nx's," 53.3 percent of the inmates either had no I-level classification, or their I-level classification differed from that which the cottage's I-level program necessitated. Likewise, the cottage presumably programmed for "Na's," showed a similar disparity: 61.5 percent of the inmates either had no I-level classification appearing on their records, or they were types not indicated for this cottage. Although both of the "homogeneous" units contained a wide variety of I-level types, some inmates who had been typed as I_4Nx and I_4Na were housed in other cottages rather than the homogeneous units.

Theoretically, I-level classification is said to be the diagnostic component of a differential treatment system. The I-level diagnosis becomes the starting point of differential treatment planning—more specifically, the setting of treatment goals for an individual that are based on the problems identified by the I-level diagnosis, and the specifying of the method to be used to reach the goals established. Clearly, homogeneous assignment is not differential treatment, nor is I-level diagnosis a treatment method in itself.[11]

In most institutions, even when the inmate's age is used in making cottage assignments, the available bed space is taken into account. Western was no exception; cottage assignments were always made on the basis of convenience, notwithstanding the official claims of "I-level cottage programs." Not only were the cottages not composed of the homogeneous types specified, but the cottage team members had not received the training that presumably was required to "work with the types."

The task of establishing treatment goals for the inmates had become part of the administrative process at Western because of the Board's insistence on concrete criteria of institutional treatment. This posed a dilemma for Western's staff: A statement of goals could always be made, but the matter of providing evidence that the goals had actually been accomplished in the institution was quite a different matter. Academic school grades could be shown; but other treatment claims were based on sheer speculation. Behavior modification techniques which utilized operant conditioning principles appealed to the Western staff precisely because of the possibility that "tangible data" could be marshaled before the Board to assess any inmate's institutional adjustment.

Treatment by behavior modification techniques presumably focuses on the specific behavior to be changed and the environmental contingencies or mental images related to that behavior.[12] At Western, however, the general medical model that considers delinquency to be a symptom of an organic or mental disease was retained; the behavior modification techniques had been added to, but did not replace, the existing cottage routine. Thus, community counseling, small group meetings, and individual therapy were part of the program in the "behavior modification cottage" as they were in the other cottages; however, the team "contracted" with the inmates to behave in certain specified ways.

The official approach to operant conditioning at Western may be briefly stated. Goals were to be diagnosed and established for each inmate. When the appropriate goal response or behavior was received or observed, reinforcing rewards were to be given to the inmates. The assumption was that through continued reinforcement of a "certain behavior" or goal, the inmate is gradually "locked into" the behavior that had been "set" for her by the staff. Delinquent behavior was defined as "critical behavior deficiencies"—that is, "all the behaviors related to delinquency which the ward performs in the community, but because opportunities are not present, seldom if ever performs in the institution."[13]

The contracts were designed to provide three types of information: (1) The inmate's written statement indicating the behavior that she was contracting to demonstrate; (2) the payment to be received by the inmate if the terms of the contract were completed (contracts did not run beyond one week, but inmates usually received partial payment); and (3) verification of the indicated behavior. The date of contract completion was shown and the signatures of the inmate and the staff member(s) were also required. Contracts were sometimes renewed for several weeks until conformity was observed.

Typical examples of contracts drawn up by the Western inmates in consultation with the staff are shown below.

I will behave in a way that will not require extra supervision. I will not be disrespectful in my responses and not complain when told to do something. Payment: 250 points and $3.00 per signature.

Approach or join in on a conversation with the staff. Payment: $10.00 per signature.

Be helpful and offer my services to Y.C. and other staff as needed. Contact each staff listed by next individual on Friday, else no points and no pay. Payment: 100 points and $100.00 cash.

I will not get any Special Incidents, Behavior Management Report slips, or any complaining phone calls from my details. Or be questioned about dorm details. Payment: 300 points and $5.00 per signature.

Write at least six ways I can discourage Chick Business. Payment: $5.00 for each listed.

I will write 10 times my curse words. Example, I will stop using shit. Payment: 100 points.

Wear a clean ironed uniform each day as per my noon server position. I will have all my buttons sewed on. Payment 100 points and $15.00 per signature. When contract is presented to youth counselor, $50.00 bonus for all signatures.

I am going to obtain a job. Payment: 150 points; $100.00 bonus.

To hold off any rash actions or hasty decisions on any immediate problems till youth counselor returns from days off. Payment: $100.00 per day

I will not involve myself in talk or show action about homosexual actions or talk in any manner. Payment: 150 points and $3.00 per signature, not to exceed two signatures per day.

I will not show rudeness, irony, or sarcasm when asked a question. I will answer properly. Payment: 300 points. $5.00 per staff signature.

I will bring my grade up in history class. Payment: 200 points and $100.00.

I will speak up in small group. Payment: $100.00.

Arrange my own individual session at least two hrs. in advance, not more than one day. Preferable days, Friday, Saturday. Payment: 100 points.

Will not receive any negative remarks in the chrono book. [cottage log] Payment: $200.00 if completed. $20.00 a day. If go full week w/o any remarks, $40.00 bonus.

Contribute and/or respond to individuals in small group at least three times next meeting. Contribution and/or response must be more than a yes-no. Must be verbal. Payment: 150 points.

I will not use profane or unladylike gestures at any time. Payment: $3.00 per signature, $15.00 bonus for all signatures, and 150 points.

Talk with each staff listed below at their convenience for ten minutes about anything but be serious. Payment: First step toward youth counselor recommending my off-campus privilege. $5.00 for each signature.

Agree to grow my eyebrows and keep them after they have grown where they look nice to my satisfaction and Y.C.'s satisfaction. Payment: 10 points weekly.

Western's contract methodology was explained during a meeting held between the staff members of the behavior modification program, and another cottage team (designated here as Cottage Z) who were interested in implementing the same program in their own cottage. In the written material provided to the staff assembled by Western's training officer, contracts were described in the following way:

> Contracts are useful tools in setting limits and *shaping* behavior. As you both get more expert, you may have more than one behavior—maybe a whole *chain* of them—lead to the "Pay Off." You can look at the steps involved—called progress checking—to see how she is coming along. Is she really performing and are you really reinforcing? You *confront* her, provide her with *feedback, model* behavior you want her to develop. . . . The time has come for her to be referred. She has earned her assigned BCU's [behavior change units]. You will know where she was when she first arrived and what she has accomplished. You will be able to report this briefly, concisely, and understandably to the team and the Board. Both you and the ward can feel good when she leaves. Her departure demonstrates that the set of procedures you put in motion and implemented produced behavior changes beneficial to her. This is called *Behavior Therapy.*

As to the "why" of contracts, the staff members who utilized operant conditioning techniques explained:

SPOKESMAN A (BEHAVIOR MODIFICATION PROGRAM). Behavior modification principles work. This is not theory. This is a fact. I call this list a workhorse series. It's simple and it works like this: [*The following series was written on the blackboard.*]

1. See behavior you want—*maintain* (or increase).
2. See behavior you don't want—*quit.*
3. Don't see behavior you want—*produce.*

When I think of contracts, I like to think of trouble behaviors. They may not be for these things only, but I like to keep these at the top of the list. The girl should do as much as she can. If you can get her to do it all, that is good.

SOCIAL WORKER (COTTAGE Z). Parole officers have criticized behavior modification as it emphasizes institutional behavior. This is what the girls mean when they say, "What does this have to do with my problems outside? I don't want to do this. This has nothing to do with my problems outside! This isn't going to help me out there."

SPOKESMAN B (BEHAVIOR MODIFICATION PROGRAM). Some couldn't care less about the program. The ones that are on *welfare*. They have everything they need. Others say, "Why should we have to pay for these things?" They've got them coming. Why should they have to pay to go off campus? They should be able to go when they have a chance! Why should they have to pay to go to the nurse? Bettyanne said she was sick and wanted to go to the nurse, and raised a rumpus because she didn't have the money to go. I checked it out with other staff people and none of us knew what to do. *It was on the menu.* We finally let her go. She raised such a rumpus.

SPOKESMAN A (BEHAVIOR MODIFICATION PROGRAM). Behavior modification principles *work. We want desirable behavior to happen, but we can't sit around and wait for it!* We have to contract for it.

In general, the inmates' contracts were linked to the institutional rules rather than to the behavior deficiencies indicated in the "printouts." The fact that the latter were received many weeks after the checklists were completed cannnot explain the lack of importance that the staff placed on the information provided (nor, indeed, by the manner in which they were completed). Rather, the staff were influenced by the following concerns: First, they little understood the sample contracts in the manual that were to guide their own "contracting"; presumably, these examples were related to factors indicating specific behavior deficiencies. What they did understand, however, was an inmate's nonparticipation in the institutional routine and the violation of institutional rules. More important, they could design contracts to correct nonconformity to the institutional rules without any difficulty.

In practice, the behavior modification program was organized specifically to deal with institutional management problems. The contracts which presumably were the vehicles whereby the inmates were to accomplish the "treatment goals" that had been set for them related specifically to internal management concerns, but only rarely with the delinquencies leading to incarceration. Some of the institutional rules were designated as *convenience behaviors*, and fines for each rule were established. Moreover, the disposition of the institutional rules that appeared on other lists, separate administrative directives, and the rules that were communicated verbally, could also include a fine, arbitrarily determined by the staff.

An example of a convenience behavior list that was in use during the time of the field work is shown in Appendix D.

A set number of parole points (called behavior change units) was determined as the basis for referral to parole. Determination of the points was based on the Board order and an estimate of the inmate's period of incarceration. The points were in the areas of critical behavior deficiencies, academic grades, school behavior, and job performance; the greatest emphasis was placed on job performance. Once the determined number of points to be earned was assigned, the information was given to the program auditor (an inmate) who maintained the many records that were required. The points assigned were at different grade levels of operation. The expectation that the inmate would be motivated to increase her level proved to be altogether unfounded.

Points earned could not be taken away, but an inmate could fail to earn points in any week; or she could decrease her "level of operation," in which case referral to parole might be made at a lower grade level. Finally, points could always be added when rules were violated, which could increase an inmate's stay. For example, an inmate who escaped and was returned to Western automatically had eight weeks added to her stay. Parole referral was defined as a "major reinforcer," but it was viewed as a long-range goal, and immediate reinforcement was considered to be essential.[14] Hence, each job assignment had a "salary" attached to it. In addition, money and/or points could also be awarded for the completion of contracts. To develop purchasing power, a monetary system was established whereby each inmate received a "salary" for the work performed in the cottage (or elsewhere in some instances); many of the jobs paid $50.00 a week, but a few jobs paid more. The amount earned (no money exchanged hands) was deposited in the inmate's *bankbook*; any points accumulated for working were tabulated separately each day and credited weekly.

To ensure that "real" deprivations would be included as "reinforcers" for appropriate behavior, the cooperation of the inmates was obtained to set up the reinforcement "menu" of purchasable items. Reinforcement rewards were based upon a few material things—they were actually institutional supplies, staff services, the use of certain cottage facilities, and the rental of designated cottage areas such as a front row seat to view television. To cite a few examples of menu items: An off-campus trip with one's parents—staff approval was possible after two months—was the most expensive item, listed at $275.00; $45.00 for a bedspread; $5.00 for a chair for one's room; $25.00 for permission to use the laundry after 8:30 p.m. or to shower at this time; $10.00 for the use of the ironing board and steam iron; $30.00 for a "special service" requested of the staff (for example, when an inmate forgot to sign the nurses' list and the cottage staff was asked to telephone the hospital nurse in order for the inmate to receive clinic service). The price of each item was based on the staff's perception of its importance to the inmates. Items and services that by law must be provided (such as meals, medical service, and clothing) were not placed on the menu of reinforcers. In a mimicry of the external society, the inmates who could not afford the menu items were said to be on "welfare." Many of the menu items appeared every week, but changes were made as reinforcers were thought to lose their appeal, and prices were changed to reflect the "state of the economy" within the cottage.

Despite the many reinforcers, group management procedures and conventional disciplinary measures also were widely used. Theoretically, the infraction of rules should have resulted in making contracts with rule violators to correct behavior deficiencies, and hence function to decrease the widespread use of such "adversive stimuli" control measures as detention rooms and group punishment. At the three institutions studied, however, the staff dealt mainly with problems that were generated by a large group of girls living in a closed setting, rather than focusing upon "extinguishing" the delinquent behaviors that had brought the inmates to the institution.

PROBLEMS OF PROGRAM IMPLEMENTATION. The process whereby mutual trust and confidence is developed through a series of casual, unstructured contacts between staff and inmate, is a long and frustrating process. The accommodation of behavior modification principles to the organizational routine made it possible to bypass this lengthy process altogether, while at the same time it functioned to formalize the structure of the interaction process. The responsibility to initiate the treatment process was reversed—that is, it was shifted from the staff to the inmates themselves. When an inmate did not approach a staff member to "talk" or did not participate in group therapy, a contract was drawn up immediately to set the inmate's behavior in the direction of conformity as administratively defined.

Although the behavior modification program had been in operation in the cottage housing the older inmates for almost two years, many administrative problems remained unresolved—some of which lent themselves to abuses on several organizational levels by both the staff and the inmates. First, the matter of work assignments posed a problem of major dimensions. Some jobs were difficult to fill even when the cottage population was at its maximum. To overcome this difficulty the role of *volunteer* was created, but this proved to be fruitless in many cases. Thus, it became necessary to *draft* inmates for kitchen duty in order to prepare and serve the meals. Moreover, volunteers could earn points and purchasing power without holding down a "regular" job; working on a regular basis could actually be put off for some time, because points also could be earned through other contracts. Second, an inmate could receive fines for rule violations to the extent that she would be "wiped out," a situation that rendered the menu reinforcers virtually meaningless. Third, rule violations not only resulted in a fine, but often incorporated room confinement in either the inmate's room or the "holding room." "Aversive reinforcement" was a legitimate part of Western's behavior modification program; indeed, such reinforcement was readily understandable to the Western staff—they were not put off by the new terminology, and they recognized that what had always been labeled as punishment was now called aversive stimuli or reinforcement. Yet the staff had not resolved satisfactorily whether the inmates should be released from room confinement to complete their work assignments. Allowing the inmates to work would, in some cases, neutralize and reduce the impact of negative reinforcement (the inmates earned money to buy and points for release when they worked). Yet it was important that each task be done, and volunteers were not always available. A few staff members simply allowed only the inmates who were "wiped out" to work, but no clear-cut pattern could be discerned as to why other staff members occasionally did so. The inconsistency exhibited by the staff caused frustration and bitterness among the inmates. Fourth, some inmates were on welfare, but food, clothing, and certain institutional supplies and personal services could not be placed on the menu of reinforcers, thus creating a situation where—except for off-campus trips with one's family—the inmates did not feel in the least deprived if they lacked "money to buy." In any case, scarce goods and most services could be had for the asking from friends. Fifth, to administer the program and maintain the daily records actually required the full-time services of a staff member. To relieve the cottage staff of the bookkeeping in connection with the points and money earned, two inmates were hired as auditor and banker to keep all records current. Not unexpectedly, some inmates were credited with money and points they had not actually earned. At one point when this state of affairs was discovered by the staff, all inmates' possessions that had been purchased from the menu were withdrawn. Group punishment procedures were as widely used in this cottage as they were throughout the entire institution, although theoretically "aversive stimuli" would have been appropriate only for specific individuals.

Unless *paid* to do so in points and/or money, the inmates often refused to participate in recreational activities of any kind. To the limited extent possible, inmates withheld a reinforcer of their own over which *they* had some control.

Finally, no criteria had been established as to how many points and/or dollars were to be awarded to complete the contracts, although each of the major areas in which inmates were to be paid did have a ceiling. As a result—under the guise of "individual treatment"—the matter was handled arbitrarily. Moreover, intake pressures also resulted in the staff "giving" points to the inmates in written or verbal contracts. Unearned points were also awarded because staff members were not always present to observe the inmate's behavior, or they did not actually observe the behavior in question even when they were present. In some cases, inmates were made to repeat certain forms of behavior simply because a staff member insisted she had not observed the inmate acting in a certain way.

Despite the many administrative problems, the Western staff were enthusiastic in their praise of the behavior modification program because it made it possible for them to state the reasons for determining an inmate's eligibility for parole by an "objective performance scale." The procedure provided the staff the wherewithal to observe conforming behavior without having to "sit around and wait for it." Points could be recorded and summarized for the benefit of the Board. Both in staff meetings and in Board reports, the assertion that treatment goals had been accomplished could be substantiated by pointing to the evidence—namely, that the inmate had "completed her contracts" and that she had received the required points. But the procedure by which the points were earned and the relationship of the latter to actual changes in delinquent behavior— that is, to the so-called "behavior deficiencies" attributed to the inmates— were not determined by this method. The nature of the behavior called forth in the contracts and its relationship to the behavioral events leading to the inmate's incarceration was not examined by the staff. Perhaps more important, the program lent itself to punitive ways of handling the inmates, under the umbrella of learning theory based upon scientific methods.

CHAPTER EIGHT

Patterns of Social Control

Custody is an integral part of an institution's function and is given first priority, whatever official and unofficial pronouncements may be made regarding treatment. The community feels strongly that institutionalized youngsters are afflicted with a kind of immoral influence that is contagious upon contact. That the few social events planned for the inmates of all the schools studied were with adjudicated male delinquents in training schools was not chance, although all the institutions for boys were located some distance from Eastern, Central, and Western and posed a major transportation problem for all the schools involved. Ironically, the same girls on parole would be expected not to fraternize with such boys, and in many cases their relationships with males of this type had led to incarceration.

Only at Central had the staff raised the question whether the inmates should be limited to contacts with adjudicated delinquent boys, and they had tried in the past to schedule a few social events with boys from the local community. The infrequent contacts that Eastern, Central, and Western had with the schools in the local community were of a formal nature, such as a band concert in the institution's auditorium and invariably involved only a few members of the student body.

The task of getting the individual to conform to the institution must

121

be given the highest priority because institutional administrators are held accountable for custody but not for treatment. Running away is regarded as a serious rule infraction in institutions of this type because it represents, in the last analysis, the ultimate negation of authority. Furthermore, inmate escapes are always a source of potential embarrassment to an institution head due to the kinds of activities an inmate may engage in while on unauthorized leave. Also, it is embarrassing when individuals in the community learn of an inmate's escape before the institution head obtains the information. A recent event experienced by the superintendent at Central and recounted in the memorandum below provides a ready example.

To: Switchboard and Administrators

From: Vernon James

I have not become too old nor too important to be advised of runaways or any other serious disturbances at the institution during my absence from the institution, such as night time, weekends, and holidays. I am requesting that I be notified of all AWOL's or other such situations. . . .

Day before yesterday we had two runaways. I was not notified and had two calls from the press early the following morning, still unaware that we had had these runaways. This put the institution, as well as me, in a rather embarrassing position. Realizing this is the exception to the rule and that I am generally notified, I am asking a concentrated effort on these situations so that we can run a tight ship and I will be in a position to answer the press or any other parties concerned.

If in the opinion of the administrator on duty, the situation is not important enough to advise me, then I would at least expect a note on my desk before the administrator goes off duty to make me aware of any situation.

Your cooperation in this matter is most important if the overall institution is to function smoothly and the channels of communication are to flow properly.

Most institutions for juvenile delinquents are not completely enclosed with walls and fences, nor is the physical movement of the inmates so closely regimented as in a former day; nevertheless, security and discipline are still very much in evidence. In spite of the attractive physical plants of most schools for juvenile delinquents, the way custody and discipline is handled indicates that they operate mainly as punitive agencies.

The institutions included in this study—often pointed to as among the best in the nation—are not exceptions in this regard.

The guiding philosophy of each institution is officially defined as treatment. But all the schools fell considerably short of the officially defined goals. The preoccupations with concerns of a custodial nature took precedence over and preempted all other goals; and the daily routine of all the schools studied was predominantly custodial. Any difference that existed among them was a matter of degree, but not of kind. However, the most restrictive policy was observed at Western where all the inmates were to be kept in "visual sight" of the staff at all times. The type of surveillance expected of the Western staff by the administrative head is set forth in the memorandum below.

August 24, 1970

To: All Program Staff

Recently there seems to be a rash of escapes from the institution. In each case the factor of staff inattention is present.

The supervision of girls in this institution is dependent on surveillance of the girls for whom one is accountable, and by communication as individuals move from one location to another.

A group of girls should remain in visual sight of a staff member and not be permitted to wander off from the main group because it is impossible to supervise them. When a girl is called to a different location, it is absolutely necessary to check to see if the girl has arrived within the time the movement should take. If she hasn't arrived in the time allotted, Control should be notified immediately so the necessary staff may be activated to search *before* the girl can get away.

It is imperative that *each* staff member assume this responsibility which is inherent in each position in this institution.

Be alert ! !

Bertha Whitehead
Superintendent

A measure of the type of supervision expected of the cottage staff in all the institutions is partially explained by the data summarized in Table 8.1.

Table 8.1   Type of Inmate Supervision Expected of Cottage Staff

	Eastern		Central		Western	
Supervision Expected	Number	%	Number	%	Number	%
To keep all the girls in sight when they are with the girls	38	25.8	34	21.5	60	63.8
To allow any girl to be out of sight if she can be trusted	104	70.8	115	72.8	33	35.1
To allow any girl to be out of sight if the girl wants to	3	2.0	2	1.3	—	—
It doesn't matter here how cottage staff regulate the girls' movement	2	1.4	7	4.4	1	1.1
Total	147	100.0	158	100.0	94	100.0

Sixty-four percent of the Western staff indicated that the cottage staff were expected to keep *all* the inmates in sight, compared to 26 percent of the Eastern staff and 22 percent of the Central staff. In response to another questionnaire item concerning job expectations held of the staff, 82 percent of the Eastern staff, 91 percent of the Central staff, and 87 percent of the Western staff maintained that they were expected to "let the girls have some freedom to express themselves, but keep close supervision so things won't get out of control." These responses, however, obscure the empirical reality of the situation at Western and of the other schools. When the Western staff did not have the inmates in sight, it was because they had delegated the surveillance function to the security staff; moreover, all movement of the Western inmates –even when escorted by the staff—was reported to the control center staff and to the security officers. Similarly, the responses of the Eastern and Central staff require qualification in order to understand properly the extent to which the inmates' movement was restricted. In actual fact, approximately ten Eastern inmates (campus privilege girls), and perhaps twice that number at Central, had some limited freedom of movement at designated times without escort or other direct staff surveillance. In all the institutions, the staff's presence was required to supervise the inmates in the cottages. But only the Western staff members were expected at all times to sit in the cottage dayroom; and wall mirrors were placed near the desk in order to aid them in their surveillance of the bathroom and corridor. Such unrelenting surveillance was not expected of the Eastern and Central staff, although they were certainly expected at all times to *supervise* the inmates. In some cottages at Central the inmates rollerskated, danced, listened to the record player, or washed personal clothing in the base-ment; the staff member on duty visited there occasionally, but did not remain long because she was also responsible for the inmates who were watching television on the first floor. The Eastern and Central inmates could obtain staff permission to go out on the cottage porches, but the Western inmates were not allowed to sit outside unless they were accom-panied by the staff. Even the inmates who lived in the cottage with an attached fenced-in yard could not venture out alone because the yard area was not within the security officers' direct range of vision.

To be sure, the Eastern and Central security staff patrolled the grounds and telephone calls were sometimes made to them to record the movement of inmates; passes were used at Eastern; and the Eastern and Central staff were expected to escort and to supervise their cottage group when they attended campus-wide functions such as school assemblies, movies, and athletic events. Taking into account the various security measures utilized, there was more unescorted campus movement at East-ern and Central than was the case at Western, but the differences were a matter of degree.

There were no more escapes at Eastern and Central than there were at Western. But to some extent this was due as much to the method of handling escapes as it was to staff supervision. Few staff members—even

Table 8.2   Opinions of the Staff Concerning
Supervision and Inmate Escapes

If Supervision Not Close	Eastern		Central		Western	
	Number	%	Number	%	Number	%
Almost all would run away	—	—	2	1.3	4	4.3
Many would run away	7	4.8	14	8.9	24	25.5
Some would run away	53	36.0	66	41.8	35	37.2
A few would run away	82	55.8	75	47.5	31	33.0
None would run away	5	3.4	1	0.6	—	—
Total	147	100.0	158	100.1	94	100.0

at Western where the staff had no direct experience with open exits—
thought that all the inmates would run away if they did not supervise
closely.[1] (See Table 8.2.)

At Eastern and Central where the staff were accustomed to open exits,
fewer staff members indicated that all the inmates would run away; only
5 percent of the Eastern staff and 10 percent of the Central staff responded that almost all or many of the inmates would run away if they
did not supervise closely, as compared to 30 percent of the Western staff.

RULE VIOLATIONS AND DISCIPLINARY ACTIONS TAKEN. All
the departures of the inmates are expected to have their starting point in
administrative decisions, rather than to originate from the inmates themselves. It is hardly surprising, therefore, that the disciplinary policies and
goal priorities of an institution are likely to be revealed clearly in the
way that its runaways are processed.

When we examine the disciplinary actions that are actually taken by
the staff, compared to the range of possible actions that are available to
them, the clearest expression emerges of an administration's implemented
operation as opposed to its defined philosophy.

At Eastern, Central, and Western, all operations came to a virtual
standstill when it was discovered that an inmate had escaped. The inmates were recalled immediately to the cottages from their work details
and school classes so that an accurate head count could be made. To
facilitate this task, the inmates usually were locked in their rooms. Escape plans were put into action, and the staff on all hierarchical levels—
including the chaplains—joined in the search to "capture" the individual
and return her to the institution.

Runaways are handled similarly at Eastern, Central, and Western. The
majority of the staff maintained that when the runaway was returned to
the institution, she would be removed from the general population. (See
Table 8.3.)

It is not clear why the responses made by some staff members to the
escape item indicated the removal of privileges as the most likely action
that would be taken. Privileges were always taken away when an inmate
ran away, not only during the confinement period but usually thereafter.
A few staff members explained after they had completed the questionnaire that they would "do both"—that is, place the inmate in isolation
and remove privileges. This would appear to indicate that either the first
response to this item was not read in its entirety, it was not understood
fully, or isolation in the case of runaways was taken so much for granted
by some staff members that they made note of the fact that privileges

*Table 8.3   Most Likely Action Taken When an Escapee
Is Returned to the Institution*

Action Taken	Eastern		Central		Western	
	Number	%	Number	%	Number	%
Place her in isolation for a few days, or perhaps in a closed program with more supervision	57	38.8	69	43.7	73	77.7
Have her stay in her room for a few hours, but keep her in the program	18	12.2	13	8.2	5	5.3
Remove her privileges, such as movies, dances, or smoking privileges	55	37.4	49	31.0	12	12.8
Give her an extra work assignment	15	10.2	6	3.8	—	—
Talk to her about it, but take no other action	—	—	21	13.3	4	4.3
No response	2	1.4	—	—	—	—
Total	147	100.0	158	100.0	94	100.1

were removed. In fact, the same procedure was followed in Eastern, Central, and Western: the inmate was placed immediately in an isolation room. If Eastern's hospital security rooms were occupied, the inmate's own room would be stripped and used until the inmate could be moved to the seclusion facilities; at Central and Western, the disciplinary cottage facilities were used.

Inmates who ran away from Eastern and Central also stood a good chance of being transferred out of these institutions to closed facilities; perhaps the transfer from open to closed facilities may have been interpreted by some staff members as a "removal of privileges." More than likely, all of these factors may have been operative to some extent.

The most severe disciplinary measures were imposed at Western. Not only was a Western runaway's term of confinement extended for two or three months, but she was confined in the maximum security cottage for a longer period of time—for several weeks or months, in some cases.

Sanctions imposed upon runaways at Western also included the loss of off-campus privileges; and inmates who admitted that they had known of an escape plan—the inmates were all expected "to be on top of the situation"—could also lose off-campus privileges because they had not informed the staff. An inmate who refused to provide the staff with this information was accused of not "assuming responsibility." The mere hint of "split talk" by a Western inmate—whether overheard by a staff member directly or learned indirectly from the inmates—would mean confinement in a holding room and the loss of off-campus privileges. The Western staff tried to control the number of runaways by threatening the entire cottage population with the loss of off-campus privileges if any *one* of the inmates ran away; and it was implied that the entire inmate population would lose off-campus privileges. Justification in this instance was based on the conviction that some inmates always have knowledge of another's intention to run away.

The runaways at Eastern and Central were placed in isolation for four or five days, and only in rare cases for a week or more. The Eastern inmate would be confined in one of the stripped cells in the hospital; when she returned to the cottage, room confinement might be continued for a brief period of time; sometimes the room was stripped and the window removed. The Central inmate would be restricted in the maximum security cottage (whether the room was furnished at all depended upon her behavior), but she resumed school classes immediately upon return to her cottage. The Eastern and Central inmates who ran away more than once were transferred to other closed facilities, although inmates who were first-time runaways were sometimes transferred, depending upon the circumstances surrounding the incident. For example, consideration was given to the amount of time the staff had to search before they found her, hence the outcome in some way depended upon the disposition of the staff. However, any factor could be justified simply by stating on the transfer request that the inmate "cannot adjust to an open setting." In addition, if the staff had been called to give chase at the "wrong time of day" (or night), she might very well be transferred. Finally, the inmates who "made it"—even for a few weeks—were transferred because it was thought that they would have a "negative influence" on the rest of the population. Inasmuch as the term of confinement in the closed institutions was considerably longer than was the case at either Eastern or Central, it is reasonable to assume that any inmate transferred to these facilities was incarcerated longer than if she had remained at Eastern or Central. Hence it is probable that runaways at all the institutions were institutionalized longer.

At Western, the staff interrogated the inmates following an escape. This was not done at Eastern or Central. The subject was taken up by the team and assistant head group supervisors in the cottage group therapy meeting until the details of the escape were revealed, including the names of any inmates who had prior knowledge of the event. To speed up the process, the cottage would be "grounded" and/or "locked"— that is, all the inmates were confined to the cottage, and classes cancelled for the cottage residents. After dividing the cottage population into several groups, the staff would question one group at a time—or sometimes the inmates were questioned individually—until the information sought was obtained. This type of interrogation was also used at Western to solve other problems besides escapes; the *incident chrono* appearing below provides an example.

Date: 8/25/70   *Name:* Webster, Jane

Location: Cottage _____

Others involved: May Elliot, L. Bryon, Theresa Hardy

Description of incident: Since Sunday, 8/23/70, rumors have existed on the dorm that L. Bryon had brought a "joint" of "weed" back to the dorm from her visit 8/25/70. I confronted the group during C/C [*community counseling*] and asking for any and all information. All backed down from commenting. After C/C I asked the team for a vote of confidence in my desire to lock the dorm and interrogate each girl individually. They agreed.

The interrogation uncovered that Bryon had returned from her visit with a "joint" and given ½ of that "joint" to Jane Webster. Webster smoked her half in her room Sunday night. Webster admitted to all of the aforementioned facts. Elliot is guilty of threatening girls. Told a few girls she was going to stick with Bryon and "Bryon's trouble was her trouble."

Hardy has joined the Bryon-Elliot Group and has been lying and throwing her weight around. She was confident that with those two behind her, she could harass and agitate her peers without fear of reprisal.

Signed: Barker Towers
Senior Youth Counselor

Recommendation: Bryon and Webster placed in holding rooms; Elliot and Hardy placed on Security Hold in their rooms.

Disposition: As above; released 9/2/70.

At Eastern, Central, and Western institutions, disposition of runaways always included punitive segregation in stripped security rooms. I know of no case where a runaway was simply returned to the cottage, talked to by a staff member, and then allowed to mingle with the inmate group. At all the institutions, room restriction was couched in treatment terminology by the staff and labeled as a "special program," although at the same time it was held that the inmates were not "in the program."

The disposition of an Eastern runaway was reported by the principal children's supervisors in their official "Daily Log." This account details the way that "privileges" were partially restored as compliance was assured:

9:30:   Friday, January 31, 1969. Went with Mr. Merris (*social worker*) to look for Mary Faris from Cottage _____, who had run on her way back to the cottage from school. While out we followed several leads to the whereabouts of the girls, but failed to locate them. Returned to campus 11:45. M. B. (*Matilda Brown*)

12:30:   Friday, January 31, 1969. Mary Faris and Rosalind Baker were brought in by three maintenance men and taken to campus hospital and placed in security rooms. M. B.

Friday, January 31, 1969. Called to hospital because Mary Faris was refusing to remove her clothing. She had on shoes with hard heels and nurse is afraid she will break the glass. Took two men from shop [*maintenance shop*] with me as nurse said Mary was very hostile. Mary absolutely refused to remove her own clothing, so the two men from the shop and Mr. Blair held girl's arms and legs while the nurse and I pulled her clothing off and put PJ's on. M. B.

Friday, January 31, 1969. Mary Faris will remain in security in hospital over weekend. M. B.

Saturday, February 1, 1969. Mary Faris very hostile at the hospital, so she will be given a combination breakfast and lunch today. M. B.

(*Later in the day*). Mary Faris given her breakfast and alerted she would be remaining in security until Monday by writer, depending on her behavior by then. J. F. (*director of cottage service*)

February 1, 1969. Mary Faris in security room refused her dinner and refused to go to B. R. (bathroom). Very hostile and refused to talk. R. H. (*Robert Horton*)

February 1, 1969. To hospital to give Mary Faris her supper. Tried to talk with girl, but she started to get loud again. Will try later on. Will let her have shower privileges if she is cooperative. R. H.

February 1, 1969.   To hospital to give Mary Faris shower and bathroom privileges. Talked to girl a few minutes. At first she was resentful, but she
soon started to respond. Told her if she acted all right and showed she
could live with a bed, perhaps by tomorrow we would talk about it. R. H.

Sunday, February 2, 1969.   While at hospital (on another matter) talked with
Mary Faris. She had quieted down and was calm and cooperating. We
moved her to a room with a bed. R. H.

Sunday, February 2, 1969.   To hospital to feed Mary Faris. Talked with girl
a few minutes. Girl very cooperative. She asked to speak to Mr. Merris.
Told her I would relay the message. R. H.

February 2, 1969.   To hospital to give Mary Faris supper and bathroom
privileges. Girl was very cooperative and sorry for the things she had
done. Wanted to go back to her cottage. I again told her Mr. Merris
would see her tomorrow and talk with her. She was satisfied with this
and promised to be good. R. H.

February 2, 1969.   To hospital to give Mary Faris medication as she was complaining of pains. No problems. Girl also given bathroom privileges. R. H.

February 2, 1969.   To our hospital at 6:15 to give Mary Faris a shower and
bathroom privileges. Girl cooperative. R. H.

Monday, February 3, 1969, 7:30. To hospital to give Mary Faris her breakfast. R. H.

[*Note:*   The inmate was released to her cottage unit later that morning.]

This case occurred during the weekend when the social workers and
other treatment staff were not present; hence all the decisions concerning
disposition were made by staff members who were charged more specifically with custodial functions. Even when the social workers were present, the procedure did not differ appreciably at any of the institutions; a
social worker might talk to the runaway in seclusion status, but if she did
so it was not likely to occur during the first day or two.

Inmates at Eastern and Central were segregated until conformity was
observed and a promise to "be good" was exacted. In all the institutions
a variety of "privileges" were withheld, such as letterwriting and visiting
privileges, smoking, and participation in all institutional activities, including attendance at the academic school. Meals were served in the
seclusion rooms and food had to be eaten with a spoon. The inmate had
to remove her street clothing and change to night apparel. (Ostensibly,
the reason for the clothing change was so that the inmate could not harm
herself.) Shower and bathroom privileges were "allowed," but the timing

of these events depended upon the "cooperation" of the inmates. At Western, the holding rooms and other seclusion rooms had toilets, but the staff would sometimes shut off the flow of water if the inmate were "loud," or "defiant." At all the schools, the provision of a bed, mattress, or blanket depended upon the "cooperation" and "attitude" of the inmate. At Western, where the inmates were kept in punitive confinement for extended stays, the staff gradually relaxed the withholding of some privileges when an inmate demonstrated compliance.

The basic custodialism of Eastern, Central, and Western is also apparent by the manner in which the staff processed other rule infractions. In all the institutions, actions that the staff perceived as potentially group-disruptive always resulted in immediate isolation of the inmate(s) engaged in the deviant act. Data in connection with the most likely action to be taken by the staff in connection with fighting and complaining about institutional practices are presented in Tables 8.4 and 8.5.

Individuals who are not familiar with the day-to-day operation of institutions for juvenile delinquents naively assume that the staff in so-called treatment institutions dispose of situations involving rule infrac-

Table 8.4   Most Likely Action Taken by Staff When
            Two Girls Are Observed Fighting

Action Taken	Eastern		Central		Western	
	Number	%	Number	%	Number	%
Place one or both girls in isolation for a few days	55	37.4	46	29.1	20	21.3
Have one or both girls stay in their rooms for a few hours	50	34.0	78	49.4	56	59.6
Remove privileges such as movies, dances, or smoking privileges	18	12.2	17	10.8	7	7.4
Give one or both girls an extra work assignment	8	5.4	10	6.3	1	1.1
Talk to both of them about it, but take no other action	15	10.2	7	4.4	10	10.6
No response	1	0.7	—	—	—	—
Total	147	99.9	158	100.0	94	100.0

*Table 8.5   Most Likely Action Taken by Staff When
an Inmate Complains of the Food and Treatment*

	Eastern		Central		Western	
Action Taken	Number	%	Number	%	Number	%
Slap her	—	—	2	1.3	—	—
Call the PCS office[a] and give her room confinement	12	8.2	29	18.4	6	6.4
Send her directly to her room	106	72.1	105	66.5	69	73.4
Tell her she will get an extra work assignment for her behavior	7	4.8	13	8.2	5	5.3
Talk to her about it, but take no other action	22	15.0	9	5.7	14	14.9
Total	147	100.1	158	100.1	94	100.0

[a] At Central, the "Administrator's office," at Western, "Security."

tions by sitting down with the inmates to talk it out. This simply is not so. At all three institutions, the initial response of the staff was always punitive segregation, and the inmate was talked to whenever it was convenient to the staff.

Sanctions as a form of social control were used for other kinds of situations. For example, when an inmate refused to clean her room, a majority of the staff at all the institutions would order the inmate to comply with the request and sound a warning that privileges would be taken away. (See Table 8.6.)

However, observation indicated that none of the staff members tolerated such behavior very long. The task of cleaning individual rooms and the public areas of the cottage were scheduled at specific times to enable the staff to handle the inmates *en masse*. The inmate would be asked to clean her room *once*—in a few cases twice—and if she did not respond immediately, she would be locked in her room until she complied. If the inmate continued to exhibit "defiance," she would be removed from her own room to a security room. In none of the institutions was the inmate given the option of setting her own time schedule for this or related tasks. All tasks were routinized at a designated time. Getting up, going

Table 8.6 Most Likely Action Taken by Staff When an Inmate Refuses to Clean Her Room

Action Taken	Eastern		Central		Western	
	Number	%	Number	%	Number	%
Order her to do it, and warn her that privileges may be taken away	103	70.1	80	50.6	48	51.1
Give her room confinement immediately; this attitude can't be permitted in the cottage	22	15.0	73	46.2	36	38.3
Tell her that she doesn't have to clean her room if she doesn't want to	5	3.4	2	1.3	2	2.1
Talk to her about it, but take no other action	17	11.6	3	1.9	8	8.5
Total	147	100.1	158	100.0	94	100.0

to bed, and going into the dining room for meals were all scheduled as group activities, with no opportunity for the inmate to exercise individual choice and responsibility.

Only when an inmate refused to attend an institutional function or to participate in scheduled activities did the staff enter into a discussion with the inmate, although handling the situation in this way was by no means the rule. In the questionnaire, staff members were asked, "Suppose one of the girls refuses to attend an institutional function in which she is enrolled, such as academic, vocational, or group therapy meetings, which of the following items comes closest to what you would do in this situation?" Thirty-one percent of the Eastern staff, 27 percent of the Central staff, and 40 percent of the Western staff maintained they would isolate the inmate from the group.(See Table 8.7.)

At Eastern, Central, and Western, an "ideal" inmate was described as one who "has been willing to work on cottage assignments and participates enthusiastically in all activities." If an inmate refused to participate in institutional activities, the cottage staff first might talk to her to discover the reason for her action. However, work assignments were not

Table 8.7   *Most Likely Action Taken by Staff When an Inmate Refuses to Attend Institutional Function*

Action Taken	Eastern		Central		Western	
	Number	%	Number	%	Number	%
Place her in isolation for a few days	8	5.4	6	3.8	2	2.1
Have her stay in her room for a few hours	37	25.2	37	23.4	36	38.3
Remove privileges such as movies, dances, or smoking privileges	44	29.9	66	41.8	36	38.3
Give her an extra work assignment	11	7.4	6	3.8	2	2.1
Talk to her about it, but take no other action	47	32.0	43	27.2	18	19.2
Total	147	99.9	158	100.0	94	100.0

"refusable," nor were the other activities voluntary; hence, an inmate could not refuse to engage in any of them indefinitely. At all the institutions, refusal to attend a specific function meant that the inmate could not go to any other scheduled activity that day and another "privilege" might be removed, such as a weekend movie. Inmates who did not participate in activities were usually sent to their rooms. They did not have the run of the cottage when they refused to go to school, church, gym, or movies.

To some extent, differences in the staff's responses are a reflection of occupational position and work shift. As a rule, staff members who worked during the night shift either were new employees or they could not assume a great deal of responsibility for one reason or another. They were given little information concerning procedural matters because it was felt that they were not directly involved; this holds true for the recreational staff—especially part-time workers, nurses, and some vocational staff members; and the same may be said for the academic teachers who were really cut off from the cottage life.

The staff in all the schools did not include room restriction and other social control isolation techniques as part of their "program." It was as if these punitive measures were not imposed by them; or perhaps it was because the inmates who were in room restriction were left to their own resources without any staff members present. The latter view seems to be implied in the following memorandum issued at Western.

June 8, 1967

To: All Psychiatric Treatment Unit Staff

From: Arthur Payne, PTU Supervisor

Subject: *Escorting Cottage Groups to Special Activities*

Some different approaches to escorting were discussed at Coordinating Committee this week:

1.   Thinking of it as a custodial function and making it the primary responsibility of the group supervisory staff;

2.   Leaving it to the teams to work out their own coverage.

The first alternative was ruled out. It was the thinking of the Committee that escorting is not only a custodial function but a treatment function in that it also involves "doing something" *with* the girls. It was felt that this is good use of staff time, regardless of the profession of the staff member.

It was recognized that some staff members may have other, more productive ways to use their time, depending upon the circumstances. The second alternative was discussed with this in mind. However, making escort coverage the responsibility of the teams presented a number of mechanical problems. Therefore, for the time being it was decided that teachers and therapists would be expected to help with the escorting, generally. However, any staff member may be excused if her work load demands it, and if there are at least two escorts for the cottage.

RESTRAINT PROCEDURES.   Although tranquilizers were used in all the institutions as a social control mechanism, handcuffs and straitjackets were used at Western but could not be used as control aids at Eastern or Central. The Western staff's view on this matter, summarized in the minutes of the Administrative Staff Meeting held on January 21, 1963, indicates that these control techniques were of long-standing tradition.

Mr. Bedelict brought up the problem of restraining girls who are out of control and suggested that this area be reviewed by the staff. The use of either tranquilizers, handcuffs, or restraining jackets would be helpful.

Although such instances are not too frequent, some girls do occasionally become so out of control and violent that more than one man is required to restrain her.

Although the staff generally felt that handcuffs should not be used, some method of restraint is needed to prevent injuries to girls as well as staff. It was felt it might be best to simply keep the girl in her room until she has either calmed down or a jacket has been obtained for her before proceeding to move her. In addition, metal shields should be installed over the light bulbs in all holding rooms to eliminate any means whereby a girl might injure herself. It was also felt that it would be helpful if the Security officer and maintenance men could receive some training in how to handle violent girls, and Mrs. Webster [assistant superintendent] will make arrangements for this.

The officially approved restraint procedures in force at Western at the time of the study appear in the policy directive below.

March 13, 1964

To: All Staff

SUBJECT: *Discipline*

Policy

Use of physical force other than to restrain in any form as a discipline technique is prohibited.

This prohibition of the use of physical force does not preclude the use of approved methods of restraint for protective purposes and in all instances an employee has the *right to protect himself from assault* with reasonable force (Youth Authority Administrative Manual).

Action shall be taken against any staff member using physical punishment and/or cruelty and violation of this policy may be grounds for suspension or dismissal. Such prohibited punishments are, i.e., snatching, slapping, gagging, arm twisting, denial of food or curtailment of standard menus, loss of sleep, mental cruelty and degradation, including use of profanity or epithets in reference to a child, etc.

Restraint Procedures

1.   *Room Restriction* is the method most desirable to remove girls from the program when their behavior so indicates. Staff members will make every effort

to verbally direct the girl to her own room or holding room. If the girl balks at this direction, a security officer should be summoned at once so as to avoid any physical conflict between a woman staff member, particularly, and a ward.

2.   A security officer, if necessary, will restrain the ward in such a fashion so as to minimize any physical hurt to the ward or himself. If the ward is too violent for rapid seclusion, handcuffs may be used to secure the ward while moving her into a holding room. The cuffs *must* be removed when the violence is over and they may be safely removed. If, in the opinion of the security officer, a situation is beyond his capacity to handle by himself, other male help shall be summoned immediately.

3.   If there is a threat of the girl becoming dangerous to herself or others, she may be placed in soft camisole with the consent of the Superintendent or Officer of the Day. She must be exercised every two hours and released when the episode seems to be over. All this information must be recorded in the log provided.

4.   If a girl has attempted to escape and is still recalcitrant upon being apprehended, handcuffs may be placed on her wrists until she has been safely returned to the institution.

Fights and Atttacks

1.   If girls are fighting, a woman staff member should summon help rather than try to physically break up the fight.

2.   If another person has been attacked and seems to be in danger of being seriously hurt, help should first be summoned and then go to the defense of the victim, using any reasonable means to protect the victim.

3.   If it becomes necessary to use physical force to protect oneself or another, a full report of the circumstances should be given in writing immediately to the Superintendent with the names of witnesses when possible.

Bertha Whitehead
Superintendent

Less social distance was expected of the Eastern and Central staff; indeed, the immediate response of the Eastern and Central staff was to separate any inmates who were observed fighting before principal children's supervisors or administrators were called to the cottage. By the time the latter staff members arrived, more than likely the inmates had already been placed in room restriction by the cottage staff. By contrast, a call for a security officer at Western was the cue for all the inmates to go to their rooms and their doors were locked by the staff. When the security officer arrived, the cottage staff and the inmate(s) to be attended to were the only individuals present. Although this method of handling the situation made it easier for the Western staff to deal with the problem of social control, it also added to the amount of time that the Western inmates were confined to their rooms.

The practices at Western contributed to the staff's greater attention to and emphasis on the custodial aspects of institutional administration; they stand out sharply when one considers that the architecture of the cottages at Eastern and Central in many respects made management of the inmates more difficult, as the inmates might be on several levels. Sometimes the Eastern and Central inmates also were locked in their rooms after the cottage staff had called for help; however, it was a consequence of the developing situation and to help the cottage "settle down" rather than as a direct response to an institutional rule.

The events described throughout this chapter are an inevitable concomitant of the social organization of prison systems.These situations tend to wear out the staff and the inmates alike, as it usually takes many days to process most of these events. Not unexpectedly, all the time and energies of the staff are directed to normalizing the situation. During this period, no pretense is made by the staff to use "new treatment" techniques; indeed, no matter what the usual treatment routine, it is shelved until organizational equilibrium is reached, at which time the treatment goal is once more held out as legitimate.

ROLE OF CUSTODIAL PRACTICES FOR GROUP MANAGEMENT. Other social control patterns at Eastern, Central, and Western were not only similar, but they have their parallel in prisons for adult offenders. Despite frequent protest to the contrary, institutions for juvenile delinquents function as miniprisons. The institutions studied, for example, had long lists of written rules that were given to the inmates. Many other rules were transmitted verbally, especially at Eastern where the number of written rules had been decreased as a consequence of a recent policy change. However, the change in Eastern's policy did not *eliminate* any rules; rather, the responsibility to inform the newcomer of the existing rules was shifted to the cottage staff. At Eastern and Western, the rules were posted in the cottages; most of the inmates also had a copy posted in their rooms. The Central inmates received a list of the "written guidelines" that were discussed in the orientation cottage, as well as another set of rules when they were assigned to a permanent cottage. Examples of the written rules at Eastern, Central, and Western appear in Appendix D.

Numerous head counts were made during the day and evening, and all the cottage personnel had to phone an "all is well" to central points at designated times during the night. All the inmates' doors were locked when the inmates went to bed; at Eastern, however, the doors were unlocked when the night staff came on duty at midnight. The Western staff's routine was exactly the reverse: when the shifts changed at midnight, the night staff checked to be sure that the inmates were locked in. Central was similar to Western in that the inmates' doors were kept locked all night; but Central's cottage staff simply unlocked an inmate's door whenever a request was made to use the bathroom. The same procedure was followed by Eastern's cottage staff; however, since they usually remained in the office on the first floor (the few rooms for inmates on the first floor were not locked), the inmates on the second floor often disturbed the other inmates because of their loud knocking. By contrast, a Western staff member could not open an inmate's door after they had been locked in for the night under *any* circumstances unless a male security officer was beside her. This meant that every time an inmate had to use toilet facilities during the night, the security officer was called to the cottage; in some cases this meant a long wait for the inmates, especially when he could not be located or was simply tardy in arriving. The security practices that the Western staff were expected to follow are set forth in the administrative directive below.

> When it is necessary for a ward to be excused to the lavatory during the night, the Control Office should be called and the Security Officer will be sent to the cottage to stand by. Wards should not be encouraged to use their wastebaskets for lavatory purposes unless it is an actual emergency and the security officer is busy in another area of the School. Lights are to be turned on at 6:15 a.m. Kitchen detail and cart girls may be awakened earlier if need be but should not be released from their rooms until the a.m. supervisor arrives on the cottage.
>
> The above policy is to safeguard the security and safety of staff and wards and should be adhered to strictly at all times.

Although the Western inmates consider it an indignity to use their wastebaskets as urinals, an inmate might still go into the lavatory when the security officer does arrive, to avoid what she perceives to be possible punitive sanctions. An inmate explains:

It's kind of an indignity having to go in the trash can. But it's been going on for a long time. When I was here before [1966], you peed in the trash can. At night you bang on your door and the staff says: "I've got to see if I can get Security." That sometimes takes a while, so you end up using the trash can. Then Security comes up, and if you don't go, you get fined or get written up for defiance. So you go into the fuckin' bathroom and you pretend you're going, and you fiddle around washing your hands, and you go back to your room. It's weird.

Other prison-like features in evidence were the censorship of mail, and the extremely limited contact with the outside world. Mail was censored at Central and Western and had been at Eastern until a few months prior to the study. The Eastern inmates' letters are now opened to remove any checks or money enclosed, but the letters are not read. Except for a few visits from relatives and the infrequent off-campus institutional activities, other forms of contact with the outside world were virtually limited to the television set in each cottage.

All the administrators were especially fearful of race riots and the loss of internal control that might stem from similar events taking place in the external society. The Eastern and Central inmates could subscribe directly to publishers for magazines, but they could not obtain them through any other means. At Western, only newspapers or magazines received by mail subscription were acceptable, as the superintendent maintained that the staff did not have enough time to inspect newspapers, magazines, and books for contraband.

Current reading materials were extremely limited at all the institutions, although the Central inmates had some of the current magazines in their school library. None of the inmates received any newspapers or magazines, and at all of the schools they complained about their inability to keep abreast of what was going on in the world outside.

At Western, extreme measures were utilized to control contraband. The inmates' visitors had to deposit their cigarettes at the switchboard upon their arrival; neither the inmates nor their visitors were allowed to smoke during visiting hours. At Eastern or Central, however, the inmates could smoke along with their guests. (In fact, this is one of the ways that the inmates occasionally obtained a few extra cigarettes.) But Western's obsession with security is revealed most dramatically in the fact that all the inmates were completely searched after they had visitors or when they returned from community furloughs. Specifically, before the Western inmate could go to the visitors' area, she had to go to the control office where she left a shopping bag containing a muumuu (to be put on when her guests left); all the clothing she had worn was minutely inspected by designated staff. The official policy concerning the search procedure to stem the flow of contraband is set forth below.

August 28, 1970

To: Assistant Heads, Superintendent, Control, All Cottages and Areas

From: Martha Baleston, Head Group Supervisor

In spite of an effort to thoroughly search girls coming in from visitors, off-campus, and furloughs, it appears contraband is still coming in. Effective immediately the following procedure will be initiated:

1.   Upon returning to the institution from off-campus trips and visiting, girls will be taken into the restroom in Control, given a muumuu and asked to remove their clothing for a thorough search; Control Supervisor or Assistant Head (female) to be present at all times during the search.

2.   When girl has the muumuu on, check her hair carefully, looking behind the ears and through the hair. If a large hair clip or barrette is worn, check it carefully.

3.   Check the girl's underwear carefully.

4.   Check all clothing, hems of skirts or dresses, collars, sleeves and all areas where contraband could be concealed.

5.   Check socks and shoes.

6.   Girl may put her clothes on as you finish checking them. Girls coming in from furlough are to be checked in the same manner and then sent to the Hospital. Their belongings are to be kept in the Control Office for a searching by Mrs. Talcott.

This procedure will make it necessary for the Assistant Head to be in the Control Office either to answer phones and supervise any other girls in the area, or in the case of female assistant head on duty, she may do the searching.

I feel this search is most important and it should be carried on consistently to ensure seizure of any contraband girls may be bringing in. I realize that on heavy visiting days this will be a time-consuming procedure, but it is necessary.

Cottage staff should be aware of this procedure and assist by explaining this is necessary and mandatory due to the incidents of contraband being smuggled in.

At Eastern and Central, search procedures were not conducted routinely, although they might be made in rare cases. The administrative staffs of Eastern and Central tried to control the flow of contraband by appealing to the inmates' sense of responsibility, threatening them with the loss of privileges or transfer to other institutions. Neither the search procedures instituted at Western nor the appeals made to the Eastern and Central inmates, however, proved to be very effective in halting the flow of contraband into these institutions; drugs, cigarettes, glue, and other items occasionally were brought in.

Clearly a disparity exists between the administrative rhetoric concerning the "individualized" treatment programs and the actual procedures that guide the day-to-day operation of these institutions. The frequent use of group punishment at Eastern, Central, and Western also belies the myth of individualized treatment. "On silence" or "quiet time" was used as a tool of group control for varying periods of time at the three institutions. The staff had only to say, "Everybody in!" and inmates would be locked in their rooms. At Western, the "quiet time" period was sometimes extended for several hours to suit the convenience of the staff.[2]

At Eastern and Central—and Western until the early part of 1970— none of the inmates were allowed to speak Spanish in the cottages. This not only functioned as a means of group management, but it also served to mark as somehow inferior the culture of some of the inmates. None of the institutions exploited this cultural difference as an opportunity for some staff members to learn the language and other aspects of the Mexican and Puerto Rican cultures in order to be more effective treatment agents. No attempt was made in any of the institutions to hire staff who spoke the language and were familiar with the social worlds of the inmates.

The general focus on group management and group punishment is also reflected in the reward structure.[3] For example, cigarettes could be—and were—withheld for violation of any rule. At a time when the Surgeon General was urging the American population to stop or curtail smoking habits to safeguard their health, Eastern and Western institutions actually *relaxed* their smoking rules. The fact that in none of the institutions was an attempt made to encourage the inmates to "kick the habit" attests unequivocally to the limited rewards at the disposal of the staff.

In response to the questionnaire item, "One of the things a delinquent needs is a chance to express her feelings without being punished," 93 percent of the Eastern staff, 89 percent of the Central staff, and 85 percent of the Western staff indicated their agreement (the greater proportion of the remaining responses indicated indecision rather than outright disagreement). Certainly, the inmates could express themselves in *some* matters to the staff; but at the same time, they were expected to abide by the rules. The actual expectations of the staff are more accurately indicated by their responses to the statement, "The best way for a girl to get along here is to do what she's told when the staff asks her." Eighty-three percent of the Eastern staff, 86 percent of the Central staff, and 96 percent of the Western staff indicated agreement.

When the inmates deviated from the established rules, the staff would justify any measures taken as indicative of the inmates' need for "firm controls" (the term "punishment" is not used very often). Custodial techniques were frequently couched in treatment terminology—even by the cottage staff. In part this is a reflection of the increased number of treatment staff in all institutions, the presence of whom has stimulated the diffusion of the "appropriate" treatment responses. The fact that the inmates often parrotted the treatment jargon indicates the extent to which these responses have been institutionalized.

The disciplinary practices outlined give us an excellent picture of the custodial emphasis at these institutions. In one sense, group punishment techniques are a logical extension of the way that the inmates are handled routinely—that is, the inmates rise and retire at the same time, watch television at designated times, go to recreational activities in groups, march into the dining room in a group. There is little correspondence between the way in which routines are organized in these institutions and the claims that are made concerning individualized treatment. Organizational discrepancies and contradictions are also apparent in the official reports that are made to justify sizable budgets to governmental legislatures, claiming that all the institutional activities are essential to "treat" and "rehabilitate" the inmates. Yet any or all of the institutional activities may be redefined as privileges to be withheld when conformity to institutional rules is not observed. However, the correspondence between the elimination of the so-called treatment measures and the impact on the inmate's rehabilitation is not spelled out.

In every sense, the chasm between the public claims made of the institutions' internal organization and the way in which they actually operated was wide. Within this framework, the inmates interacted not only with the staff but, also, with the other inmates.

CHAPTER NINE

The Eastern Inmates' Social World:
The Racket

At Eastern institution, the inmate informal social system consists of family groups of varying size. Relationships among the inmates are defined primarily in kinship terms. Almost all of the inmates are part of family groups. The kinship network functions to structure groups of varying size and interlaces the inmates into a cohesive group. The homosexual dyads consisting of culturally defined sex roles, and the kinship ties formed by the inmates are referred to as "the racket."

The Eastern inmates have structured their social relations through courtship, marriage, and kinship ties to provide functional substitutes for normal relationships with family and friends of both sexes. The marriage relationship in particular provides the inmates with companionship and a feeling of belonging and meets their needs for love and affection that normally would be satisfied through heterosexual contacts.

For many inmates the *fem* role is an important means by which they may preserve an identity relevant for civil society. In an attempt to seek continued fulfillment of former satisfactory roles, their behavior may be termed "substitute role *conformity*." For other inmates, the fem role provides an opportunity to function in a role that would very likely have been assumed in a heterosexual relationship in civil society. For this group of inmates, the fem role is a "substitute role *experience*." The *butch's* role incorporates many innovative features to complement the fem in a marriage relationship.

The informal social system is not of recent vintage. Although many inmates have been released and other inmates have replaced them in a steady and unending stream, the structure of social relationships formed by the inmate body has persisted.

TRUE BUTCHES AND TRUE FEMS. The Eastern inmates distinguish between the individual who is lesbian—that is, gay and part of the gay life in the external society—and the inmate for whom homosexuality is a temporary adjustment to incarceration. The latter is labeled a *trust-to-be*.

The "true butch" is the inmate who is said to be "gay on the outside" and intends to continue homosexual relationships when she is released. The true butch acknowledges a serious commitment to homosexuality and consistently assumes a male role in the institution. She is said to be "hard," which translates to mean manly. The true butch who consistently exhibits distinctive masculine qualities, and demonstrates considerable adeptness in playing the male role is sometimes referred to as "stone butch" or "big" or "hard daddy."

The complementary role to the true butch is the "true fem" who assumes a female role in the gay life. Like the true butch, the true fem acknowledges a preference for sexual relationships with girls and confirms her intention to continue this type of behavior when she is released. Both the true butch and the true fem exhibit stability in their chosen roles. In short, the true butch and true fem are members of the lesbian community in the external world, and they may be expected to return to this community upon release.

At Eastern, the true butch and true fem set the norms of permissible behavior in connection with homosexuality for the inmate population. Many of the inmates are inexperienced in homosexual relations and must be socialized to this phase of institutional life. The lesbians set the standards because of their knowledge and expertise.

TRUST-TO-BE BUTCHES AND TRUST-TO-BE FEMS. The inmate who assumes a male role while incarcerated but prefers to "go with boys outside" is a "trust-to-be butch." While the trust-to-be butch enjoys romantic attachments with girls in the institution, most inmates who assume this role maintain that they intend to resume relationships with boys when they return to the community.

The "trust-to-be fem" is the individual who assumes a female role in a homosexual relationship while incarcerated, but who maintains that she is not committed to homosexuality.

Eastern inmates understand that the trust-to-be person is *trusting herself* to act in a way that would be consistent with behavioral expectations of her assumed sex role. She is also "trusted by" the other inmates to act in a way that is consistent with their expectations of the role. A trust-to-be may be viewed as an institutional recruit to homosexuality, but with the possibility always present that she may graduate to true butch or true fem; this is determined by the adeptness demonstrated in her role behaving and a verbal expression of commitment and preference for this behavior. The majority of the inmates at the Eastern institution are occupants of trust-to-be sex roles.

The lesbians at Eastern have higher prestige than those who are institutional converts. Two factors contribute to this: (1) the neutrality of the staff with respect to this form of behavior; and (2) the general attitude widely held by the juvenile girls at Eastern that "time is short" and one should have a wide variety of experiences, including different forms of sex experiences. The logic expressed by the inmates is, "Don't knock it if you've never tried it." True butches and true fems look down on the trust-to-be. The lesbians argue:

> Trust-to-bes want to be in the in-crowd. They come in here and they want to be in the in-crowd. And then they go out with boys and get pregnant.

JIVE TIME BUTCHES AND JIVE TIME FEMS. Two other roles that differentiate the Eastern inmates are those of "jive time butch" and "jive time fem," sometimes referred to as "jive butch" or "jive fem." The jive time butch and fem tend to move from one partner to another without forming a serious attachment. The jive time butch is referred to contemptuously as a "playboy" who "fools around" and "raps with every girl he sees." Moreover, the jive time butch has the reputation of going with several girls simultaneously, whereas the Eastern inmates maintain that one should "go with" an individual for a period of time to determine whether they would be compatible in a marriage relationship before selecting another inmate. The occupants of both these roles, however, have a reputation of breaking up within a week or two.

The jive time fem and the jive time butch are not defined as "sincere." Family members—especially the parents—advise the other family members not to become involved with a jive time fem or jive time butch, saying, "Don't pick someone you know is going to jive on you and has a bad reputation."

STRAIGHTS. The "straight" inmate at Eastern is one who does not participate in homosexual activities, courtship, and marriage. However, straight inmates may be—and often are—members of family groups. Straight individuals form kinship ties such as sister, aunt, or female cousin. Many inmates who begin as straights move into butch and fem roles of the trust-to-be type. Usually, the straight forms kinship ties then drifts into a "going with" relationship which later may be transformed into marriage, depending upon her preferences and needs. The inmates maintain that most girls come to Eastern straight and then "turn."

SQUEALERS. The "squealer" is an inmate who divulges information to the staff about inmate activities. At Eastern, inmates have little trust in other girls; trust is reserved for a few close family members. In fact, inmates maintain that most inmates "squeal" at one time or another. While they sometimes acknowledge it is for the "person's own good" (such as in the case of a plan to escape, because running away will increase an inmate's stay), divulging information to the staff about the informal social system is bitterly resented by the inmates.

Among the Eastern inmates there is no social role for the inmate who changes sex roles, although sex role instability does occur occasionally. However, this is more apt to occur before marriage; rules regulating marriage between the inmates specify that all marriages are to last six months. A marriage cannot be terminated except for good cause. The inmate who exhibits instability in her sex role is ridiculed, and she will be bitterly reminded by the other inmates that her behavior is not consistent with expectations of the trust-to-be role. Particularly, the butch who switches to a fem role earns the most severe ridicule.

SYMBOLS OF COMMUNICATION. The Eastern inmates distinguish individuals occupying male and female roles by the use of campus names—colorful fictitious names which inmates adopt soon after they arrive. Almost all the inmates have campus names, including the few straights. Inmates have complete freedom in the selection of a campus name, but an inmate who assumes a male role selects a name that would be considered masculine. The inmate is known by her campus name during the entire period of incarceration.

A campus name becomes the exclusive property of the first individual who decides to call herself that. A new arrival to the institution may select any name she wishes; however, if an inmate selects a campus name by which someone else is named, she would have to change it slightly. For example, if there already is a "Moon" on campus, another inmate may name herself "Lil Moon" or "Little Moon."

Campus names are widely known by all the inmates. Inmates usually learn the campus names of other inmates before the legal names are known. The girls introduce each other by their campus names. Examples of campus names which were in use during the period of the field study appear below.

Feminine Names		Masculine Names	
Heatwave	Asia	Little Man	Lefty
India	Toketto	James Brown	Frenchy
Granny	Sakina	Larry	Johnie
Yogi	Pretty Woman	Honey	Percy
Flyness	Pee Wee	Josie	Butchy Boy No. 1
Double Eyes	Twiggy	Rusty	Butchy Boy No. 2
Poochie	Sugar	Kado	Ray
Sad Girl	Fidget	Ricky	Major
Teddy Bear	Bunny	Tracy	Lil Ace
Cookie	Tighten Up	Jay Jay	Chico
Dimples	Tango	Tokeo	Jo Jo
Pussycat	Lil Bit	Lucky	Buckweat
Sunny	Peaches	Country	Shamrock
Little Heart	China	Smokey	Stacy
Precious	Tenderness	Deco	Torch

A few inmates said that their campus name was their nickname before they were incarcerated. Most of the inmates, however, select a name shortly after their arrival. Although the final choice is left up to the individual, other inmates may make suggestions.

Nobody knows you by your real name. You have a campus name. Everybody on campus has a campus name. It's a name that fits the person. You might be Dimples because you have dimples. You might be called Shyness because you're shy. Or something that you like for a name—a name that you make up. Usually it takes a week. A lot of people suggest names, and you pick one that you think suits you.

The inmate learns which names are not to be used because they belong to other inmates. As soon as an inmate is released, however, other inmates may use the campus name. Recidivists almost without exception use the same campus name they had formerly, unless it is presently in use.

In addition, all family groups at Eastern have surnames. The name may be a fictitious campus family name or a butch's last name. If an inmate has been a member of two or more families—either during the present or previous incarcerations—the names of all the families are proudly carried. Thus, one's campus name could be "Country," together with a campus family name consisting of three surnames—"Dovell Capri Monticello." This name would indicate that the inmate has been a member of three families, perhaps as a result of marriage.

An individual continues to use a campus name even though she may change her sex role. But inmates who are "stone butch" rarely change their sex role, as to "turn fem" carries no prestige. Ridicule serves importantly to maintain the stability of sex roles; only the trust-to-bes sometimes change roles.

Inmates are quick to pick up relevant cues when an individual deviates from the normative structure. Everyone understands the implications of accusations hurled at an inmate who changes from a male to a female role: "How pretty you look with your earrings on today"; "Your makeup is crooked"; "You got a run in your stockings."

Perhaps more important than ridicule in contributing to role stability, however, is the fact that marriage is an important relationship for the inmates, and this exerts a powerful influence in maintaining the stability of sex roles. The inmate who exhibits instability in sex roles may have a profound impact on the structure of kinship ties, and may disrupt the need structure of particular inmates. Hence inmates who switch sex roles may have difficulty in becoming members of family groups.

> If you keep switching from one sex role to another, nobody wants you in the family. Well, hell, you don't know what you've got. Once, you think you got a mother, or a sister, and then the next thing you know, it's a father or a brother. Then you'll be without a mother, or you could have two mothers if they both get married again. It's like a fem turns butch, and she was your mother. If the ones that were your mother and father both get married again, you could end up with two fathers and two mothers when you don't want them.

The Eastern inmates maintain that there are fewer butches than fems on campus because girls find it easier to "be themselves." But there is also thought to be more risk involved in assuming a male role. First there is the possibility of detection by the staff; second, one may leave oneself open to ridicule (from one's partner as well as the other inmates) when the proper role behavior has not yet been learned. For inmates with little or no financial resources, however, there may be an economic advantage in assuming a male role.

> Some like themselves more feminine. It's easier to be a fem. But butches get a lot in some ways. There are always girls right at your back with candy or a cigarette, to do things for you.

It's harder to play the butch than the female role. The fem—the way she acts and dresses are natural, as if straight. The butch, she would be found out. It's not as easy to play the male part.

The sex identities appropriate to male and female roles are overtly assumed. Inmates who assume the female role wear make-up and dress in clothing that is considered feminine attire. The Eastern inmates who assume male roles are distinguished by such symbols of communication as dress, behavior patterns, and language. (The masculine pronoun is used—even by the straights—to refer to anyone assuming a male role.) Inmates playing the butch role strive for masculinity and assume many stylized symbols of masculinity. For example, because the Eastern inmates cannot cut their hair short to emphasize masculinity, they create other symbols to indicate the chosen sex roles. Inmates assuming the male role part their hair on the left side, brushed back and slightly elevated in front.

Masculinity is also communicated by the length of skirts. Butches at Eastern wear A-line skirts below the knee. The skirt zipper is left unzipped, making it possible for the inmate to place her left hand through the opening as if it were a pocket. This subtle cue, combined with all others, gives the appropriate masculine stance. Both ankle-length and knee-length socks are worn; a few inmates wore two pairs of socks to make their ankles appear less slim, which they think is more masculine. Fems also wear socks, but the inmates occupying male roles wear them almost exclusively. Butches do not wear shoes with heels; they wear sneakers, preferably boys' sneakers (if they can purchase them). They also wear the black and white saddle shoes provided by the institution. Blue jeans and slacks are worn whenever possible in the cottage and during certain recreational activities. They cannot be worn to school; and at no time can jeans which zip in the front be worn.

Inmates at Eastern are allowed to wear inexpensive wrist watches. Consistent with their concept of masculinity, the campus males wear a man's watch with a wide bracelet, but wear no other types of jewelry except marriage rings.

To avoid detection by the staff, a few inmates assuming male roles will occasionally wear their hair in a "fem part" or put on a pair of nylon hose. Once firmly committed to a male role, however, such concessions are not likely to occur.

The most difficult feat for the individual to accomplish is to learn convincingly how to act out a male role, consistent with the expectations that other inmates have.

To be a butch, you have to learn how to walk, how to talk, how to act and how to dress.

Most of the girls like a stone butch—one that wouldn't turn fem at all. But any butch should act like a boy. They act like a boy. Bullying a girl, pick on you like a man. They act tough. They push and punch girls. Fems take it because he's your butch.

Butches are expected to walk in a stride, to "bob up and down," and to "talk like a man." Most males on campus are of the trust-to-be type—that is, they are in various stages of perfecting their maleness. After a period of "testing" herself in the role, an individual may come to the conclusion that she is psychologically suited to the role and may become a true butch. According to the inmates, this stage is reached when the inmate states a commitment and preference for homosexual behavior upon release to the community.

MATE SELECTION, COURTSHIP, AND MARRIAGE.   Induction into the inmate social system depends to some extent on the number of acquaintances one has. Some of the inmates have already met in other places and at other times; for example, they are from the same home neighborhood, are recidivists of Eastern, or have been remanded to youth house juvenile center or another detention facility.

All of the inmates, except those that are from upstate, usually spend at least one month at youth house juvenile center before they go to Eastern. Some inmates had been at youth house juvenile center for three to five months before coming to Eastern; the implications for the inmates' entry into the informal social system are obvious. One inmate already knew nineteen individuals who had preceded her to Eastern—four of whom were in the cottage to which she was assigned. An invitation to join a family may have been extended to her the first day she arrived.

You could start in youth house, and somebody's there who's your brother, and he says to you: "When you go to [Eastern], so and so's up there. She's your mother, and so and so's up there, and he's your brother. When you get up there, tell them I said, Hello!" They're your relatives because they're related to your brother. Then when you get to [Eastern], you find that they're in other families. They've got other relatives, and so you get more relatives. Then *you* start a family, so the family gets bigger and bigger. Some people here don't know it, but everybody on this campus is related. If you go back far enough, everybody's got a common mother. Some girls get married in youth house, and then they come up here. When they come up here, they get a bigger family.

There is no orientation unit at Eastern; after a few hours in the hospital, the inmates are moved directly to the cottages. The induction process into the informal social system begins almost immediately. Many inmates join family groups as a "daughter" or "son" first, then over a short period of time form romantic and marital attachments.

A new arrival is approached by a few girls in each cottage to determine what she is like. She will be asked her name, age, home town, and whether she originates from upstate or downstate. Inmates at Eastern who are from the metropolis downstate are especially interested to learn whether any of their friends are in youth house juvenile center. The newcomer will also be asked what her offense is, whether she has used any drugs, and if so, the kinds of drugs. If she is not an Eastern recidivist, she will be asked, "Do you know what the racket is?" "Are you in the gay life?" The latter question is to ascertain whether her experience is limited to institutions or whether it extends to the community.

If the inmate is already familiar with the informal social system of the Eastern inmates, she would be placed in a different social context. If she is not familiar with this phase of campus life, how quickly she learns "how things are done at Eastern" depends in large measure on how she relates to the inmates in her cottage and on campus. If she is extremely well liked, she may learn within the first hour.

Whether the individual is presently involved in the racket or has been in the past is of considerable interest not only to the inmates but also to the staff. When the inmate arrives at the cottage, the staff member on duty spends a few minutes with her in the office. She informs the inmate that if she "is in it" or "gets in it" at Eastern, she will be kept longer at the institution.

Inmates at Eastern are not allowed to talk to other inmates who do not live in the same cottage.

> When you're with your group [cottage group], you can't say "hello." You could be walking by in a group in the evening, or alone, and you pass someone that you know, and you're not even supposed to say "hello"— just pass on.

Despite this restriction on communication, inmates have an opportunity to contact other inmates when they meet in school, at the clinic, work assignments, church services, at the gymnasium, and at other recreational activities such as movies. When it is to their purpose, they find other means of communication even if it means feigning illness and going to the clinic on a specified day; or they may roam—go somewhere on campus without official authorization.

Inmates also communicate with one another by letter—an "issue" in the inmate argot. Issues are an important means of communication, especially in connection with romantic interests both within and outside of marriage. Even inmates who live in the same cottage often write an issue to communicate their feelings.

Most of the letters follow a conventional pattern. A corruption of the date and address appear to be standard; and hopes, aims, and reasons for writing are expressed in terse phrases. Many letters tend to be quite lengthy (which indicates that inmates at Eastern spend much of their free time writing issues). The Eastern issues usually contain a list of popular song titles or short phrases of popular tunes expressing what the inmate hopes will be the outcome of her writing and conveying her deepest feelings.

A number of abbreviations are used in the margins of pages, at the end of the letter, and on the corners of the envelope (when one is used). The most frequent combinations are noted below.

T.L.A.	True love always
T.D.D.U.P.	Till death do us part
H. n W.	Husband and wife
H. n W.S.	Husband and wife soon
H. n W.A.	Husband and wife always
H.O.L.L.A.N.D.	Hope our love lasts and never dies
T.H.A.W.	True husband and wife
G.B.O.M.	God bless our marriage
G.B.O.L.	God bless our love
T.F.A.D.	True father and daughter
D.T.K.L.A.M.F.	Down to kill like a mother fucker
D.T.K.A.M.F.T.M.W.M.W.	Down to kill a mother fucker that messes with my wife
F.E.A.E.	Forever and ever
F.E.A.E.A.E.	Forever and ever and ever
S.W.M.T.K.	Sealed with my tongue kiss
S.W.A.T.K.	Sealed with a tongue kiss
L.Y.	Love you
S.L.	Secret love
H.N.W.F.E.A.E.	Husband and wife forever and ever
B.A.S.A.	Brother and sister always
T.B.A.S.A.	True brother and sister always
T.B.A.S.	True brother and sister
E.T.	Everything
T.M.A.D.	True mother and daughter
T.F.A.D.	True father and daughter

The Eastern inmates also make use of a numerical code. Several numerical combinations are widely used by the inmates, especially "110" (pronounced one-ten), which means, "I love you" and is understood by all the inmates. This number appears frequently in letters; and it is often used as a concluding remark between intimates, relatives, and friends. An inmate may be asked to give someone a message: "Tell Lil Bit I said 110." Inmates sometimes increase this number by doubling, tripling, quadrupling, and so on, to indicate the intensity of the feeling expressed. The code "225" (two-two-five), meaning that a relationship is terminated, also is understood by all the Eastern inmates. To "call the numbers" indicates to the individual that she has been replaced by another inmate.

Other code numbers frequently used and understood by all the inmates are "115" (I like you); "143" (Will you go with me?); "333" (kiss); "711" (marriage); and "117" (divorce).

These numbers have been part of the inmate culture for many years. Recidivists have no difficulty recalling the code numbers, as they had used them all during their previous incarcerations.[1] Letters that had been intercepted by staff members prior to my study also contained evidence of this numerical code.

When inmate movement was more restricted than it is at the present time, the Eastern inmates may have used the code to conceal their activities and motives from the staff. (There is some evidence that the code was more extensive in the past.) This does not explain its continued use, however. Some staff members know the meaning of some of the numbers. Moreover, inmates in some of the cottages are allowed to keep letters in their rooms, although they must destroy them before being released. But a few inmates keep their letters carefully hidden or destroy them soon after they are read. By contrast, marriage certificates are never destroyed by the inmates because they must be presented as evidence when one seeks a divorce.

While verbal expressions could be used to convey the same meaning, the numbers have the advantage of being direct and completely unambiguous. To call out "711!" or "225!" has a particular dramatic force. It is never necessary to elaborate on the meaning intended. Moreover, in some inexplicable way, "using the numbers is just more fun" for the Eastern inmates.

The issue has a wide variety of functions in connection with dating, courtship, and marriage. Issues also are used to express grievances, give advice, secure and retain mates, and to make arrangements to "live together" after release. Many of the letters are written on paper which inmates appropriate from school. A few issues are enclosed in envelopes, but most of them are simply folded by a method which renders them small enough to be hidden easily. They are not to be found in the inmates' case folders, but I had no difficulty in obtaining letters from the inmates.

The following examples illustrate the typical style and content of an issue. All are uncorrected copies of the handwritten originals. In the first letter, the introduction is much longer than the actual body of the letter; the song titles and other conventions used by the inmate in the introduction have already spelled out the important reasons for writing. This letter also illustrates the use of formally scheduled activities by the inmates to give messages to one another.

To: Lucky

From: J.W.

Time: Forever I hope
Place: In my heart
Reason: I really love you
Because: You act it anyways
Realized: Your love is strong (I hope)
Why: Your love is amazing
Aim: I want you back
Wish: You take me back
Hope: You realize it
Want: Your sweet loving
Tempt[ation]:   Your sweet lips
Mood: Lonesome for your love
Desire: To have you in my arms

Songs:

My desire
Your love is amazing
What love has joined together
Two lovers
It's just a matter of time
I really love you
I do love you
Unchained melody
Just let me know

143—again
225—never
117—never

711—I hope (maybe)
225—never
500—always
643—??? Up to you

My Dearest Darling:

Why don't you answer all my letters. I know you probably have something on your mind. But even if you do. You could at least send a message. Betty in the morning, and Clarissa Steward is in my class in the afternoon. So please answer my letter. Have to go now.

Love you always

J.W.
-n-
Lucky

T.L.A.
H.O.L.L.A.N.D.

P.S. ans back soon

The letter below, written by the same inmate, was sent after the "numbers had been called" and the relationship terminated. The song titles have been selected to convey the change in mood and the outcome desired.

To: Luckie

From: J.W.

Place: In my Heart (always)
Date: Forever: I hope
Mood: Lonesome
Desire: To hold you in my arms
Why: I really do love you
Realized: That I can't live without you
Because: My love is to deep for you
Want: You come back to me
Aim: At least to try and get you back
Tempt[ation]:   To at least mack
Hope: We do go back
Wish: You say yes

Reason: My love for you is tearing my heart apart
Butch: J.W.
Fem: Luckie
Love: You (Only)
Songs: The fem's alright with me
         Going out of my head (over you)
         I just can't help myself
         Nothing can stop me (from loving you)
         As I sit here (thinking of the love we could positively have)
         This can't be true (that we have parted)
         I'm a hurting inside (for your love)
         Any old time of the day: (I'll come running back to you)
Why: Because this is how strong my love is
         When a man loves a woman
         When a woman loves a man
         Just let me (and don't keep me in mystery)
         I made a mistake (at least I hope I haven't)
         Are you there (waiting for me to come)
         Take me back (because I want you back to)
         Tears on Pillow (these I definetly have for you; not knowing what your
              doing; or who your with)
         Anyone who had a heart (yes I positively do)
         It's just a matter of time (when we shall find out the stone truth)
         Unchained melody.
         My Baby loves me (at least I hope you do)
143:   again
Reason: I want you back
Why: My love is definetly deep for you
Because: Your the only one I really want on campus
Realized: That you really do love me
Hope: You say (YES) not (NO)
225—never again
Why: It should have never happened anyway
Because: love does just separate because of certain things
Reason: I don't care what the people say, the point is I love you
711:   Soon I hope
Because: I hope it comes soon
Why: So I can always have you
Reason: Because if we get married and you want me on the outside I'll
              always be there
Hope: This answer is (yes) not (no)
117—Forget it
Why: That's for people with problems
Wish: You never ask for it

Because: I wouldn't give it to you anyway
89—Never
Reason: Naughty
69—Never
Reason: Only for people who don't care
110—Always
Why: It's really there
Place: In my heart
When: Deep down inside
Date: Forever; no nopes about it
Dedication to you: Every Little Bit Hurts
Why: Especially when its deep down inside
Because: It can really tear a person apart
Hope: You don't hurt me twice in a row
Wish: We remain together for always
Want: To take this song into stride

143—Again
225—Never again
333—Always I hope
711—Soon I hope
117—Never
69—Never
89—Never
110—Always
375—You never know
500—Always

My Dearest Love:

While sitting here in my lonesome room. Thinking of the questions you ask the girls today. There was nothin wrong with me in the dining room. I was just hot and tired. Because I cleaned my room and all that mescelleanous Bullshit. Luckie I love you so god dam much that I definetly want you back. And if I can't have you back, I think I'll go crazy. And let me tell you something I'm not jiving with you. I really and truly and deeply love you. I heard this—about you and etc. But I don't let it stop me from loving you the way I do, because sometimes it is hard to find someone you really like; or I must say really and truly love. Because let me tell you. You fascinate me a great deal. You had best to believe this statement I have just made because it's no lie. It's only fact which I'm writing you in this letter. See I don't think shit. I believe I know. Especially I know I love you. And there is nothing that can break my love no other kind of girl. There is no other girl on campus that fascinates me as much as you do. Just give it one more try and see what really happens. I think I have explained my self clear enough for you to understand. Excuse the hand writing. Ending my letter but never my love.

Love Always
J.W. Capri

P.S. ans. soon
  J.W.
   n
  Luckie
    Soon again   Yes or No
    I hope   Please don't say no

In the following letter, a fem points out to a trust-to-be butch that the appropriate procedure is for the butch to propose marriage. The expressions at the end of the letter reflect the writer's wishes concerning both enemies, friends, and relatives; they are typical. Similar expressions may also be found in graffiti on many walls and other surfaces throughout the institution.

143—Always (open)	To: My Dearest Darling Dino
225—Never	From: Nita
110—I really do	Date: for-ever
333—soon	Time: to answer your sweet letter
711—It's up to you, not me to ask	Place: in my Heart
117—never if 711	Reason: I really love you
115—more	Hope: you mean what you said
375—never again	Want: you only
220—Always	Need: you only
73 —you are	Tempt[ation]: your soft sweet lips
116—never	Aim: To keep you
500—People should	Song: What love has joined together
	Butch: you
Songs	Fem: me
	Mess[age]: It's growing (fast)
Close your Eyes	Ded[ication]: "Stay together young lovers"
Dry Your Eyes	
Just Be Sincere	
Stand By Me	
I've Got a feeling	
I do love you	
The Whole World is a stage	

The Girl don't care (I do)
Just be True
The Hunter Gets Captured by the Game
I gonna miss you
I dig you, Baby
RainBow 65
You've Waited too Long
Danger She's a Stranger
Ain't to proud to Beg
I love you 1,000 times
Message to Michael

Tramp
Respect
Funkie Broadway

Dear Sweet Dino,

While sitting here with Time on my side and *only* you on my mind, I decided
to drop you these few lines of love. That was a sweet letter you wrote me.
but I don't understand on thing. When you wrote in the numbers (711—It's
up to you). It's not my job, it's your job. Understand? What I really want to
say is that I love you with all my Heart and soul. I love you more that I *loved*
Skeeter. And that's a lot. I always did like you even when I was going with
Skeeter, but then you understand. All I want is to make you happy and not
regret that you asked me. Just stand by me darling, and I'll never leave you.
And if you should ever leave me it would feel like a part of me was also gone.
But if you should find out later that you don't love me, it would be better for
you to tell me, than to go on playing me for a Dam fool. Okay? If I act like I
don't like you, it's Because sometimes I get shy. So I'm closing now saying I
love you forever & ever.

                                          110 Baby,

                                          Nita

                                          DINO
                                          -N-
                                          NITA

                                                    T.L.A.
                                                    H.-n-W. *Soon*

P.S.   Tell lil-Brown Eyes, Lil Joe say 110 forever. and Tell lil-Brown Eyes I said 110 too.

Skeeter	Flame
-n-	-n-
Maria	Gidget
H. & W.	T.L.A.
(Hope their love Dies)	H. & W.A.
Happy	Lil-Joe
-n-	-n-
Chiffon	Lil-Brown Eyes
	T.L.A.
	H.-n-W.S.

Although fems do not take the initiative in proposing marriage, a fem who finds a butch attractive may write to the individual expressing her interest. In the letter below, an inmate who has been on the campus three days writes to an inmate who lives in the adjacent cottage.

Sugar City
Lemon State
This letter needs a date.

Dear Lefty,

I'm a new fem on campus but I've been here since Tuesday and I've been watching you since Tuesday and I'm writting you to let you known that I think you are the finest Butch on campus.
You can recognize me because I'll be wearing a pink & white suit to the movies in cott. #10.

Love Always
Tanya

Issues are sent not only to establish romantic relationships but also to settle misunderstandings between husbands and wives. An inmate's apology to her husband in the letter below illustrates this practice.

Time: To Say I am sorry

Reason: I Love you

Disire: To Prove it to you

Hope: You understand

Song: What have I done to make you mad
Song: I've been good to you
Song: Baby Baby Please
Song: Love makes me do foolish things
Song: Darling Forever
Song: For your love
Song: Selfish One
Song: God Bless our Love
Song: Baby let me be good to you
Song: Give my love a try

Dearest Love,

I know I shouldn't even write to you. But I feel that in a way I was wrong too. But I'll make to up to you if I can. Honey these little arguements that we've been having are not at all necessary, and I'm going to see that we don't have any more of these stupid arguements. Honey I'm really very sorry. I think that the only reason we've been acting this way is because of me. because I'am alway's worrying about what other people in the cottage are saying about us. And I know at times I hurt you but I will try to be good to you for you are my man, my Husband and I love you. "all of you" An I don't want to do anything to make you unhappy. for I married you because my love was far to strong to just be going with you I had to marry into this Love. and now that we are united I'am going to make you a happy man. And I'll be a "Do right all *day* women, If you will be a do right all *night* man. And there is nothing in this world that I wouldn't do for you. for your precious love means more to me then anything in this world. for when I first met you I was lonely and so blue, but now I have a love that's true. And I'll do anything "yes i would to have your precious love. Please don't be mad. I love you for what you've made me. and that's a *Women*. Your women"

Love always your Wife.

For some of the inmates who have children in the external world, involvement in the informal social system may create special problems. This is expressed clearly in the following letter.

To: China
From: Tango
Time: To Write
Place: From the heart
Reason:. I do love you
Desire: To keep you always

Hope: you feel the same
Can't: Do without you
Need: you every hour
Want: this to stay like it is now
Why: I can't bare these pains alone
Butch: Tango
Fem: China
Mess[age]:   Never never leave me

Songs

Baby you're my everything
This can't be true
Follow your heart
Never leave your baby's side
S.O.S.
Whisper you love me
Danny Boy
Nothing can stop me
Fading away
Hurt so bad
Doo Baby, baby
Rainbow "65"
Every little bit hurts
Choosey begger
Thats when it hurts
Cry no more
Street of tears
Someday, someway
Rainbow
My girl
Love
Come to me
Opportunity
Cry baby
I've got no time to lose
Going out of my head
Pain in my heart
Long long Winter
I love you (yeah)
A sweet woman like you
Kiss, kiss, kiss
Tonight's the night
My vows to you

I had a talk with my man (Fem)
Love makes the world go round
This heart of mine
My world is empty without you
You're my soul & high insperation
Man's temptation
Greetings
My prayer
Reap what you sow
Sitting in the park
You really got a hold on me
Good night my love
Two can easily do
Don't have to shop around
I have faith in you
I found a love
My baby loves me
Stay together
I do love you
Temptation bought to get you
I need you
You'll never walk alone
Maybe the last
Lost some one
Please, Please, please
Try me
I got you
I can't help it
Strange feelings
This old heart of mine
A changes gonna come
For your precious love
Precious words
Save the last dance for me
I'm hurting inside
I'm hurt
Any one who had a heart
I'm the one love forgot
Cry baby

My dearest darling China,

While sitting here tonight just thinking that today was a most dreadful day of ever on this campus. You see I thought for sure that I was going to get shipped so I told the girls to tell you so that in case you didn't see me on campus any more you would no why. Because yesterday I had a talk with [*staff member*] and thats why but now I know that I'm not. China there are going to be a lot of changes around here for one thing I'm too deep in the racket and if I don't cool it I on my way an that's the gods honest truth so if you see me look different on somedays you know why. And for another thing I don't want to get you in any kind of trouble you see I'm looking after your warfare as much as mine. I love you too much and couldn't bare the hurts and pains it might cause for you nor I. You know after I heard that you were going to get shipped I got sicker by the minutes. You are the only one I love and hope to for the rest of my life. I want you to understand one thing before I go any farther. I have to make a chose between you and James and my three year old daughter this as you know is a descession that I have to make on my own and with the decession I will make I have to live with it for the rest of my entire life *You James* and *my daughter* remember that its up to me and me alone what ever I decides is a matter of my future and my life god only knows its his descession as well as mine. But whatever it may be its hard to decide. China I love you more than you or I really relieze it but every word is a known and true fact. I just can't do without you to me you're my life my reason for laughing, crying for living and dying you're every breath that I take my ice cream my coffee my sugar my tea my reason for living each and every day if you ever turn your back my life would fade away. To me you're gods only gift to the world beyond its like another demention into a world unknow these are steps we have to take without them theres nothing no people no earth nor world or outer space there would also be no Heaven nor Hell these we must think about to me love is some thing on so great something no man could ever explaine this is how much I love you. I need your love as well as you need mine and this no one can help not even god above. Well I guess now that you really know how much I love you I guess theres not much more than I can say or express my self to you you have to take it from here its up to you to prove you love me as much as its up to me so you think about this and think dam hard because these are things I want you to relize also it concerns our love affair so you have to help understand this too. So I'll close my letter for now but never my love for you.

Tango   Love Always
&   Tango
China
T.L.A.
T.D.D.U.P.

                                               Ronnie
                                               &
                                               Chickie
                                               T.L.A.

There is a great deal of competition for partners at Eastern. Hence, it is not unusual that inmates try to break up relationships before they are finalized by marriage. An inmate, aroused by jealousy, may call out the numbers in a rash moment—only to regret it seconds later—because the one she is going with pays special attention to another inmate. These situations result in both verbal and physical attacks. Some inmates strive for a reconciliation after calling the numbers, but efforts in this direction usually prove futile.

To: Jojo
From: Lil Bit
Time: To write
Place: In my heart
Reason: Because your still on my mind
Because: I care about you
Desire: To have and to hold
Hope: We do get together one of these day's
Wish: You will understand me
Song: Let it be me

Dear Jojo:

just a few lines to tell you that I read your letter, but for one thing I think you are wrong because I know you love Popeye but Popeye really is not in love with you and I wouldn't want you to be played for her fool because she isn't worst it and when I was going whit you, you know for a fact I din't play you for a fool and you know I din't do you wrong. All I did to you was called 225 and that was because you were looking for it. and I know Popeye is doing you wrong because she use to come to me everyday and tell me thing's, and she even said herself she din't love you, and you can belived what I have just wrote you in this letter because every thing is true and I think you all ready know it. And Jojo I do love you very much and if you think you can keep Popeye you can try it, but after you find out for yourself she's doing you wrong you will want me and at that time I will be with someone else. So I will advise you Jojo take me while you got me, because if you don't your just messing up good things while you got it.

Love Alway's
Lil Bit

Mate selection among the Eastern inmates is based on romantic love. All of the homosexual relationships are established on a voluntary basis, from going steady to marriage. However, at all three schools, homosexual attacks sometimes occur, usually involving adolescent inmates who have expressed an unwillingness to participate in homosexuality and who are zealous in ridiculing inmates who engage in this behavior.

The Eastern inmates make a distinction between inmates who are "married" and those who are "just going together." Going together refers to the process of "dating and getting to know" the individual to determine whether they would be suitable in a marriage relationship. It is the equivalent of a girl "going steady" with a boy in the external world. (Thus it also functions to give the inmates the kind of social practice that they most likely would have had in the external world.)

> Going with a girl is like a boy and girl. The same pattern as outside. You go with a lot of boys outside and you do the same thing here—except with girls.

In matters of courtship, rules of etiquette prescribe that the "males" on campus take the initiative.

> The boys ask the girls out. It's just like outside. The butch asks. The butch is supposed to ask. The fem has to wait. But the fem can do something. She can write an issue to let him know she'd like to go out. Then she'd wait to see what would happen. She'd wait until she'd see the person in person, and then they could talk. If he don't write, there are others around—later for it.

The period of courtship may vary from a few days to a few weeks. If the two individuals find that they are compatible—that is, they can "make it"—they will marry. A few inmates limit all their relationships to "going with" and never marry, but most inmates get married after a short period of time.

In matters of courtship, parents play an essential role. First, the Eastern inmate must have a set of parents before she can marry because parents must sign the marriage papers if children are under sixteen years of age (they often do even for those who are older). Parents also must make the arrangements for marriage. This means that individuals who are going together are constrained to become members of families if they intend to marry.

> You can't get married with somebody else that is still married. You can't get married unless you have a father and a mother. . . . It's impossible to get anyone without a mother and father because it's the mother and father who handles everything. It's their responsibility—the signing of the papers and everything like that.

Hence the Eastern inmates usually establish kinship ties before they engage in courtship relationships. Some parents suggest individuals; a mother may say to a son or daughter, "Roadrunner would be good for you. Why don't you look into it?" If parents disapprove of a child's choice, they do not hesitate to make this known. Parents have veto power concerning additions into the family. A child may always establish a relationship with someone in a kinship tie, but they will not be related to the other family members unless the parents express approval.

In addition to giving advice, parents speak to other inmates in their child's behalf to promote a romantic interest, or they may request another family member to act in this way if she knows the individual better. Parents also shield a child from disappointment whenever plans do not materialize.

In a few very prestigious families, almost all mates are selected within the family. The members believe that through a careful screening process they have recruited the "cream of the crop" in their family, and therefore need not go out of it in search of mates. In these families, a child may also go with one of the peripheral relatives. Parents, however, are not allowed to go with their children. Incest involving parents and children is strictly prohibited, but it is not unusual for brothers and sisters to marry. In fact, this is encouraged by some parents.

Lack of expertise may have an important effect as to how desirable one appears to others. Gay people prefer to go with other gay people or at least those inmates who have had prior experience either at Eastern or elsewhere.

I don't want to go with her, because she's just starting and she don't know what she's doing. Some that are stone butch won't want to be bothered because she won't know what to be.

One family on campus (perhaps the largest and most prestigious) is composed entirely of lesbians and other inmates who have stated a commitment to this way of life. To be part of this family, commitment to homosexuality is all important.

The Eastern inmates want their world *inside* to be as much like the *outside* world as possible. The strain for realism is particularly expressed in marriage and divorce proceedings. Marriages and divorces are *formalized* by family surnames and "legal" documents. Inmates prefer to have marriage certificates and divorce papers typed because they are thought to be more like printed documents, thus more realistic. In this regard, the inmates who are enrolled in typing courses perform a valuable service. If marriage papers cannot be typed, they will be handwritten in ink.

Information appearing on marriage papers includes the date the marriage took place, the location where it was performed, names and signatures of the couple, and the signature of the inmate who performed the ceremony. If a child is sixteen years of age or less, the parents also must sign the marriage papers.

Marriages at Eastern must be performed by a duly authorized person, who is usually referred to as a "preacher" but occasionally as "judge" or "priest." A butch always acts the role of preacher. The preacher must know "the Eastern way" of doing things, including the slight variation in ceremony that is made depending on the wedding site. The preacher must also understand the rules of divorce procedure, because only the preacher who married a couple has the authority to grant them a divorce.

The inmates are not recognized as married unless they go through a formal marriage ceremony; and proper witnesses must sign the marriage certificate. The number of witnesses varies from two to as many as six, but most inmates seem to have four witnesses—"two on each side." Witnesses are recruited to represent "both sides" to provide *proof* that the marriage actually took place.

The parents work closely with the preacher until the marriage is performed. Apart from granting their permission, parents handle such details as where and when the wedding will take place. They also obtain the signatures of the witnesses. Inmates use campus names to sign the marriage papers.

Marriages take place on the Eastern campus wherever the inmates can assemble together. Inmates of different faiths do not get married in the chapel because the inmates cannot attend all church services; similarly, if the couple do not live in the same cottage, a cottage wedding must be ruled out. In an effort to stabilize marriages, the Eastern inmates maintain that they prefer to marry individuals who do not live in the same cottage. This is based on the conviction that when one sees too much of a marriage partner, it inevitably leads to fights which would strain the marriage relationship, and in addition, it would make the relationship visible to the staff.

Nevertheless, after going with one or more inmates who live elsewhere, many inmates do marry individuals who live in their cottage. In many ways (although the staff is present), it is easier to perform a wedding in the cottage because many family members are likely to live in the same cottage. But the inmates change wedding plans to fit the exigencies of particular situations. Marriages on the Eastern campus may take place in the gym, bathroom, auditorium, school building, administration building, or the hospital clinic. When it appears to be the best solution, all the inmates who are to be present at the wedding may make arrangements to be at the clinic for medication on a certain day. Such arrangements may provide solutions to the inmates' informal activities, but they create serious organizational problems for the nursing staff.

When marriages take place in the cottage, a favorite setting is the recreation room as the preacher, the couple to be married, parents and other relatives, the witnesses, and their friends may all assemble there. Relatives frequently act as witnesses. The entire gathering stands, and the ritual follows the procedure of the traditional wedding service. The preacher says the familiar words, vows and rings are exchanged, and the bride is kissed when it is over. If staff members appear to hover about on the day a wedding has been scheduled, the procedure is modified to ensure that the wedding is not apparent. Thus, although it may appear that several inmates are merely peering out of a window, a wedding may actually be taking place.

After the wedding, the two copies of the marriage papers are signed; both the husband and wife receive a copy.

A few marriages take place in the chapel, but inmates tend to rule out this location because members of the wedding party may be of different faiths. Also, because staff members tend to get "more upset" when inmates marry in church, discipline may be severe. For a church wedding, ritual behavior is modified. The inmates cannot speak to one another in church, hence the preacher must recite the crucial words silently and give cues to the couple getting married when the words have been said, so that they may rise, face one another, and then sit down. To avoid detection, inmates rise in a manner as if they were arranging clothing or looking for an object. The act of rising is important, and the butch and fem are not considered married if they do not rise from their seats. Standing up proves to everyone that they are serious because they are willing to take the risk involved.

During the summer months, when organized recreational activities take place on the quadrangles between cottages, marriages are sometimes performed in the open area. But most inmates at Eastern are married in the auditorium during a movie. Going to the movies fits the important criteria that would be associated with a wedding in the external world—the most important of which would be "dressing up and going out."

But there is another reason: The number of inmates who may be present at a marriage depends upon where it takes place. If the marriage is performed in the cottage, all the family members may be present if the entire family lives in the same cottage. But most Eastern inmates have kinship ties in other cottages, and most couples prefer that their family and friends attend their wedding. Because all the inmates go to the movies on the same day, it is possible for friends and relatives to be present.

The ritual procedure varies slightly when a marriage takes place at the movies. When the inmates do not sit together (they may live in different cottages), the ceremony resembles a chapel wedding in that the couple must stand, face each other, and then sit down.

The Eastern inmates display a keen sense of pride—and in some instances triumph—when they are to be married. Word concerning weddings spreads rapidly throughout the campus. The sentiment of the fems was put in these words:

> No marriages are secret. If you want to keep it a secret, there's no sense getting married. If a butch is proud of you, that's what's important.

The inmates who marry are those who have been successful in their respective roles. The major goal for the Eastern inmates is marriage; hence to attract an individual and to marry—in the face of considerable competition on campus—is an achievement of sorts. For this reason, inmates sometimes make it a special point to invite rivals to the wedding.

Time: Ours

Dear Love,

While sitting here with you on my mind, I decided to drop you these few lines.

Well, as you already heard, that me and you are getting married. How the staff no, I don't know.

But if you love me like you say you do, you won't let anyone break us up. Not even Brenda, Betty, or Anna. I just found out that Anna like you also, and she is trying to break us up. They will try or say anything to fill your head with something which isn't true.

You got to believe me, that I really but truly love you, and that no one can stop my love for you.

Don't let anyone fill your head with that Bull————, because that just what it is and it is getting me mad.

If there is a wedding for me and you, I'll make it my business to give all these damn girls in here who is trying to break us up an special invitation.

Because I ain't giving you up, for a damn fool. Please excuse the handwriting, but I'm mad and crying at the same time.

So until I hear from you. I love you.

Love Always and Forever
DECO

All Eastern marriages require that the couple being married wear clothing of the same color; indeed, sometimes every member of a family will wear something that is the color worn by the couple. This small detail contributes to the occasion for the inmates, as it helps to make it different from the routine day.

Marriage ceremonies on the Eastern campus are carefully planned events, the details of which may take several days to complete. First, witnesses who can be trusted have to be recruited to sign the papers. Family members usually perform this important task. The father, as head of the family, sometimes assumes the role of preacher, particularly in the families where all mates are selected from within the family.

The prominent factors of most of the Eastern marriages are demonstration of affection and love, sharing of experiences, companionship, loyalty, and mutual aid. In all matters, the Eastern wife is expected to defer to the husband and to *obey* the latter's requests—including requests to wash and iron. Contacts with all butches on campus are expected to be minimal and brief, except with males who are family members.

Once a relationship is formalized by the wedding ceremony, it cannot be terminated except by signing "legal" divorce papers. An important function of the marriage papers is to keep the marriage intact.

To be legally married, you have to have papers. The papers are important because if she's doing anything wrong you can say, "I've got papers on you." Or if someone tries to break it up you can go and say, "I've got papers on her."

The *papers* serve as a reminder that there are certain rights and obligations that attach to the marriage. The papers also serve as a symbolic weapon which may be used if an inmate tries to break up the marriage.

DIVORCE. The rules governing the structure of marriage and divorce are communicated to the inmates before marriage. The most important socializing agents are the parents of the couple and the preacher who make it clear that they must remain married for six months. The Eastern marriages remain relatively stable, although a couple may become estranged and "separate." When a separation reaches its most developed stage, an inmate will *go with* other inmates. Even so, the marriage is still considered intact, and unless a divorce is officially granted, neither the husband nor the wife may marry again. Before a divorce actually takes place, the parents and other family members attempt to "sit down and talk out the problem."

Under some circumstances a divorce may be obtained before the six-months period has elapsed. Yet divorce is not automatically granted simply because it is requested by either the husband or wife. Both the husband and wife must agree to the divorce. They must go to the preacher who married them. If the preacher has been released from the institution, one of the male parents grants the divorce. Furthermore, divorces are granted only when just cause can be shown; and the preacher must make this judgment. In a sense the preacher acts as a marriage counselor.

> You have to ask why they want a divorce. "What's wrong? Are you sure this is what you want?" And you have to ask them the reason why. I talk to each one separately, then I get them together. I might say, "No!" if I think it's something stupid like a fight, or something like that, and you know that in five minutes they'll be lovey-dovey.

The most frequent reasons given for divorce are: (1) the husband and wife argue; (2) a spouse talks with another inmate for what is perceived to be an intolerably long period of time; (3) an informant tells the husband or wife that her mate was kissing another inmate; (4) a mate sends an issue indicating that her interest has shifted; and (5) because of nonconformity to institutional rules, a mate spends too many evenings and weekends in "locked" status. But whatever the stated cause, the major reason for most divorces is that an inmate finds another individual more attractive and decides to go with that individual.

Divorce may be communicated with no preliminary statement to soften the news. One's intentions may be declared by simply walking up to the mate and calling out "225!" But many inmates prefer not to be so direct. For example, a butch who wants to terminate a marriage may wait until the wife engages in an act contrary to the norms and then will confront the individual with "225!" This strategy is more desirable because inmates who have acquired a reputation for frequent break-ups not only weaken their kinship ties but also are less able to attract other inmates.

Even when an inmate utters the fateful numbers face to face, divorce is not automatically certain. The inmate addressed may not agree to the divorce; then the inmate has little choice but to play a waiting game. If she chooses not to wait, she may resort to a method that will almost certainly guarantee the outcome, but will make her unpopular—she may delegate the task of communication to a third party.

You can tell one of her friends to tell her. This really hurts when you have somebody else tell her. To get somebody else to call the numbers makes you lose face.

To such impersonal communication, almost any inmate will agree to a divorce on the spot.

After six months of marriage, a couple is *automatically* considered divorced; it is not necessary for them to go through the formal divorce procedure. Both the husband and the wife are free to go with other inmates. If they decide to terminate their relationship after six months, the marriage papers are torn up and kinship ties are adjusted. For example, a son-in-law may now be a son—or might not be related at all, depending upon the individuals involved and whether a change in sex role occurred at this time.

In the few prestigious families where mates are selected within the family, divorce is granted before the expiration date when it is clear that a couple cannot "get along," as it is feared that discord may jeopardize the family structure. The father usually acts as the preacher in these families; if a divorce is granted, the individuals are restored to the kinship roles that they occupied in the family before they were married.

An inmate may also obtain a divorce shortly before the termination of the six-month marriage period if she is to be released, in order to relieve her partner of all marriage responsibilities; otherwise the marriage would still be intact.

Even after a discharge you're still married, unless you get a divorce. Most girls do not remarry after their partner is discharged. Some might go with a girl—especially the butch—but most don't get married again unless you have a divorce.

The structure of divorce is formalized by written documents, made out by either the butch or the fem. The divorce papers are typed whenever possible, for the same reason noted earlier in the discussion of marriage papers. All divorce papers contain the names of the couple; reason for the divorce (a common "cause" listed is "adultery"); signatures of the couple, the witnesses, and often the parents; date of the marriage; and date of the divorce. The papers must be signed by the preacher, now acting as judge.

The divorce papers also may contain a short statement of the events leading to the divorce. Campus names are used by all to insure anonymity in the event that the documents should fall into the hands of staff. The marriage papers are torn up after the signatures are affixed to the divorce papers.

THE STRUCTURE OF KINSHIP TIES.   At Eastern institution, all relationships among the inmates are defined primarily in kinship terms. Kinship ties span all the cottages and cross racial lines and social classes. A family begins with a set of parents, and children are linked to this dyadic structure almost immediately after the butch and fem have been "united" in marriage. To enter an Eastern family as a child is in a sense to be born into it, as one is automatically related to all the individuals to whom one's parents are related. This holds not only when one first joins the family, but for any subsequent kinship ties the parents may establish.

The Eastern inmate community may be viewed as a large network of loosely structured nuclear families, matricentric and patricentric families of varying size, and other kinship dyadic configurations or family fragments which result when inmates are divorced or released to the community. But all are linked in an intricate pattern of kinship relationships by virtue of the fact that some inmates have overlapping membership in two families.

The Eastern inmates do not specify that kinship ties other than marriage are to be sustained for a definite period of time; nor are they formalized by written documents. Yet the family groups among the juvenile girls are not disrupted easily; in fact, they are relatively stable structures, but more options are available to the individual as to the kinship ties she wishes to sustain at any time. An inmate may move out of a family group or terminate other isolated kinship ties when her needs change or when she disagrees with the behavior of individuals with whom she is linked in kinship bonds.

The family group that social scientists refer to as the nuclear family consists of eight roles: husband, wife, father, mother, son, daughter, brother, and sister. Almost all of the Eastern family groups exhibit all of these roles. The interaction between the members of family groups is characterized as warm and close.

Apart from the social functions of protection, mutual aid, and affection which parents provide the family members, they also help to maintain social control in the institution. One of the important conditions of sustained family membership at Eastern is that one abides by the institutional rules. Indeed, if an inmate continually breaks the rules, she may be "disowned" by the parents; this action would mean exclusion from the entire family group. For most of the inmates, the emotional and social support gained within the family is of such magnitude that they conform.

Kinship roles are based principally on sex and to some extent age. Some kinship ties are formed to fill the inmate's social and psychological needs. For example, an inmate may ask another inmate to be her aunt simply because she "reminds" her of an "aunt outside," or to be her mother because the inmate "acts like a mother would."

The inmate implicitly expects that both she and the individual to whom she is related will act out the appropriate behavioral prescriptions. Therefore, if an individual who is "supposed to be a sister" acts instead "like a mother," the behavior would be contrary to role expectations. The relationship between them might then be changed to that of mother and daughter, or it may be terminated.

For the Eastern inmates the structuring of kinship ties in a family group occurs prior to marriage. As put by an inmate:

> You have to have parents before you can have brothers or sisters, because the way we feel about it here: "I want to know who my mother and father is."

All Eastern couples "create" families soon after they are married. Usually the newlyweds ask other inmates to be part of their family within a few days after they are married. The number of inmates they recruit depends upon their personal and social characteristics—whether they are popular on campus, have pleasing personalities, and possess the qualities that would enable them to "act as parents should." Usually, one or two daughters will be selected first, then other children may be added; rejection does not occur frequently because the inmates ask their best friends to join their families.

Inmates do not deliberately set out to form families of any particular size. To have more than three or four children is to run the risk of detection by the staff. Nevertheless, the basic family groups are usually considerably larger, and they increase in size as children "grow up" and marry—all of whom will add at least three children to their family. Moreover, their children may be expected to marry, and the cycle is repeated.

Families at Eastern also grow through sister and brother kinship bonds established by the parents. When a family member is released, another inmate may be added as a relative to fill the void. The parents decide who enters their family, and children are related to all other inmates that their parents claim as kin. When parents adopt someone into the family, the rest of the family honors the kinship tie. A parent may simply inform a son or daughter, "This is my sister, and you have an aunt."

A third way in which a family may increase in size is by accepting an inmate who has asked to join them. At Eastern, if an inmate is not asked to join a family group it may be because she is not a close associate of any family member, is a new arrival on campus, lacks the qualifications deemed necessary for membership, or inadvertently may have been overlooked. Therefore she may take the initiative; for example, she may ask an inmate to be her mother or father. The acknowledgment of the inmate's request depends upon the family's assesment as to how well she will fit into their family.

Another procedure often followed is to initiate the aid of a friend: "You go to the best friend you have in the family, and ask if you can get in." This procedure has an obvious advantage; if the individual is not acceptable to the family, this fact may be communicated in such a way that she will not be offended and the parents need not be involved directly.

Inmates may be motivated to join a particular family because of its popularity on campus. An inmate also may want to join a family because of its potential marriage mates. She may try to attach herself to a popular butch as a sister, in the hope that one day the butch's romantic interests will be directed to her.

> If there's a well known butch in a family, others try to be in that family. They think: "I will be well known, too."

> If you have a popular figure in the family, the others try to get in. They try to make friends with you. But we try to keep the families small so the staff won't know.

Peripheral kinship ties are occasionally added when the individual is not quite acceptable to the family members; then the inmate would be accepted in the general role of "cousin" or, as in a few cases, in a foster child role. The latter role is quite within the inmates' frame of reference because many of them have been in foster homes.

Parents expect their children to obey them in all matters, and the children expect their inmate mother and father to act as surrogate parents; therefore the inmates choose inmates who will "act as parents would." Although the Eastern inmates believe that you should have only one set of parents at any time—"because you respect your mother and father"— a few inmates do have more than one set of parents. An inmate may select a second set of parents when her mother and father do not live up to her expectations. Most parents object to this, however, and a child's acknowledgment of a second mother and father may be reason enough to disown her. But most relationships with dual parents come about as a consequence of divorce. In any case, an individual's membership in two families contributes to the linking of the family groups throughout the campus into a vast network of kinship ties.

The kinship ties may be terminated whenever an individual decides she will not honor the relationship with any inmate to whom she stands in kinship bonds; she simply informs the inmate to whom she is related as a daughter, brother, sister, or whatever, that she no longer wishes to continue this relationship.

An inmate may terminate a kinship tie for several reasons. An inmate's parents may refuse to consent to her marriage, and she may drop her parents and seek another mother and father. But the most common reasons are related to the inmate's personal habits or personality.

You lose interest. You think you know someone, but sometimes you haven't known them very long. You get them in the family, and two days later you find you don't like their ways.

Sometimes you think someone is nice, and you ask them to be in the family, and then you find you don't like them. So you just tell them, "I don't want you in the family, anymore." Would she still be related to everyone else? Oh, she'd still be related, and in a way, she still would be related to you. You have the same mother and father. If you fight with your brothers and sisters, you could be kicked out of the family. But you wouldn't be so close after you told them.

If you don't like a person you don't *accept* them, but you would still be related. But you usually respect the choice of other family members. You might not consider yourself related, but everyone else on campus would.

All kinship ties are established with individuals who are "trusted-to-be"—either as a sister, brother, mother, father, or in another kinship role; hence whenever an individual is convinced that a relative is not living up to role expectations, she may "drop" her. This would almost certainly be the case whenever a change in sex role is made.

When kinship relationships are terminated, inmates usually seek to establish the same type of relationship with someone else. The inmate may want to have a sister or a brother to complement her needs, and isolated kinship links may be established at this time.

Generally, an inmate does not terminate kinship links indiscriminately because she would be defined as "hard to get along with" and would have difficulty establishing other kinship ties.

If an inmate breaks a kinship tie with a sibling she experiences no difficulty in establishing the same type of relationship with another inmate. But if she terminates her kinship ties with her parents, the consequences may be more serious. Dropping a parent would mean that the individual is literally out of the family and she is related to no one.

An inmate may be *disowned*, although it does not necessarily constitute a permanent break with the family. An individual may be welcomed back into the fold if her behavior improves. The individuals who are disowned may become part of other families, however. In short, one family's loss becomes another family's gain.

> When you say, "I'm your daughter!" it's like taking a vow. They can disown you. It's the person who asks another to be a relative that has the right to disown the other person. All they'd have to say is: "I disown you for a daughter!" and the two of you wouldn't be related after this.

Inmates who violate institutional rules always stand the risk of being disowned by their parents. This negative sanction is used only as a last resort when counseling and warnings by parents and other family members have proven unsuccessful.

Divorce usually has more serious consequences for the kinship structure because often it involves parents with children. Yet divorce is not a frequent phenomenon. Many couples go through a period of "separation"; during this period the family remains intact, and sometimes the members become reconciled. In addition, most inmates go with several individuals before they get married; and parents discourage marriages when they have reason to believe that the two inmates would not be compatible. The normative rule stipulating that a couple must be married for six months before a divorce may be granted also contributes to the stability of marriage.

The prestigious families on campus attempt to maintain the structural integrity of the family unit. Old and new members alike are socialized that they "have to keep the name up" and they are reminded occasionally to "keep the family going." Understandably, inmates are reluctant to disrupt their kinship ties in a family that has considerable prestige on campus. To restore harmony in these families, the father will grant a divorce to anyone whose behavior threatens to disrupt the structure of social relationships in the family.

When the parents in a family are divorced, the impact may have far-reaching consequences. For example, a husband's brother would no longer be a brother-in-law to the wife, but they would probably remain friends. The children may decide to drop or disown their parents and become drawn into a number of different families; or an inmate may choose to remain in kinship status to her parents, and thus may have stepparents as well. Finally, an inmate may decide to "go on her mother's side," hence all her important relationships would be through the mother.

When divorce disrupts established relationships, existing kinship ties must be restructured. The family is fragmented into small discrete units which are in turn incorporated into larger family structures. Small families retain partial structure—especially when the family members are married, as these family units become larger with the addition of children. But some families may become completely disrupted to fragmentary kinship linkages that are further fractionated as individual members are released. Most families continue to exist, however, because of the marriages of the family members and by the recruitment of other relatives, especially children.

If an inmate changes her sex role after a divorce, kinship roles are adjusted within the family. In some cases, all to whom she is related will acknowledge the change in sex role and define kinship relationships accordingly; for example, a brother may now be a sister, but if the brother is unwilling to acknowledge the inmate as a sister, they may continue to relate to one another as brothers. In this case, the inmate who changed sex roles occupies a dual sex role. But changes of an even more dramatic nature sometimes take place. An inmate related, "Annie Beck is my sister. She used to be my father. When she switched sex roles, we decided to be sisters."

THE SOCIAL FUNCTIONS OF KINSHIP TIES. The role content of the family units is that which we associate with the nuclear family in American culture. The group structure of the nuclear family is importantly related to the inmates' social expectations in connection with their needs—emotional reciprocity and emotional security, mutual aid, and protection against other inmates when necessary.

The most important members in the Eastern family units are the mother and father. Authority is vested in the parental role, although other family members voice their opinions in some matters. But the parents—and especially the fathers—are the undisputed leaders. Leadership in this context is defined as a social process in which a person (or persons) organizes and directs the interests and activities of a person, group, or persons, through securing and maintaining their more or less voluntary approval of the goals of the community.

The campus parents socialize their children to conform to the institutional rules. Parents expect their children to "cooperate"—that is, they are admonished to use "common sense" when violating any rule. An inmate who does not use discretion may be disowned by her parents—a state of affairs that would disrupt her relationships with everyone else in the family. The threat of expulsion from the group serves as an important social control to structure conformity.

Although children are expected to accept their parents' views uncritically, brother and sisters may be unwilling to accept criticism from each other.

> If she's in my family, and I'm the father, I expect some respect from her. I wouldn't do anything to get her in any trouble. Like there's one daughter in my family—she gets in trouble with the staff, and I keep telling her to cool it. Girls are always arguing with the staff, but when I tell her to be quiet, I don't expect her to argue or talk back.

> Like Martha and the way she's been acting with Clara. She told me to mind my own business. For what we're supposed to be, brother and sister, I don't appreciate it. I didn't appreciate it, because it *is* my business. If you're supposed to be a brother, you're supposed to tell someone when they're wrong, and not get hostile. You try to help each other—to help each other out. It means a lot to have a family. I have something of my own.

The parents also play an important part in connection with dating and courtship. Inmates turn to their parents for advice in connection with marriage partners.

> Mothers want you to tell them, and they advise you. If they don't like a girl they'll tell you, "That's not the person for you." Sometimes a campus mother will give you advice about picking someone. She'll point to someone and say, "That would be a nice wife or husband for you." Or she knows someone, and if you want to get married, she'll tell you who would be good for you.

The family also functions as a nucleus of intimates who can be trusted with delicate matters concerning one's dating and courtship interests. The entire family may be recruited to lay the groundwork for an affair.

You can talk over your romantic problems with the family, and the family won't carry it to someone else. They'll tell you what they think, and sometimes this can help you. The family will cooperate with romantic problems. You can ask them to do things for you—with issues, or to talk to the person.

Obviously the inmates are vitally concerned about their release dates. Members of their family who have jobs in the administration building are expected to obtain information concerning the inmates.

You get information. If someone works in the main building, you find out things: "Your reviews are not today." "Your field worker is coming to see you." How do you find out? You'll be looking! You'll be listening!

An inmate probably never runs away without talking to someone in her family. Most likely, she will turn to her mother and her father. Because running away will not only extend her commitment but will mean transfer to a maximum security facility, the advice she is apt to receive will vary.

If you're thinking of running away, you tell your mother that you're thinking of running. Sometimes she tells you, "Go ahead!" and sometimes she tells you, "No!" If she thinks you'll be going home soon, she'll say, "You better not. You're only hurting yourself." It all depends on how things are going.

While most of the Eastern inmates agree that they have *enough* food to eat, they do voice some complaints about the way in which it is prepared. Also, there are some scarce goods and services that the institution does not provide; and not all the inmates have the private funds to purchase them (even if that were possible). In providing extra food and services, cooperation between family members is as varied as are the needs of the inmates.

You do things together, You share things. A girl goes to the storehouse [inmate commissary], and she picks something for the family. You do more for girls in the family than you do for other girls.

If someone in the family works in the kitchen, you might get the piece of meat you want—extra sugar, or you get your toast a certain way. If someone in the family works in the laundry, you get starch in your clothes. If you're in the same cottage you get to borrow clothes.

You share candy. It's like a family. You have an adopted mother that treats you like a daughter. It's like a regular family. If you're in room confinement, they'll slip issues, candy, gum, magazines and cigarettes under your door.

The family makes me feel more wanted—more liked. Not everybody gets in *a family*, although most everybody here belongs to a family. It makes you feel like you're part of it—like you're part of things. Plus you trust people more—the ones that are in your family. They're there when you need them. When you have friends, they're your friends all right! It's, "Hi" and "Goodbye" and all that jazz. But when you ask them to do you a favor, they're not there. But with the family, if you're not feeling good— if you're not feeling like doing your job, they'll wash your dishes. The family will wash them for you. If you want to borrow somebody's clothes, somebody else might say, "No, you won't take care of them." But in the family, you feel closer to one another, and they let you take their things.

Inmates who are fortunate enough to have visitors often receive packages of food, which is shared with other family members. Visitors also provide an avenue for contraband, although staff members unwittingly cooperate in this regard.

You can do things that other persons can't do like smoke an extra cigarette, because someone is bound to have visitors, and this is one way of getting extra cigarettes. The other ways to get them are to steal them from staff who sometimes leave cigarettes on their desks; you can get butts if you work in the main building. Or, you get the staff to think you're trustworthy, so she tells you to get the box. [Cigarettes are kept in a shoe box in the office.] While you're at it, you might slip one or two extras.

While members of the family are expected to share things, it also is expected that they should use prudence. To give without regard to the consequences raises questions concerning an individual's motives.

Some of the girls here, they try to buy other girls' friendship. Like for example, the type that's like this—she'd give you her last stamp if you asked her. This is bad because you need it yourself. Some girls never say, "No!" to nothing!

The family protects its members against direct verbal and physical attacks as well as the indirect attacks made against any family member in the community group meetings held daily.

> Sometimes in the group meetings a girl will bring up somebody that's in a family, and right away her family will come to her aid. They'll say, "I don't think she's bad." The family acts as a shield. Girls are in the family because it gives you a certain amount of protection, and, also, to be in the in crowd.

Parents carry the major responsibility to protect the family against physical attacks. They expect their children to keep them informed of any such problems they encounter.

> You don't like a girl, and she's been bothering you, so you might talk to your parents about it . . . They might tell you to fight or ignore the girl. If they're a good mother and father, they'll tell you, "Don't fight!" so you don't get in trouble. But if *they* fight *you*, the whole family will jump in and fight the girl.

When an inmate is accused of a deviant act—the family members protect her either by outright denial or by minimizing the seriousness of the behavior. Also, when any member of the family wants to retaliate against another inmate, her family lends support to her arguments (whatever they may be) and exhibits a united front.

> They help you out when you need help. They stick up for you. They stick up for you in group meeting, and if you want to get at someone in the group meeting, they'll help you because they agree with what you say. If you say a girl did something, they might not be there, but they'll say they were.

For the adolescent girls, the most serious deprivations of incarceration are separation from family and friends and the concomitant loss of freedom. The comments below reflect these concerns, as well as the inmates' problem with the passing of time.[2]

> Before I was in a family, the days were long. *Time stood still.* I felt like I was never going to leave here. If I didn't belong to a family, I would feel lonesome.

> To belong makes you pass the time away. You belong so you'll have somebody. It helps to pass the time. *Time goes slow here.*

The Eastern inmates are not able to resolve their sense of isolation in the formal organization and, therefore, seek a solution to confinement through the informal organization—the family group.

> The family makes me feel accepted and that someone cares. It makes you feel closer to the girls—the warmth that you feel at home. At home you have friends and your family—you have nobody here. You get lonely once in a while. It doesn't make you feel so lonely.

> It means that you have a family. A lot don't have a family at home. They want a real family to pretend.

> It makes you feel more secure. It takes the place of a girl's family—the one she has, or if she doesn't have one, she has one here.

> Your real family is home. You feel lost here, so you go into the family racket—and for a few, they just want to be in it. It makes you feel good, more secure, to have parents. A regular family has to have brothers and sisters. You have a mother and father here, and they're just young girls when I go out. We want a mother and father here. You want for a sister and a brother.

In the impersonal atmosphere of the institution, the adolescent inmates want above all to be accepted as human beings and to interact in primary social relationships that are similar in nature to those which they had with some individuals in their civilian lives. To this end, the informal group is shaped in the image of the nuclear family. Only in this context can one begin to understand the seriousness with which the inmates declare their kinship ties and the special joy and satisfaction that the inmate reveals when she interrupts a conversation with another inmate as a member of her family approaches: "Hey, this is my brother!"

> Once you live with a person for a while, you get attached to them—they're like your brothers and sisters. It makes you feel happy, not lonely. Before I used to be lonely, but now I can pretend that I have sisters and brothers, and it makes me feel better. When I was on my trial visit, I *missed* them. That's strange for a girl like me who's in an institution. They usually want to get out—but me, I wanted to come back.

Hence the social relationships formed as a temporary substitute may acquire a meaning for the individual that extends beyond the boundaries of the inmate social world. For a small unknown number of inmates the substitute social relationships may compete with the social ties they have in the external world.

The Central Inmates' Social World:

The Sillies

The informal social system of the Central inmates is called the "sillies." The term *sillies* is used in a broad sense by both inmates and staff to refer to the family groups, kinship ties, and homosexual alliances formed by the inmates.

Before a Central inmate is permitted to participate in the informal social system, she must "turn into a sillie." Rumors about the sillies at Central are widespread in the diagnostic center; indeed, recidivists engage in "sillie behavior" while they are in the diagnostic center. Although this behavior is visible to everyone, most of the first offenders do not become involved in this phase of institutional life until they are committed to Central:

> At VDC [diagnostic center] you find out a lot about the sillies, because they do a lot of talking about it. They'll say, "Watch out for the sillies!" "I wonder if they're in the sillies yet?" And when you come here, in the orientation cottage, you hear about it, too. You were scared of the sillies and you kind of look around and say, "I wonder who in here is going to turn into a sillie."

> Being in the sillies is fine. It helps to pass the time. At first I hated to talk about it, but now, if they respect others, it's up to them what they want to do. Just about everybody is in the sillies.

187

The Central inmate's socialization to the institutional rules begins in the orientation unit. Because the educational program at Central is emphasized, each girl is assigned to school classes while she is still in the orientation cottage. Of the three institutions studied, Central most nearly approximated the curriculum found in high schools in the community in terms of the number of courses offered and the opportunities afforded the inmates to belong to other school activities. Apart from their intrinsic value to the inmates, all of the scheduled school activities provide many opportunities for interaction among the inmates.

Although most inmates do not establish kinship bonds in the orientation unit, they do learn a great deal about the sillies. As a matter of fact, due to their experiences in the diagnostic center or other detention facilities prior to their commitment to Central, many of the first questions raised by the inmates are about the sillies. That recidivists are not housed in the orientation cottage does not decrease the possibility that first offenders are socialized to the informal culture within a few days. They are placed in the school program within a week after they arrive, and school attendance facilitates interaction with other inmates. The use of two or three inmate helpers—as extended staff in the orientation unit—means that some peer influence is immediately transmitted to new admissions in this cottage. All the orientation helpers were very much a part of the informal social system. In short, the organizational procedure of separating the new arrivals in the orientation unit functioned only to delay, perhaps for a week or two, their sustained participation in the informal culture.

The process of induction into the informal social system at Central is very similar to the process observed on the Eastern campus. The old-timers in a cottage ask the recent arrival the same kinds of questions about social background, knowledge of the sillies and whether she is interested in being in the sillies. These questions are important because they enable the inmates to place each individual in a certain social context.

STUDS, PIMPS, AND FOXES.   The inmates of Central school make a clear distinction between homosexual behavior originating within the institution as an adjustment to incarceration and homosexual behavior in the outside world. The inmates who form homosexual alliances as an adjustment to incarceration are sillies in differentiated sex roles. Girls who are lesbians in the external world are referred to as "for reallies." They are identical to the gay people at Eastern and prefer to establish sexual relationships with members of their own sex in the external world although boys are available.

The term stud refers to any individual who prefers homosexual relationships in the outside world. The inmates emphasize that the stud "came in that way," and furthermore, "will stay that way when he gets out."

> The stud is *for real.* He went with girls on the outside and not ashamed of it. They don't care who knows it. The others—sillies—aren't ashamed, either; but most of them—when they go home—they cut it loose.

No distinction of sex role is made; the stud "can take the part of either the boy or a girl," but she does not exhibit instability in her chosen sex role. Few individuals occupy the stud role, but those who do are looked upon a knowledgeable individuals who understand the appropriate role behavior in homosexual alliances. For this reason, studs set the standards for appropriate behavior in the institution.

The inmate who prefers heterosexual relationships in the external world but assumes a male role at Central is called a "pimp." The Central inmates stress that the pimp is "playing a boy's part," but they hasten to add that "he is not *for real.*" Depending upon the degree to which the pimp conforms to the masculine ideal held by the inmates, the pimp may earn the reputation of a "big" or "campuswide" pimp. A campuswide pimp would be well known on campus and "looks and acts like the real thing." At any given time, two or three inmates at Central fall into this category. They are very popular and are known to have "foxes in every cottage." In contrast, most of the other inmates have one fox; or, in some cases, two foxes, depending upon the extent of their exploitation of other inmates. In any case, only a few individuals at Central earn a campuswide "reputation."

A "fox" is an inmate who assumes a female role and is the counterpart to the pimp. The sillie who *foxes* at Central is said to "play herself." For this reason, the role of the fox is not considered to be an inversion because the inmates insist that

> She is playing her own role—a girl; she is playing herself. For the fox what is important is being able to handle the responsibility of a woman. The pimp lays down the rules. To be a pimp you're supposed to be truthful, honest, act masculine. The fox is supposed to iron his clothes and give him respect.

With the exception of the inmates who are recidivists of Central school, all the inmates spend two weeks in the orientation unit. The recidivists, however, go directly to the discipline cottage for a few days. Although some inmates in the orientation unit establish relationships with other girls within a few days, or indeed a few hours, most inmates tend to wait until they are assigned to a permanent cottage:

> The majority wait to turn after they leave the orientation cottage. Half of the time, they'll fox first. They come up here and they already be a girl, so they'll think they'll be more of a lady and they'll fox for a while. If they decide to change, they'll try to pick up the habits that pimps have and do it themselves.

First offenders usually enter the social system as foxes. Newcomers constitute a resource pool that oldtimers, especially studs and pimps, seek out and pressure into becoming a sillie; in addition, the appropriate role behavior must be learned, but expectations of the fox role are compatible with the familiar girl-boy relationship in the community. Of course, she may graduate to a pimp role, but she must first learn the appropriate behavior. It is unlikely that the young girl with no understanding of the behavior expected of the pimp will occupy this role until she has observed other inmates for a period of time. Regardless of the role that the inmate assumes, degrees of involvement and commitment are recognized by the Central inmates:

> Those who are deeply involved are *serious*. They think about girls all the time. They don't talk about boys. Most girls when they see a boy walking by, they'd be head over heels over that boy. "Oh boy, a boy!" Whereas for the others, they'd just walk off.

POPCORNS. Once an individual selects a sex role, she is expected to remain in the chosen role, either as a pimp or a fox. At Central institution, the "popcorn" is an inmate who switches sex roles indiscriminately. The popcorn has low status among the Central inmates. As they put it:

> They do one thing and then do another—they switch around. People don't like it. They pop from one thing to another.

> One minute a girl is a fox, and the next minute she calls herself a pimp. Then everybody talks: "Oh man, she don't know what she's doing!" One minute she wants to pimp, and one minute she wants to fox. "You go get yourself together, and you let me know what you're gonna do, whether you're gonna fox or pimp."

Thus inmates who switch sex roles may find difficulty in securing a partner, because instability in sex roles is viewed as a poor basis for beginning a relationship that an individual reasonably anticipates will complement her own chosen sex role. Popcorning is frowned upon by the inmates, and the popcorn leaves herself open to ridicule.

Because there are fewer inmates occupying male roles, the Central inmates are likely to view the behavior of a popcorn pimp as a more serious act of deviance than to switch from a female to a male role.

In addition to factors of individual choice and experimentation, economic factors sometimes precipitate a change of sex roles. Although the inmates express strong disapproval of the popcorn's behavior, they tend to be more understanding if there is an economic reason. For example:

> They foxes one week and pimps another week. Most pimps like to see how many girls they can get. Some girls start pimping because their parents don't send them nothing, so they get a fox! So sometimes they got no choice. But it's better to stay what you are.

Other roles that characterize the informal social system of the Central inmates are the customary kinship roles. Some features of the inmate social system at Central are identical or similar in structural form to the informal social system evolved by the Eastern inmates. To avoid repetition, I only point out the existing similarities but describe in more detail the important differences in structural form that obtain between the two inmate social systems.

SYMBOLS OF COMMUNICATION.   Symbols are selected by the resident population to communicate certain aspects of their culture, and the individuals who enter the inside world, are taught the meaning of the symbols. The symbols are changed when they become obsolete, either because the staff has learned their meaning, or perhaps because the institutional rules have been changed.

The inmate entering the institution becomes integrated into an already established structure, although—as is true of any social system—redefinition of existing rules sometimes does occur. The newcomer becomes socialized to the existing practices of the inmate body. Recidivists are brought up to date on all important changes that have come about since their former stay so that they will know how to proceed. The inmate becomes an integral part of the existing group structure or she remains an isolate. Only a few of the Eastern, Central, and Western inmates remain isolates.

The Central inmates, like the Eastern inmates, distinguish between inmates occupying male and female roles by the use of nicknames. The inmates refer to them as "sillie names," and they are adopted soon after the individual's arrival. A recidivist may choose a sillie name within a few hours of arrival; if she has selected a sillie name at the diagnostic center, she simply tells it to the other inmates. The nickname selected by an inmate is used during the entire period of incarceration; a sillie name is concrete evidence of an inmate's participation in the sillies.

The girls strive for originality, but an inmate is free to choose any name she fancies—consistent, of course, with cultural expectations of appropriate nomenclature for male and female roles. An inmate may receive assistance from other inmates; those living in the same cottage are frequently helpful in making known the names by which other inmates are identified. The Central inmates do not have exclusive rights to a particular sillie name. Inmates have no difficulty distinguishing inmates with identical sillie names because the person's own last name and her cottage unit suffice to keep matters straight.

Inmates occupying pimp roles sometimes change their given name to sound masculine; for example, *Jane* may be changed to *John* or *Jack*. On the Eastern campus, however, the cultural tradition is that the nickname selected bear no resemblance to one's given name. When a Central inmate changes her sex role, a new name is selected that would be considered appropriate; the Eastern inmate uses the same nickname even when she changes her sex role. Examples of sillie names which were in use during the period of my field work appear below:

	Feminine Names		*Masculine Names*
Misty	Country	Diamond Dick	Bone
Frosty	My Heart	Slick	Eli
La Sawanda	Ravina	Batman	Tom
Margo	Bootsie	Sonny	Mike Anthony
Tanya	Tootsie	Danny	Donny
Bunny	Bally	Tony	Tyrone
Tina	Sunshine	Afro	Iceberg Slim
Miss Lady Panther	Kitten	Gus	Dupree
Moonbeam	Shawnita	Hawk	Shawn
Angel	Princess	Apache	John
Beauty	Buttercup	José	Michael
Starlight	Tango	Joey	Terry
Tammy	Snowflake	Larry	Slim
Blondie	Green Eyes	Smoke	Tonto
Hotlips	Sheba	Carl	Fred
Slim Goodie	Pumpkin	Jerry	Rudy

Inmates use their sillie names as terms of address and as reference terms; they usually appear on the *hunks*—the letters inmates write to each other—indeed, they are preferred at any time an inmate is interested in disguising her identity.

The symbols adopted by the Central inmates to communicate sex role differentiation are similar to those for the Eastern inmates. The task of the pimp at Central (as for the butch at Eastern) is to look masculine— "as much like a real boy as possible." The pimps who best approximate this ideal are likely to be more popular with the foxes. They do not wear dresses, except when a dress is mandatory, as in the chapel; then they wear simple skirts and tailored blouses. At other times, slacks and shorts are preferred. Shoes worn by males have low heels, and frivolous styles are avoided. Knee length socks or ankle socks rolled over once at the ankle are appropriate.

Pimps are also differentiated from foxes by hair style: a white pimp must not have any suggestion of curl, whereas a black pimp wears an Afro. A short time prior to the study it was contrary to the rules for black inmates to wear their hair in an Afro because the staff members understood the symbolic significance. With the heightened demands of blacks in American society for self-identity, however, the administration recently reversed itself, and black inmates may now style their hair without pressing it. At Central, an Afro hair style is always associated with masculinity.

Central males do not wear make-up, and jewelry is taboo except for rings which may be worn both before and after marriage. The Central inmates' conversion to the male role is also accompanied by certain patterns of behavior. They are expected to incorporate in a general way the cultural expectations of the male in American society. They should "walk" like men, speak with deliberation in a low-pitched voice, and assume an unemotional facade at all times. The pimp is expected to exhibit strength—to "act tough." The transformation to maleness is complete when the individual has assumed the semblance of maleness to the degree that it is convincing to the other inmates. At this point, the other inmates relate to her as if she were a male.

Expectations of the inmate who assumes the female role are consistent with the expectations for the female in American society. As in the external society, great store is set on physical attractiveness and personality. For the inmate playing a female role, success in the dating and courtship game depends upon the degree to which she possesses these characteristics. Indeed, the length of time that elapses between her arrival and her initiation into the sillies is, to a considerable extent, dependent upon her physical beauty. As the inmates maintain:

> It's just a matter of a couple of hours for some. It depends on whether they're good looking—their shape. If they're good looking, right away

everybody wants you. If they're real ugly, they just forget you—they don't even ask you. They don't consider that you're even in the cottage.

Inmates who do not possess the physical characteristics that are socially defined as desirable may be exploited by other inmates if they have funds in their institution account or if they get frequent visitors. Apart from this possibility, inmates who are not graced with beauty may—like their counterparts everywhere—turn to others who are similarly unendowed.

MATE SELECTION, COURTSHIP, AND MARRIAGE. The pimp assumes the aggressive role in establishing a dating and courtship relationship. When the pimp lives in the same cottage as the fox, contact is made on a face-to-face basis. If the fox lives in another cottage, a pimp would "run his line down" with hunks. Hunks serve exactly the same function at Central as the issues do at Eastern. In addition to their important use in conveying all kinds of news items, they are important vehicles to establish dating relationships that later may be transformed into marriage. The content of the body of the hunks is similar in style to the letters that the Eastern inmates write. The stylized introduction that precedes the body of the Eastern issues does not appear on the Central hunks, but the latter sometimes do contain stereotyped headings—date, place, subject, and a single song title—which takes the form appearing on the Eastern issues. No numerical code is used by the Central inmates. The differences and similarities in the letters written by the Central and Eastern inmates indicate that the inmates adopt the cultural form that exists when they enter; that is, they are socialized to certain existing literary forms and cooperate to sustain through time a particular stylized format simply by adopting it.

The Central inmates destroy hunks soon after reading them; if they are discovered by the staff, discipline may take the form of counseling, room confinement, loss of privileges, or—as is often the case—a combination of all of these depending upon the content of the letter.

After a preliminary period of "talking" to determine where a particular fox's interests lie, the pimp will ask—when reasonably sure of the outcome—if she is "ready to choose." The question is put: "Will you be my sillie?" or, "Will you be my lady?" To be asked to be someone's sillie is to be made an offer to "go steady." Put to the novice, it means that she is being asked to participate in the informal culture of the inmates—to "turn into a sillie." Although the pimp plays the aggressive role, the fox may drop a few hints to let others know that she is in fact "ready to choose."

Although the Central inmates maintain that they prefer to go with inmates who live in other cottages in order to keep the relationship intact (the reasons given are the same as those of the Eastern inmates), they usually marry inmates in their own cottage. Indeed, the inmates prefer that their family unit be located in their own cottage, but the basis for this is different from that for selecting mates outside one's own residence.

Once a pimp and fox make a commitment, they are said to be "going together." Going together is a period of dating and courtship that is patterned in the same way that relationships of this type are among the Eastern inmates. The period of courtship may vary from less than one week to one month before inmates marry. A few of the inmates limit all their relationships to the "going together" type without getting married. Marriage is defined as the end result of going together. The goal of the inmates is marriage; indeed if an inmate does not marry, it indicates that she has been unsuccessful in her assumed sex role.

An inmate playing a female role is a fox before marriage, but after marriage she is a wife. The latter is an important distinction made by the Central inmates, because after marriage it is possible for the pimp to "have" another fox but she would not be a wife. When a married pimp establishes a relationship with another fox, it is mainly for the purpose of economic exploitation.

Mate selection among the Central inmates is based upon romantic love. With rare exception, the dyad configurations—from the casual dating and courtship pairs to the "legalized" marriage relationship—are established on a voluntary basis. But an inmate sometimes may apply verbal pressure to ensure success, or small gifts may be given when such action is thought to influence the outcome. Central inmates do not select their mates within their own family group. Marriages between inmates who are mem-members of the same family are forbidden at Central. In this regard, the Central inmates are guided by the cultural norms of the external society. Their sentiment in this regard is often expressed as follows: "It's like home. You don't go with your brother outside."

While the Central inmates make a clear distinction between the inmates who are married and those who are merely courting or engaged in more casual dating, they sometimes use "going together" to include both the married and unmarried inmates. However, the quality of an inmate's existing relationships with other inmates is widely known. As soon as a couple is married, the information is disseminated within a few hours by word of mouth and via hunks to everyone on the Central campus. Changes in sex role and news concerning the inmate who has chosen recently (or is about to choose) run a similar course.

Unlike the cultural prescription of the Eastern inmates, however, the culture of the Central inmates does not require that one must have parents before getting married. Yet many inmates are actually members of the established family groups in their cottage or they honor single kinship bonds with inmates in other cottages before they are married.

Like the Eastern inmates, the Central inmates strive for realism in their social relationships; they define and pattern marriage and other kinship bonds to approximate existing cultural forms in the outside world. Marriage and divorce are "legalized" by the use of written documents. Specifically, a Central marriage is formalized by marriage papers (MP's), but the body of the marriage papers differs according to whether the marriage is performed by a "preacher" or "judge," or whether the marriage is the "legal-by-touch" type.

Both the pimp and the fox may handle the details, but often it is the pimp who makes all the arrangements; the marriage papers are usually drawn up by the pimp, although a few couples approach this project jointly. The marriage papers (actually it is one copy that is usually made out) must be signed by the witnesses—deemed necessary to provide proof that the marriage actually took place, by the judge who marries the couple, and by the pimp and the fox. When the pimp or the fox have parents, their signatures may also appear on the marriage papers, but they are not absolutely necessary. All the names appearing on the marriage papers are the inmates' sillie names. The pimp's last name becomes the surname of the family established by them. The Central inmates do not invent sillie surnames, nor do last names appear on the marriage papers. At Eastern, racket family names appear on marriage certificates.

The time limit for each marriage is stated directly on the marriage papers. The length of time is highly individualized and is made clear at the outset, by building this feature into the marriage form. One consequence of this procedure is that the inmates can experiment with more than one marriage partner, and interpersonal strain between rejected partners is minimized. It varies depending upon the preferences of the couple. To state on the marriage papers "as long as you are here" means that the marriage cannot be terminated until one of the inmates is released. Most of the marriages performed by a judge are for ninety days, but the legal-by-touch marriages are for thirty days. Once the stipulated period of time is over, the marriage contract has expired, and therefore the marriage is terminated. If the principals decide to remain married at the end of the period stipulated, they are free to do so; no additional papers are drawn up. They are free to choose other inmates if they wish. But prior to the expiration date, a marriage cannot be terminated unless divorce papers are "handed out."

Although the marriage papers of the Central and Eastern inmates differ somewhat, they serve the same function. One major difference between the marriages of the Central and Eastern inmates, however, is that elaborate marriage ceremonies are not held so often at Central as at Eastern; moreover, the rituals surrounding marriage differs at Central.

Marriage among the Central inmates takes two distinct forms: marriages performed by a preacher or judge and marriages that are legal-by-touch. Each is important to the inmates, but by far the more popular and preferred way is to be married by a preacher.

When the marriage is performed by a preacher, the procedure followed resembles the marriages of the Eastern inmates. The pimp makes out the necessary papers—often referred to by the inmates as the marriage license or certificate. Included on this form are the date of the marriage, the names and signatures of the principles, signatures of the witnesses (usually three, although some inmates have two witnesses), the preacher's signature, and the expiration date of the marriage. Moreover, marriage certificates are sometimes embellished with sprays of interwoven leaves drawn around the border of the page.

In each cottage, one or two inmates are designated as preachers. A preacher may be either a female or male and must "know what they are doing." Here, as at Eastern, the judges or preachers are lesbians. However, under some circumstances the preacher may be an inmate with extensive knowledge of and participation in the sillies (as a consequence of previous incarcerations) but who does not refer to herself as a lesbian.

Like the Eastern inmates, the Central inmates marry wherever all the principal actors may assemble. The specific location may be in the school building, the public areas in the cottage, an inmate's room, the cottage basement, on the school grounds, in the auditorium or hospital. Marriages rarely take place in the chapel, however, because the inmates are not allowed to speak to each other there.

A marriage ceremony performed by a judge often takes place in the cottage units when the inmates who are to be married live in the same cottage. In some of the older two-story cottages, the inmates are married in the basement. Put to several uses by the staff, the basement functions especially as a recreation area and as a laundry room. The youth counselors do not supervise this area closely. The inmates are, therefore, sometimes left to their own devices, and opportunities of this kind are exploited by the inmates to the extent of their needs.

The inmates who live in the more recently built one-story cottages make different arrangements in order to carry on their deviant activities; for example, particular attention is paid to staff patterning; some staff members—especially new staff members because of their unfamiliarity with established routines—are perceived to be more "lax." Moreover, the general cottage routine is taken into account when making marriage plans. Activities that involve meal preparation, cottage cleaning, and the like invariably involve many inmates, and they are sufficiently loosely structured so as to provide an effective backdrop wherein other dramas may be played with relatively little chance of detection.

There are no colors that have symbolic meaning for the Central inmates when they marry, although a "dress up" norm is operative for this important occasion. Wedding receptions are sometimes held on Sunday, even though a marriage may actually have taken place on a weekday, because everyone can dress in their best finery without the staff becoming suspicious.

After the marriage papers are duly signed, they are torn up soon after the marriage to avoid the possibility of detection by the staff. This is a very different procedure from that of the Eastern inmates who keep the marriage papers until one of the inmates is released or the marriage is nullified by divorce papers. Eastern inmates threaten to produce the marriage papers when anyone intimates interest in a married inmate. Central inmates merely circulate information regarding new marriages, but this information becomes public knowledge almost immediately. Moreover, the witnesses are testimony to the fact, as both the witnesses and the judge are physically present during the ceremony.

Legal-by-touch marriages are also formalized by written papers. A judge is not required to sign a legal-by-touch certificate, although the signatures of two or three witnesses are essential. The marriage becomes "legal" by virtue of the fact that the inmate to whom the marriage paper is given touches it. Neither the fox nor the pimp sign the legal-by-touch marriage certificate.

In the "traditional" marriage, the pimp always takes the initiative—"the way a boy would"; in the legal-by-touch marriage the pimp or the fox may make out the certificate and give it to someone, although it is usually the pimp who takes the initiative.

Legal-by-touch marriage papers differ in some respects from those that are made out for the "traditional" marriages: The heading "LBT" or "Legal By Touch" appears at the top of the page; the date of the certificate is included; and the sillie names of the fox and the pimp who are "united under the order of LBT." The time limit—thirty days—is written: "limited until 30 days" or "no divorce until 30 days."

The legal-by-touch marriage is not a functional substitute for inmates who do not live in the same cottage and want to marry; nor do the inmates utilize this form of marriage because they may have difficulty assembling in one place to be married by a preacher. As a matter of fact, the Central inmates somehow arrange their affairs in such a way that marriages can be performed at any time with a minimum of inconvenience. Rather, the legal-by-touch procedure may be viewed as a way of structuring relationships between individuals for a brief period, while they decide whether they want a permanent relationship. From the inmates' point of view:

> It's a form of marriage, yet it's temporary. It's saying, "This is mine. This person belongs to me, so don't mess around." It's over at the end of thirty days.

An important difference between the legal-by-touch and the "traditional" marriages is perhaps best seen in that the couple united by the former method are not related to other members of their respective family units. When it is a legal-by-touch union, each individual retains her kinship ties, but neither acquires additional relatives through marriage. The inmates who are united in marriage by a preacher are automatically related to everyone else in the family; hence, this type of marriage links the family groups on campus into a large network of kinship ties.

The motivation for this type of marriage may also differ from that associated with the "traditional" form. For an inmate who has doubts or vague misgivings about the possible outcome of a marriage, the legal-by-touch type may be seen to function as a trial marriage. The relationship may be terminated after thirty days, or the inmates may be married by a preacher. Legal-by-touch papers are not reissued after the expiration date.

When the Central inmates are married by a preacher, both of the inmates have agreed to the marriage. With the legal-by-touch marriage, both the pimp and the fox may have agreed to the marriage. Most legal-by-touch marriages are based on a sincere feeling, but there are instances when this is not so. Sometimes, it appears to be wishful thinking on the part of one inmate; that is, the inmate hands the marriage papers to an inmate to touch (without her knowledge), hoping that the relationship will become more permanent. Once the certificate is touched, the individuals are united according to the "orders of LBT" in the eyes of the entire inmate body. A few inmates object to this, but most maintain, "They're glad to get it."

Some legal-by-touch marriages are made out of spite to become married to someone who has refused. Most inmates know, of course, when they may be receiving legal-by-touch papers that they would rather not have, and may refuse to accept all written materials. This procedure does not occur very often because she is then bound to a person she does not love; during the thirty-day period she cannot go with or marry any other inmate. In spite of the fact that this procedure is a way of "getting back" at someone, most of the inmates maintain:

> You usually don't give them to someone unless you care for them. Who wants someone that don't want you? But you can slap LBT papers on her to prove that you can get her—on someone who doesn't like you. To prove to someone that you can get her.

The legal-by-touch certificate may also be given to an inmate who claims to be "above" the sillies.

At the Eastern school, inmates are assigned to a cottage for the entire period of incarceration, and they are transferred to other cottages only under special circumstances. At Central, inmates are transferred to different cottages for a variety of reasons: as a disciplinary measure; reward for positive behavior—the "opportunity cottage;" or at the inmate's request. Hence, the legal-by-touch marriage may function to keep the relationship intact between inmates who live in different cottages and have doubts concerning the relationship.

The social obligations of the Central inmates after marriage are similar to those of the Eastern inmates. The structure of social relationships cast in the context of courtship, marriage, and kinship function to alleviate the deprivations of incarceration consistent with the needs of the adolescent females. For the same reason that the Central inmates prefer their family groups to be located in the same cottage—so that the members will always be together—most of the marriages are between inmates who live in the same cottage. When an inmate marries an individual who lives in another cottage, one of the partners may request a cottage transfer. The fox, in the role of wife, defers to the pimp at all times, and she is expected to wash and iron for the pimp and to clean the pimp's area when they share a room. This is, of course, easier when they live in the same cottage.

DIVORCE.   Although marriage as a permanent relationship is an ideal, divorce is a common feature of the Central inmate culture. In contrast, at Eastern divorce is an infrequent phenomenon.

Marriages among the Central inmates are contracted for a specified period of time unless the wife determines that the marriage is over. The pimp chooses a marriage partner, but the wife controls divorce.

The pimp has papers over the fox, and the only way the pimp can get a divorce is for the fox to give him DP's.

In the same way that marriage is formalized by written papers, divorce is legalized by written forms. The information that appears on the divorce paper includes the date, sillie names of the couple, and the reason for the divorce. At Central, the wife makes out the divorce paper, and she alone must sign it. She "hands" it to the husband, and by this action the marriage is officially terminated.

The factors precipitating divorce, however, are sometimes considerably more complex than is implied here. Although the wife makes out the divorce form, the husband may let it be known, directly or indirectly, that it would be judicious for the wife to terminate the relationship. The hsuband's preferences are often indicated by showering attention on someone else; the definition of the situation sets the process in motion, and the wife does, in fact, make out divorce papers. Until she does, however, they are still married in the eyes of the other inmates.

The typical reasons stated on divorce papers are child neglect, mental cruelty, and adultery, although most inmates declare that the principal reason—"a change of scenery"—is left unstated. As the foxes put it: "The pimp finds another fox that looks better to him." Because fewer inmates assume the male role at Central, the pimps are very much in demand. In addition, the Central inmates' less rigid definition of marriage contributes to the more frequent occurrence of divorce among them.

The divorce procedure differs according to whether the marriage was performed by a preacher or whether it is a legal-by-touch marriage. In the case of the "traditional" type of marriage, divorce may occur whenever one of the partners decides to terminate the relationship. Some couples remain married until one of the inmates is released, when a marriage is automatically dissolved. Some do stay together for the entire term of the marriage, but in general, most "traditional" marriages last about two to three months.

Neither the husband nor the wife in a legal-by-touch marriage can obtain a divorce for the period specified on the legal-by-touch certificate, but one week after the date of the marriage, the inmate who touched the marriage certificate may issue "separation" papers. This notice declares that the inmate is "separating" from the individual to whom she is married according to the "orders of LBT." Both of the inmates are now free to go with other individuals, but they may not remarry.

Foxes tend to wait out the thirty days particularly if they anticipate even a remote possibility that the relationship may be extended beyond this period because pimps are held in high esteem. They provide the inmates with a relevant male image that is lacking.

> There are no men around here except WSC [school for delinquent boys] boys. The WSC boys empty the garbage, they mow the lawns, and they do the painting here. And these men around here [employees], they can't do for you—they're going home to their wives. And the WSC boys—they're nothing—they're in an institution. They can't do anything for me, and I can't do anything for them. And some of them are kings and queens.

THE STRUCTURE OF KINSHIP TIES. The specific reasons leading to the establishment of kinship ties are related to the inmate's interests and her social and psychological needs. Without some knowledge of the quality of the interaction obtaining between the inmates prior to the formation of the kinship tie, the relationship may appear to come about almost spontaneously. For example, an inmate may address another inmate casually, "Hi, Mama." The inmate addressed may acknowledge this greeting in the same deceptively casual manner: "Hi, who? Yeah! I'm your mama." But kinship bonds established in this way have their basis firmly rooted in the quality of the interaction that obtains between two inmates over a period of time; the specific kinship role is suggested by the way the individuals relate to each other. Thus, the inmate who gives advice, admonishes another inmate who has been caught violating an institutional rule, and comes to an individual's aid when others attempt to exploit her may be perceived to be acting "as a parent would." Therefore, she may be asked to assume the role of parent.

Other inmates may be motivated to establish a specific kinship link by the advantages of security; the entire family stands ready to provide protection for all members.

> Some want to belong to be in the in crowd because everybody else is. But some do because they don't let anybody else mess with you. One girl joined because she thought this girl would take up for her. She was scared so she joined. Another girl—they stole her clothes and was wearing them right at school right in front of her! And that's why she joined.

Moreover, kinship ties are sometimes formed when the relationship between two inmates is close, but not to the extent that the inmates want to "go with" each other:

> To someone you're close to, you can become sisters, or something else. If she would help me—if she would build you up when you didn't feel right—you can become sisters, or you can go together.

Because of the overcrowded conditions at Central, all the inmates are not housed in separate rooms. Indeed, in a few cottages, small dormitories accommodate up to four inmates; in addition, some doubling-up in a few rooms in each cottage is standard. Room partners usually establish the more intimate relationship characteristic of inmates who are going together, and they often marry. If they do not define their relationship in terms of courtship and marriage, room partners tend to establish kinship ties.

The vast majority of the inmates at all three schools participate in the informal social system. They insist that their participation in the informal social system is due to the fact, "It's the thing to do here."

> Almost everybody is in it. When they first come up here, they say, "I don't want to be in that *sillie* life." But after a while, they do. They have someone they can talk to.

> Girls get tired of being locked up, tired of not seeing their families, tired of not seeing boys, and then their mind get twisted up, and they start going with girls.

One of the major deprivations of incarceration for the adolescent girls is the loss of family and friends. Each adolescent girl must overcome her feelings of social and personal isolation as a consequence of her incarceration. Very few—if any—of the adolescent girls can "go it alone" for the entire commitment period. The kinship, courtship, and marriage relationships provide a context wherein the needs of the inmates for friendly and intimate sociability may be fulfilled.

The informal social system evolved by the Central inmates is similar in structural form to the informal social system of the Eastern inmates. The structure of social relationships formed by the Central inmates consists of courtship, marriage, and kinship ties The informal groups made up of inmates who are bound to one another in kinship status are called "*sillie families*." The vast majority of the Central inmates are part of this informal group structure and acknowledge kinship bonds with other inmates. The family groups are racially integrated, and they cut across differences in social class. The Central inmates do not establish time boundaries for kinship ties, nor are the kinship bonds formalized by written documents.

The family groups of the Central inmates usually are made up of inmates who live in the same cottage. Complete families with well-defined generations may be organized in a single night, over a period of a few days, or in a few hours. The inmates maintain that this group structure "grows out of friendship." When inmates have established that they are friends, their relationship may be transformed to kinship, depending upon individual preference. Generally speaking, if a few inmates are always together, they soon become a family group and define their relationships through kinship.

The family group at Central is a social unit that can be distinguished from all others in terms of the degree of social cohesion that exists between the members:

> Everybody is for everybody else and share each other's problems. The majority of the families are in the cottage. You want to be together; in Cottage _____ we wash in the basement and CPs don't go down there.

> Most girls prefer that the families are all in the same cottage. You don't use other people than those in your own family. With other people, it's, "Hi," here, or "Hi," there. They [the parents] have to provide for their family.

The family groups include parents, children, aunts, uncles, and grandparents, as well as other relatives. Once the basic family is established, additions to the existing structure are usually made from the ranks of new inmates coming into the cottage or from families that become disrupted through divorce. The release of a marriage mate, however, does not necessarily mean that the family will be disrupted; rather, the family may continue as a viable structure with one parent as the head of the family.

The size of any family varies. The nuclear families usually include the parents and four or five children. If the parents have brothers and sisters, the latter are aunts and uncles to the children. Any other kinship ties acknowledged by the parents are related to the children in the same way that such ties are acknowledged in the external world, unless the inmate does not want to acknowledge certain individuals as relatives.

The principle of personal selection in the formation of kinship ties is much more highly developed among the Central inmates than among the Eastern inmates. An Eastern inmate's important kinship bonds are formed through her parents. The socially recognized kinship units made up of family groups are established by the Eastern parents, and a child automatically is related to everyone that the parents acknowledge as kin. Hence the principle of personal selection in the formation of kinship ties is an option that is exercised by an Eastern inmate only occasionally.

The Central inmates are not bound by any restrictions in establishing kinship ties with any inmate: An inmate's marital status, whether the inmate has parents or indeed acknowledges any kinship ties at all, are not factors in establishing kinship bonds. Although the Central inmates need not have parents before getting married (many of them do because they are recruited into family groups soon after their arrival), parents have considerable influence and control regarding who will be recruited into the family. This does not mean that an inmate may not establish isolated kinship ties (most inmates do establish many such ties) but the parents express their opinions concerning prospective recruits for the nuclear family, including marriage partners. Each family is a tightly knit group, and therefore the inmates do not usually marry anyone who does not measure up to the expectations of the family members.

Usually you don't get married to a girl that's not approved by the family, because you go along with the family. They're [family members] ones you look up to.

When the parents do not approve of a child's prospective marriage partner and the child persists in her choice, she is still free to marry the individual. In taking this course of action, however, she may be removed temporarily from the family. In discussing the issues involved, a parent declared to a son who insisted on marrying a particular inmate, "You go your way. We'll go our way. And when you're ready to come back, you can. But you're not going to live under our household now."

Because the children who are recruited into a family are the couple's best friends and the entire family is made up of inmates who think of themselves as "best friends," most inmates conform to the parents' wishes, as well as those of the other family members. Relationships between parents and children are asymmetrical in that the parents have authority over the children, as contrasted to the symmetrical relationships of siblings, which are characterized by structured equality between the role participants.

Each of the cottages at Central has well-defined family units. Usually there are three or four families in each cottage, but the number varies. The network of kinship ties does extend beyond the cottage family units, as the inmates honor kinship ties with inmates in many other cottages. These kinship ties span and overlap all the cottages and thus merge the inmates into one social unit. To some extent this is due to the fact that an inmate may establish kinship ties with other inmates who live in her cottage, but later she may transfer to another cottage and establish new kinship ties. But she still retains her other kinship bonds which results in linking two or more kinship units in different cottages. The kinship ties of the Eastern inmates also span all the cottages, but the cause is mainly mate selection and the linkages of inmates in kinship ties to individuals outside their own family.

At Central the ascription of kinship roles is based on sex and physical size. The inmate's physical size rather than chronological age is sometimes considered in allocating kinship roles. The parents sometimes select an individual who is small in physical stature to be the youngest child in the family; when another child is added to the family, the inmate who is selected may be physically larger so is "older" than the first child. Children in a Central family never "age," although they may, in the words of the parents, "improve." The method of allocating roles on the basis of physical size makes it possible for the Central inmates to suggest, in a very general way, continuity through time.

The family unit as created by the Central inmates is an attempt to re-create the structural elements of the external world inside the institution:

It's like real life—you have children in families outside, we have children in families here. You can have a little baby and an oldest girl, or a son. How do you get somebody in the family? You might ask, "Do you want to be part of my sillie family?"

Naturally, you have to know them—be friends with them. In the same way that you don't just walk up to somebody and say, "Will you be my sillie?" you don't ask just anyone to be in your sillie family.

The physical attractiveness of a girl is also a factor in deciding to invite her to join a particular family. Inmates who are beautiful receive many invitations to join family groups. Yet inmates who possess quite ordinary features also establish kinship ties, but their relationships are formed—barring a few exceptions—with other inmates who fit into the same mold.

In short, the Central inmate community consists of a large network of loosely structured nuclear families, matricentric and patricentric families of varying size, and other kinship dyadic configurations or family fragments—all of which are linked together into a vast kinship network due to the overlapping kinship ties that inmates have in two or more families, as well as the other kinship linkages they establish with other dyadic configurations and family fragments. A few inmates have two sets of parents, but this does not occur often because the inmates view the acknowledgment of a second set of parents as a sign of disrespect to the original mother and father.

The Central inmates do not deliberately set out to form families of any particular size. Inasmuch as the families are made up of friends, the size of a family is determined at the outset by the number of friends a couple has. Nevertheless, the consensus of the inmates is that to have a large family is to run the risk of early detection by the staff. Most of the Central families have four children, but there are many other relatives. At any point in time, the families vary in size, not only when they are first established, but over the life span of any particular family, as some inmates are released, others become divorced, drop out, or are "kicked out."

The stability of the inmate families is also related to the structure of marriage, with its built-in termination date. When the husband and wife do not extend the marriage beyond the fixed time, reorganization of the structural elements is necessary if complete disruption is to be avoided. In some cases, the family is completely disorganized when the parents' marriage is over; the children are no longer related to the parents, although other isolated kinship ties outside the family may of course still be in force for the parents. The family may break up into smaller units at this time if some of the family members continue to honor the kinship ties existing between them—such as brother and sister; in addition, inmates may establish other kinship ties at this time, thereby increasing the size of existing families.

When the family is completely disrupted, the event may be the occasion for structural reorganization as a new family unit by some or all of the original members, with different individuals occupying the various kinship statuses. Thus, two inmates who were sisters in the family may become mother and daughter, aunt and niece, uncle and niece, or stand in some other kinship relationship.

Many of the family groups retain their structure until all or most of the children in the family are released; this is due mainly to the way in which the marriage certificate is drawn up and the fact that the parents are kept at the institution for a longer period of time.

If the parents continue to occupy the same statuses after the marriage certificate expires, the family remains intact. It is not necessary for the parents to go through a marriage ceremony again. Usually when a marriage approaches the expiration date, the parents have already made an assessment of their relationship. Accordingly, they may decide to remain together or they may separate. If it is the latter course, most likely one of the parents has already begun romantic explorations, which will probably result in a prompt marriage for one of the parents. This action also may have an impact on group structure; whether a child retains kinship with her mother or her father at this time will depend upon her assessment of the individual who may be her new parent, as well as which parent she favors.

The termination of any marriage—whether due to expiration or divorce —has important consequences for the size of a family. A remarriage on the part of a parent may link a fairly small family with a very large family. Moreover, for inmates whose social relations within the family have become strained, the reshuffling of kinship roles and linkages that takes place at this time may encourage her movement into another family in the cottage; it may mean movement out of the family for a few days, weeks, or altogether. However, most of the family members remain together—reshuffling and reallocating kinship roles, and perhaps adding new members.

The kinship roles are adjusted within the family when changes in sex role take place. Consistent with the principle of personal selection that governs the formation of kinship ties at Central, sex role changes would be honored only if the members are agreeable.

Divorce affects the structure of a Central family in the same way as an expired marriage. (Inmates who are united according to the legal-by-touch method are bound by different rules; the legal-by-touch relationship is limited to the fox and the pimp, without extension to the other kinship ties). In contrast to marriage, the kinship ties are not formalized by written papers, and they may be terminated at will. Relatives who acknowledge kinship ties to the couple usually continue to honor these ties after a divorce; however, the so-called in-law relationships are no longer honored, but they may form the basis for the establishment of other kinship ties.

Divorce disrupts the established relationships of the inmates, but it usually means that the kinship ties of the Central family members are restructured. In this regard, the Central family units resemble those of the Eastern inmates after divorce. Although some individuals are incorporated into other larger family units, small families manage to retain partial structure (sometimes with one parent as the head), and these may increase in size over time through the marriages of the members, as well as the recruitment of other individuals into the family.

THE SOCIAL FUNCTIONS OF KINSHIP TIES. The kinship network links individuals together by convergence of interests, social and psychological needs. The ties of kinship among the Central inmates are conditioned by the principles and values that are associated with the nuclear family in the external world. The social relations between the members of a family unit are characterized by mutual respect, trust, identification, affection, and love. This is in marked contrast to the way that the Central inmates relate to nonkinsmen, perhaps best summarized in the words of the inmates: "Most girls won't speak to you unless you have a visitor, and then they're in your doorway." The observation may be made that, in general, an inmate's actions determine how she is treated by the other inmates. As the inmates put it, "There's an old saying: 'If you see a fool, use a fool!'" In short, all inmates are exploited to the degree that they allow themselves to be so used, but the inmates make important exceptions for close family members, especially those of the nuclear family. Mutual aid is channeled through the family.

Within the context of the Central family unit, the role of the parents is similar to that of the parents at Eastern. The parents are the leaders of their family, and authority is vested in the parental role. The extent to which the children defer to the parents is put this way:

> The mother and the father—they're the ones that have the say. If they say, "Don't go to school!" you don't. You say you have cramps, a back-ache, a stomach ache, anything, but you don't go.

Notwithstanding the fact that to carry out their deviant activities parents do give such orders, they play an important organizational role in maintaining order. They socialize their children to conform to the institutional rules. All the inmates understand that the rules are to be broken—but only if the conditions are favorable. The parents also socialize the children to the inmate culture and the way in which they should relate to the staff, and they allocate certain responsibilities to the older children in the family to help "take care" of the younger children. Thus an older sister is admonished by a parent to "watch out for," and to see to it that no one "bothers" a younger sister. Furthermore,

> The responsibility of the parents is to get them up on time, to see that their clothes are clean, their hair combed, and they look nice when you go to school. If you get in trouble, they try to get them out of a fight. They also protect the kids, and they share the work.

Parents become angry with their children if they do not abide by the rules and are placed in "strict" (punitive isolation) by the staff. To get caught breaking the institution rules is not only to "low-rate" oneself, but, by extension, it "low-rates" the entire family. Consequently, parents do not hesitate to strike their children if they "act up." The threat of expulsion from the group is a powerful weapon to insure conformity.

Most inmates conform because they want to remain part of the family group.

> Once you're in the family, you stay part of the family, but you can be kicked out. That would be when the family doesn't like what a person does, or a person disgraces the family—like for example, when you instigate or you agitate. You bust somebody without a reason: You see two girls kissing and you see that the cottage parent sees them, or for some other reason like this. If you can't be cool about something, then you deserve to be busted.

The parents perform an important protective function for the family members not only in connection with other inmates, but also with the staff. Parents will talk to other inmates in the interests of "their own"; when it is necessary, verbal persuasion will be reinforced by fighting. Parents also stand ready to approach the staff with a "strong rap" when anyone in the family needs help:

> Your parents talk to your cottage parent if you're in some kind of trouble. If their rap is strong enough, you get one day's restriction instead of three. Or if somebody in the cottage is on your back, they can go to that person and talk to them.

Parents buy their children soda, powder, candy, and other items when they go to the canteen. Children also share whatever they buy with their parents, and they often buy special items for them when they go off-campus. But the children are not exploited economically. When an economic need arises, the father—with the full knowledge of the wife—will "get a fox." This additional "woman" in the household provides the means whereby the economic problems of the family will be alleviated.

The nuclear family groups, as well as the other kinship relationships, provide the broad framework for social relationships of a primary nature; they are a meaningful substitute for relationships the inmate no longer has (and in a few cases, which she never had) because she is incarcerated. All the adolescent girls must adjust to the loss they experience as a consequence of their separation from family and friends. The brief comments below express the concerns of the inmates in coming to terms with the deprivations they experience, and the meaning of the family unit for them:

> It means a lot—someone who cares. The families care about their children and don't let their minds stay on outside. They don't let their minds stay

on the fact that they're locked up. You can say it's almost like home. It's not home, but it's almost like home. It makes your time go faster. Outside they'd have their own mother and father; they wouldn't need a substitute.

Time is easier when you're part of a family. . . . It's a game—it makes the time go by faster. You don't pay attention to time. You don't think about what's going on on the outs.

When you have a family, you don't go to anybody else but your famliy for things. Children go to the parents—especially the mother. It gives you someone to talk to—to share their problems with. You share your problems wih them. Everybody here belongs to a family.

Some don't have families outside, and it helps. It makes you feel more like you're wanted. The sillies help to pass the time. If you go at it in a positive way, you can talk to someone and they help you in some way to keep out of trouble.

It gives you security. You belong to someone, or somebody, or some group of people. You're in with the group—in with the "in thing." You *belong!* Especially in a big family; they're in with somebody, so they don't care about anything as you can say what you think—what you feel—and you know they'll come to bat for you. When you're alone, what you say doesn't count with anyone. *You're nobody.* It's security.

Your parents hold bench. If the children get hurt, they got somebody's shoulder to cry on. Parents give advice—how to pimp, how to fox.

Once you leave, they're forgotten. But while you're here, you're looking up to the person *as* your father.

Some people think it's freakish, but I think it's normal. Everyone in the world needs some kind of love and companionship, and out of these families with girls, you get love and affection. After a while, everyone comes around because everyone needs love and affection. Some have never had a family outside and through the family here, they learn what a real family is like—the love and affection that you get. In the institution family, you learn what families are like, and they have their family and treat their children a certain way, and you get the kind of love and affection that you wouldn't have. The families help the girls here, yet they are against the rules. This institution is putting the only thing that helps the girls against the rules, so they have to go against the rules in order to get help.

CHAPTER ELEVEN

The Western Inmates' Social World:

Chick Business

The informal social system of the Western inmates is called "chick business." The term *chick business* is used by both the inmates and the staff to refer to all behavior related to the homosexual alliances and other kinship ties. The kinship network evolved by the Western inmates functions to structure groups of varying size, and it interlaces the inmates into a cohesive group by reconciling competing and conflicting social motives. The Western inmates are differentiated in terms of the social roles and sex roles they occupy. Almost all of the inmates are part of the family groups in the institution.

FEMS AND BUTCHES. The Western inmates (like their counterparts at Eastern and Central) make a distinction between the individuals who have chosen homosexual roles in the external world and the inmates who engage in homosexual behavior only in the institution; at Western a broad distinction is made between "gay people" and "game players." The gay people are individuals who come into the institution with prior experience of homosexuality in the outside world and who express a preference for "going with girls" rather than boys. Gay people are said to be the "serious" homosexuals. They are a small percentage of the inmates.

Gay people have considerable prestige at Western, and they establish the rules concerning marriage and divorce. Indeed, only the gay people who assume male roles may act as "high priest" to unite individuals in marriage, and only they have the authority to dissolve marriages by divorce.

Game players are the inmates who are actively engaged in the homosexual activities within the institution, but who have not yet committed themselves to engage in homosexual behavior upon release to the community; they are said to be playing "institution games," and they are held in derision by the inmates who are confirmed homosexuals.

The roles that are widespread throughout the entire institution differentiate individuals on the basis of assumed sex roles. The "fem" is the individual who assumes a female role in the institution. She can retain her identity as a female. This role is especially attractive to the adolescent girls, as it is thought to be more difficult to assume a male role.

The "butch" is the individual who assumes a male role at Western.[1] The term stud broad is occasionally used by the Western inmates to refer to the inmate who is masculine in an exceptionally dramatic way, very adept at playing the male role aggressively, and consistently displays appropriate masculine behavior. A few butches are also referred to as "big man"—a title earned by especially attractive and popular males. The big man is usually a recidivist or a "real" homosexual.

FINKS OR SNITCHERS. Although the "no finking" norm is held up as an ideal by the Western inmates, a few individuals in each cottage occupy the role of "fink" or "snitcher." The fink or snitcher is the inmate who voluntarily divulges information to the staff or who supplies information willingly when it is solicited by the staff. Because of her eagerness to "help" the staff, the fink is shunned by the other inmates, and in their words, "treated like dirt." At the earliest possible opportunity, the inmates see to it that the finks or snitchers "get what is coming to them." Occasionally, although usually as a last resort, physical force is applied to enforce the no-finking norm. Most of the Western inmates, however, wait for an opportune moment during a cottage community counseling or small group meeting to set matters right by divulging information to the staff about the fink's deviant behavior. The strategy often adopted by the inmates feigns "concern" about the fink's well-being, and they describe her behavior in treatment terminology.

> We have ways of getting back at them in small group or in community counseling. You can bring her up and say, "I was concerned about her," and then start telling something about her which will let the staff know

that she's not such a goody-goody. If she finks, we've go something on them. Everybody breaks a rule here eventually.

This means of retaliation, however, may take longer than some inmates are willing to wait. Hence, the Western inmates tend to resort to physical force as a means of social control when the issue concerns something that would result in punishment in the isolation unit and perhaps keep an inmate in the institution longer. An inmate who had aided several girls to escape, and whose part in the plot was subsequently described to the staff by an informant, put the matter in this way:

It's hard to get at the fink. You can't always get them. If you wanted to do what you'd like to do, the staff would lock you up. These girls don't realize that this is jail. This is a different world! And after all, the staff is by themselves, and we shouldn't have anyone to go to staff and tell them stories about another girl. If you're smart, you'll play it cool, and wait until you can get her ass.

While the Western inmates consider all finking serious, some types of finking are viewed as more serious than others; for example, an inmate may resort to physical force if the matter concerns homosexual activities or an inmate's escape from the institution.

Fighting is an effective means to control the behavior of particular individuals in a particular instance, but its utility is limited. To overcome this situation—although first offenders are expected to violate the normative order—the Western inmates try to draw a newcomer into some of their activities almost immediately in order to control her deviance. At the same time, a degree of social distance is observed until she demonstrates to their satisfaction where her loyalties lie. An inmate put it:

In this cottage right now we got a lot of new girls and there are five or six finks. They'll go to staff with anything, so we try to get ahead of them. We figure, "Let's keep in good with these finks because they get scared when the staff talks to them." Not real, real close; but just so she thinks she's in with the crowd and she'll keep cool.

COPS OR JUNIOR STAFF.   The inmate who tries to assume the functions of the staff is despised by the other girls. In the eyes of the inmates the "cop" or "junior staff" is

A girl who gets on the good side of the staff and does the things a staff does like sit behind the desk. They try to tell the girls what to do. Like, "So and so, go shut your door!" "You're supposed to be doing your detail!"

"You're supposed to have your door open!" We don't like it, but usually there's nothing you can do about it. We feel the girls should be on each other's side. The staff is on their side, so why should you go on their side?

The low status the cop holds in the eyes of the inmates is evidenced by the fact that she is held up to ridicule, and they ignore her remarks calling attention to cottage rules.

SQUARES AND STRAIGHTS. The "square" is the inmate who identifies with staff values and is oriented to noncriminal values. Not only is it said that she is "good friends" with the staff, but she is often accused by the inmates of "telling everything to get out faster." Like the cops and junior staff, the square is shunned and ridiculed by the other inmates. Only a few inmates fall into the square category. They do not engage in homosexual activities, and do not belong to any of the family groups. They do, however, conform to some aspects of the inmate culture; for example, squares use nickname terminology to define some of their relationships with other inmates, but the reciprocal relationships formed by them are with other squares.

At Western, the individual who assumes a "straight" role does not engage in homosexual behavior. The straight professes a preference for boys, and she often looks down upon the inmates who engage in homosexual behavior. However, straight individuals—unlike the squares—usually belong to family groups; indeed, they form many other kinship ties with inmates in other families, occupying kinship roles that would be defined as female.

SISSIES. While the informal social system of the Western inmates consists mainly of individuals who are engaged in courtship, marriage, and other kinship relationships, inmates who establish intimate friendly ties with each other become "sissies." Sissies address one another by the term *sissie*. The Western inmates frown upon having more than one sissie, as this relationship is defined as *genuine* friendship. "Friendly relations with other inmates are always on a more superficial level.

The relationship between sissies is not to be confused with the "sister" role within a family unit. Although sissies claim to be *like* sisters, they are, in the words of the inmates, "real close friends." Moreover, the Western inmates make a clear distinction between this unique relationship and the other more casual ties they form by the use of other nicknames. The sissie relationship proclaims to the inmates: "We've known each other a long time."

Sissies are best friends. They're really tight. When they call each other sissies—and everyone who is tight with someone has a sissie—it's to let everybody know that they're as close as they can ever get—like blood relationship. To let everyone else know that there is no way that they can split them up, because . . . blood is thicker than water.

The sissie role is stable; these relationships cannot be terminated even when relations between role encumbents become strained.

SYMBOLS OF COMMUNICATION. The Western inmates distinguish individuals who occupy male and female roles by the use of nicknames—"chick terms." In the most general sense, chick terms are similar in function to the campus names of the Eastern inmates and the sillie names of the Central inmates. However, nicknames are also employed by the Western inmates to isolate specific friendship dyads and paired relationships of a more intimate nature from the rest of the inmate population.

When two inmates have agreed upon a nickname, they will use it to address one another, but this privilege does not extend to any other inmates; it cannot be used by the other inmates to address them.

The procedure of "calling" each other by an agreed-upon nickname communicates the preference that two inmates have for one another. It induces certain forms of action on the part of the two inmates involved, as well as for the rest of the inmate population. The friendship dyads form a broad base from which other relationships are established. A friendship dyad may be transformed to one involving courtship and marriage, or it may be changed to other kinship ties, depending upon the preferences and needs of the individual.

The specific nicknames used to define relationships originate in the identification of any two individuals with certain social situations, things, physical attributes of the individuals, or characteristics of personality. The nickname must be one with which both individuals can identify; that is, they consider it to be appropriate for the structure of social relations between them. Two individuals who are friends may call one another "Potato," while two inmates who are "going together" might prefer "Inspiration," or something similar; but, in any case, "Potato" would not be an appropriate name for individuals who are going together. Hence, the name gives clues to the nature of the relationship between individuals; reciprocal nicknames fall into two categories: the names that identify friendship pairs and the names used to define the relationships involving courtship and marriage. Examples of nicknames that were widely used between friends at Western appear below:

Spooky	Bow Legs	Twiggy
Slim	Flatfoot	Pebbles
Gopher	Slick	Love-child
Skinny Legs	Kitten	Jellybean
Buttercup	Crazy	Cheeks
Little One	Skinny	Shorty
Steel	Big H	Big Crank
Sometimes	Potato	Blondie
Mellow Yellow	Beep Beep	Smiley
Ace	Neighbor	Trouble
Jazzy	Blimp-de-blop	Darkey
Browney	Donkey	Teardrop
Tootie	Runaway Child	Brown Sugar
Square	Ducky	Hussy
Pineapple	Sad Girl	Puppet
Shithead	Little Bear	Tiger
Secret	Mouse	Just Me
Cookie	Get It Girl	Pisces
Legs	Pressure	Namesake (both have the same first name)

Considerable care and time is spent in the selection of names which indicates the importance that the event has for the inmates. Not only must a nickname be appropriate for the relationship, but it must be ascribed and validated within the broad rules governing the process whereby names are chosen and adopted. A few examples will serve to make this point clear:

I have high cheekbones and she has high cheeckbones. She said, "You have high cheekbones like I do. Let's call each other 'Cheek.' "

We always got in *trouble* together, so we gave each other the name.

We work in the kitchen, and got pretty tight. One day we were eating jellybeans, and she said: "Jellybean!" So we call each other "Jellybean."

You give nicknames if you have a good friend. I have a "Secret" because with her I could tell her things and she wouldn't tell, so we became "Secrets." It's someone that you're close to—someone I could talk to. Not a new girl, because I wouldn't know what she's like. Nicknames are for friends. If they don't like her, they surely don't want a nickname with her.

If you say: "Be my 'Stuff' " to someone, then you both use it. To me, it means something, and it means something to the others, too. It means, they are a little different than just anybody else.

The basic rule of names specifies clearly that no more than two persons in the *same* cottage are to use a nickname. When two inmates have selected and adopted a name, they have exclusive rights to that name. To avoid confusion, everyone in the cottage is urged not to adopt it. This norm is adhered to almost without exception, and newcomers to the institution are socialized to the proper institutional etiquette. Those who violate this rule are punished accordingly:

> If someone has a name on the dorm, they don't like it when someone tries to use it. On the same dorm, they try to put a stop to it. It leads to fights sometimes, calling someone by a certain name: "That's not your 'Crazy!' Don't call her that."

> If I had a name for a certain person, no one else would call her that, they could call her something different. They would have to. The girls you give nicknames to are your best friends. If someone tries to use the same name, we'd say: "Where did you get that name? We had it first." Some make a big thing about it: "We had it first." Some might get into a fight.

The reciprocal naming by the Western inmates is a procedure that functions to isolate certain individuals into an exclusive relationship vis-à-vis other inmates; it provides a means of separating friendship dyads of solidary relations from all others in the social environment. These relationships may be viewed as dyads of symmetrical solidarity, and they remain relatively stable over time. Indeed, the use of nicknames functions to structure reciprocal relationships of varying degrees of trust between two individuals, trust that gradually may be increased as the individual is observed to display behavior that would be consistent with the other's definition of a trustworthy person. In addition, the procedure functions to differentiate all the inmates from the staff, as the nicknames identify each inmate as belonging to a specific minority.

The use of reciprocal nicknames is an effective mechanism for handling personal relations among the Western inmates. The circle of friends identified by nicknames later may be transformed into closer ties such as marriage and other family and kinship ties. A nickname that would be appropriate for friends would be inappropriate to use between individuals who are married or who go together. Hence, two individuals who become friends may decide to call each other, "Donkey," for the reason that they are both stubborn. If they decide later to go together or marry, they will confirm publicly their new social role by selecting one of the names below:

Everything	Togetherness	Wonderful One
Precious	Fascinator	Lovable
Honie	Pride	Special
Sex Machine	Sweetheart	Lovable One
Wonderful One	Lover	Inspiration
Puppie Love	Peaches	Pretty Lips
Baby Love	Heart	Honey
Irresistible	Tight	Angel

These names are never used between friends. Inmates who marry also use the terms "husband" and "wife" to address one another and as reference terms. Once a relationship is established by two individuals and appropriately named, they are expected to use the nickname. If the name is not used, it would mean either that (1) a disruption in social relations has occurred; that is, the individuals are not speaking; or (2) the relationship has changed from friendship to a more intimate one.

How many nicknames an inmate has depends on the number of inmates defined by her as friends through reciprocal nicknames. Specifically, she would have one nickname with each inmate she has singled out to be a close friend; in addition, she would have another nickname with the individual she goes with. A few inmates have as many as fifteen nicknames; yet a few inmates have only one nickname in addition to their [astrological] "sign." ("Signs" have been adopted by the inmates recently and their use reflects the current vogue that astrology enjoys in the outside society.)

The inmates discourage the use of too many nicknames, as they maintain it gets confusing "trying to keep the nicknames straight." More important, however, is the fact that the Western inmates do not go about willy-nilly giving names to all inmates in sight, because mutual aid, affection, and esteem are patterned between individuals who have nickname status with one another.

> When people come in here, they like to drop the names that they have. If you get tight with someone you give them a name. The name you give them depends on how you feel about that person. If you have the name first, you jump at another person that tries to use it. If they're not your friends, they'll try to use them. So after you get to know a person you think they should be something to you. "We should be something to each other—like _____," and you tell them the name you would like to use. Nobody is going to come up to you and say: "I want to be your friend." That's stupid.

To have someone "want to name you" is the acid test that the individual is accepted as a friend or a lover.

New arrivals are frequently approached by old-timers when their relationship has progressed to the stage that a nickname is felt to be in order; however, newcomers may also approach other inmates. They enter friendships soon after they come to Western and use nicknames. Recidivists are already familiar with the informal social system at Western, and they may establish nickname relationships with others soon after they arrive without waiting to be asked. In fact, inmates sometimes give nicknames to friends while they are all in the diagnostic reception center, and these nicknames continue to be honored.

If a new inmate makes the mistake of calling an inmate by the nickname that she overhears another inmate use to address her, she will be reprimanded as an unauthorized user.

As put by the Western inmates: "You have your name for everyone— if you want them to mean something." A crucial test of one's friendship for another becomes the acknowledgment of the nickname. If two inmates do not define their relationship in nickname terminology, given names are used; they are considered to be very *impersonal:* "It's what the staff calls them." Nicknames between friends are never "given up" even when the social relations between them become strained; they simply may not be used for a time. If the name is not verbalized, an inmate cannot respond to it.

Although any nickname may be selected, certain "stereotype" names are used throughout the institution. Indeed, recidivists recalled that these names were common and widespread during their previous commitments to Western. Examples of stereotype names are "Tight," "Wonderful one," "Precious," "Fascinator," "Lovable," "Sissie", as well as the names that fall into the namesake category.

When two inmates start going together, they select another name that they consider appropriate for their relationship; the new name indicates the important change that has taken place in their relationship.

In addition to one or more reciprocal nicknames, many of the Western inmates also use a general nickname. The latter type is selected by the inmate herself or it may be suggested by the inmates in her cottage; unless the individual forbids an inmate from calling her by the name, anyone may use it. General nicknames are frequently used to sign *buzzes* (inmate letters) to avoid detection: "How is staff going to find out who's Taurus?" Inmates who assume a male role also have a general name that symbolizes masculinity in addition to all their other nicknames. A few inmates do change sex roles, although the ratio of males to females remained quite stable during the period of the study. When a change in sex role is made, one's name is changed accordingly. With the exception of the nicknames symbolizing masculinity, the other general nicknames may be adopted by more than one inmate in the same cottage.

In the social context in which the names are created and come into being, they have a dramatic and poignant meaning to the individuals concerned. With the experience of incarceration, juveniles assume new identities: The nicknames are the symbols of these identities. As the incarcerated adolescents become part of the inmate group, they undergo a change of name that is consistent with their identity of being a different person, located in a different setting, and involved in many things that are different from those to which they were accustomed in the outside world. The casting aside of a legal name for nicknames to be used inside may be viewed as a reflection of the individual's conversion to inmate status.

As late as 1968, colors were used as important symbols of communication by the Western girls, but colors no longer have any significance.

Although they do not use word abbreviations, the Western inmates do use a numerical code. Although a few inmates use code numbers that are not widely known throughout the institution, the main code consists of assigning a number to a word according to the number of letters in the word. When numbers are combined, the meaning of the phrase must be memorized because the same number may have a different meaning in another phrase.

The sex identities appropriate to male and female roles that are overtly assumed by the Western inmates resemble the distinctions that are made by the Eastern and Central inmates. Indeed, the social system of the Western inmates is similar in structural form to the informal social systems at Eastern and Central.

The Western inmates who assume female roles strive to make themselves attractive in a feminine way. The general expectation is that fems should look and act like "ladies." They wear makeup and jewelry, and their clothing and hair styles are feminine.

Inmates who assume the male role are expected to conform to cultural expectations of masculinity. They are differentiated from the fems by their dress, hair style, language, and behavior patterns. The aim of the butch at Western is to act, dress, and "look like a boy." Slacks are worn as often as possible. Blue jeans cannot be worn; staff members maintain that this type of clothing would be "taken advantage of" by the inmates. The rule prohibiting blue jeans on campus was once relaxed—and promptly reversed—as the staff found the situation "embarrassing" whenever there were visitors. The Western inmates are allowed to wear their own clothing, but administrative rules specify that clothing must be in "good taste." Clothing that is defined by the staff as having a masculine look or that can be converted into "masculine type" clothing cannot be worn.

Yet none of the restrictions imposed by the staff really makes any difference. The inmates simply construct new symbols whenever necessary to deal with the developing situation. Western males resemble their counterparts at Central and Eastern; jewelry is not worn, except a ring or a medal; they do not wear high-heeled shoes, makeup, or nylon hose. Some of them wear boots all the time, and they tend to wear knee length socks more often than do the fems.

Masculinity is also communicated by the shape of the garments worn and by hair style. All the garments worn by the inmates who assume male roles are fitted loosely, they are longer in length, and dresses are more tailored. (The Western inmates must wear dresses to school.) The black butches usually wear Afros, and white butches either wear their hair short or brushed back smoothly and held with a rubber band.

The general stance assumed by an inmate also communicates to the general population which role she occupies. The Western inmates recognize that both fems and butches are "women," but they make several important distinctions for institutional living:

> You're both women, but he's still giving orders, just taking the place of a man. You wear slacks when you can. And you act like a man: An ash tray, a light for her cigarette, other things—you try to do it—not like a kiss-ass, but consideration.

> In chick business, to go with another girl—to mess around with a woman—you expect one to be more demanding, more violent, but you expect respect.

The butch is expected to "walk, speak, and sit" like a man; to exhibit a no-nonsense facade at all times—to act "tough"; tears are a luxury reserved for the fem. Indeed, the butch's popularity depends upon the degree to which she conforms to the inmates' general expectations of masculinity.

Instability in sex roles is discouraged at Western. The norm regarding sex role stability is enforced very effectively by ridiculing the deviant; nevertheless, sex role change does take place occasionally.

MATE SELECTION, COURTSHIP, AND MARRIAGE. The Western inmate's induction into the informal social system begins almost as soon as she enters the control room to be formally processed into the institution.

When an inmate arrives at her assigned cottage, she is often taken in hand by the inmates—one of whom will direct her to her room and give her bed linen and a copy of the cottage rules and regulations. Gradually, over a period of several weeks she learns who the cottage staff members are, but within a few days she becomes acquainted with all the cottage residents.

The Western inmates ask newly arrived inmates exactly the same questions as do the Eastern and Central inmates. The major questions include her age, county or city of origin, former institutional experience and offense history, use of drugs, and her attitudes and experiences regarding homosexual activities.

Because the Western inmates, like those at Eastern and Central, are processed through a central reception and diagnostic center, rarely does an inmate not have *some* knowledge of the informal social system before she arrives. Even the inmates who have not participated in chick business in juvenile halls or in the diagnostic reception center are not completely ignorant of the inmate culture, although the extent of their knowledge may vary. The excerpts below are typical of those expressed by all the inmates:

Chick business means that you're in the business. Even if you didn't know anything about it, you'll hear about it at State Diagnostic Center. They ask you there just like we do here: "Are you in chick business?" "Do you like girls?" Then when you come here, you sit back and study them. You see it and you hear about it, and that's how you find out. Eventually, you become part of it all—part of the group.

When you first come here—for someone who doesn't know very much about it—it gets confusing, although every girl who has been in other schools and in Juvenile Hall, learns something about it. There are very few girls up here who don't know absolutely nothing about it, although some may never have tried it before they came.

In the beginning you think: "I can't see how you can tell the difference, because they both act like females to a certain extent." But when it comes down to the nitty-gritty, he dresses and acts like a man; fights to defend her; he must fight to have her.

The newcomer becomes socialized to the existing practices of the inmate culture; recidivists are brought up to date on any changes that have taken place since their previous commitment. Each inmate conforms to the already established group.

For the Western inmate, induction into the informal social system begins shortly after she arrives at the cottage. However, the specific length of time varies; it may be a few hours for some inmates, while for others it may be a day to a few weeks, depending upon whether they already know any of the inmates. Most inmates know at least one person; they were in the same reception center or juvenile hall before commitment, or they originate from the same neighborhood.

Some girls are going together as soon as they come on the dorm. For others it takes two days or it could take one week or one month. It depends on what crowd you get into. Some get in the in crowd real fast—if they know you on the streets, and if you're friendly and hip.

It depends on the girl. Some do the first day. For some it takes longer for them to want to go with a girl. It's two weeks before you start school and knowing who goes with girls and who doesn't. On your dorm, you find out real fast who's going with who.

Yet while the inmates expect the new arrival to be friendly, there is a limit beyond which the inmates claim she should not go, or it may work to her disadvantage.

When a new girl comes in, she should be cool. There was a girl that came in, and the first day, she let a girl finger-bang her; and that's not good to be known as the campus whore. They were playing truth and dare—four girls in a big group. The first day, it's just not cool. They can get anything they want. If they want some pussy, they can get it anyway.

Success for the Western fems also depends upon physical attractiveness and personality. The recidivist is in an altogether different situation; already knowledgeable in the ways of the inmate culture, she need only make a decision as to when she will be actively involved and what strategy she will follow to achieve desired ends. Within one month, however, all but a very few of the Western inmates are active participants— at least at the level of courtship. Moreover, some inmates may have married and established their own family groups by this time, while others may have joined existing family groups.

While the staff members in all the institutions are expected to keep the inmates under supervision, the movement of the Western inmates is much more restricted and the inmates are under constant surveillance. One important consequence of these factors is that the Western inmates usually go with and marry inmates in their own cottage. Some inmates do go with individuals in other cottages, but almost all inmates eventually marry someone who lives in their cottage. Inmates at Western remain in the same cottage for the entire period of incarceration unless they are moved to the maximum security unit for disciplinary reasons. Kinship ties span all the cottages as many inmates establish kinship bonds with inmates who live in other cottages as well as in their own living unit.

Western inmates have many opportunities to interact with one another outside the cottages. They meet in school, the outdoor pool, the movies, gym activities during school hours (and sometimes from 6:30 to 7:30 in the evening), work assignments, and at the infrequent activities billed as special events.

The courtship procedure of the Western inmates resembles that of the Eastern and Central inmates. The inmate assuming the male role is expected to take the initiative, with the fem pursuing an indirect approach; fems sometimes enlist the help of friends or relatives to advance their cause in the ways described previously for the Eastern and Central inmates.

Buzzes are often used to establish these relationships, although this form of communication is prohibited by the staff. The letters are usually torn up after they are read because the Western inmate could earn an evening's room confinement for violating the rule. Nicknames are used to sign the letters. Except for the elaborate stylized preliminary matter—characteristic of the Eastern issues, the letters of the Eastern, Central and Western inmates are indistinguishable from one another. Code numbers appear on many letters written by the Western inmates. The inmates write song titles on the envelope, or at the beginning of a letter; (although they rarely list more than five song titles). They are called "dedication songs," and they are appropriate only on chick business buzzes. While two girls who have a "going with" relationship are listening to records, one will turn to the other and say, "Dedicate!" The song becomes their song, and the title may appear on their letters to each other.

The Western inmate responds to a buzz the same as her Eastern or Central counterparts. An affirmative reply results in the public acknowledgment that the inmates are "going together." (The Western inmates sometimes use the latter term to refer to inmates who are married, a designation that is unambiguous because everyone knows who is married.) Sometimes proposals are rejected.

If you're not interested, you can let them know: "I'm involved with a girl." "I don't go that way. Get out of my face!" But not too often because there could be a payoff. It could be detrimental to your stay—like one of my letters turned in to staff.

The going together relationship for the Western inmates is similar to a "going steady" relationship with a boy in the external society. The length of time inmates go together varies. It may be a few days or a few weeks before some inmates marry; other inmates may terminate their relationship after the same period of time. A few inmates simply go together with other inmates for the entire period of incarceration without ever getting married, but the vast majority of the Western inmates eventually marry. These relationships are for the most part established voluntarily.

Unlike the Eastern inmates—who may select marriage mates within the family—mate selection within one's family is taboo for the Western inmates. In this respect the culture of the Western inmates is the same as that of the Central inmates. Moreover, a Western inmate is free to go with and to marry anyone on campus, but if she belongs to a family, the other family members may counter the individual's choice of a mate. Marriage always has an impact on the structure of the family, and, therefore, it is of considerable interest to the members.

Some inmates first establish a casual nickname relationship and gradually focus the relationship to the going together stage. Yet, if an individual misreads the signals, it may result in the loss of a friendship.

I liked her as a sister but she liked me in another way, so I told her; but she was really hurt. You could have a best friend here, and it would turn out to be love. It's never been the same between us. Sometimes you start out by being friends. It usually breaks up your friendship when you start going with a girl.

The decision as to which sex role a Western inmate will assume is often determined by the sex role preferred by the inmate whom she wishes to court. A few inmates exhibit masculine or feminine role behavior to such a marked degree that the possibility of any other role behavior is never raised. If two inmates are newcomers to chick business, the problem of sex role choice may be solved by one inmate saying to the other, "I want to play the man. I want you to play the woman."

The inmate who assumes the butch role takes a more aggressive role in the courtship procedure. Fems must wait to be asked, although they may, and, indeed, often do, take many steps (short of an outright proposal) to bring about the desired result. In short, courtship is patterned according to the inmates' cultural expectations of male and female roles in the external world.

It's like a man and a woman. It's the same as going steady. If they decide that they're going to go together, then they exchange rings. It's just like being engaged. You're not supposed to go with anybody else, or write to anyone else.

Recent converts to the male role sometimes go with inmates in other cottages because it facilitates the degree to which they can convey an impression of role stability. As the inmates explain:

If your girl is on your own dorm, you have to act more mature. It's like outside—you have to make an impression. The fem is supposed to act like a young lady. A butch is supposed to act tough. They don't like their girl friends to see anyone push them around, so they get into more fights. They have to act like a man—like the boss

However, most inmates select mates from the cottage population. In general, a married butch is likely to exploit inmates from other cottages for food packages and other items that may be purchased during off-campus trips with visitors.

Marriages at the Western institution are formalized by written documents and by a marriage ceremony. At Western, however, many of the marriage certificates are handwritten, but the younger inmates prefer and often insist that they be typed. (The terms *marriage papers, marriage license* and *marriage certificate* are used interchangeably.) A few of the inmates specify the number of months the marriage is to last based on the couple's evaluation of how long they can "make it." Thus, some inmates will "sign up for four" or "sign up for five" months. Most of the inmates, however, do not specify the number of months; rather, their general expectations are that a marriage lasts until one of the inmates is released.

The inmate who has the authority to marry the Western inmates is called a "high priest." To be "legally" married, a couple has only to go to a high priest and request to be married. The majority of the marriages are performed in the cottages, and the proximity of all the inmates facilitates matters. A high priest rarely has to postpone any request for more than a day or two. The high priest makes out the marriage certificate with the following information: the nicknames of the couple; their birthdates; date of the marriage; place the marriage was performed; and the signatures of the couple, high priest, and witnesses. Three copies of the marriage certificate are made out—one each for the fem, the butch, and the high priest.

At least two witnesses must be present at a marriage ceremony, although they do not necessarily represent "each side." At a "big wedding," however, there may be as many as four witnesses. They are the couple's best friends and are probably related to them in kinship bonds.

The high priest assumes a male role and claims to be a homosexual in the external world, that is, "gay and not just in chick business." The high priests tend to be older inmates because only the inmates who have had several years' experience in gay life activities in the external world may assume the role. Usually, there are two high priests in each cottage (a maximum of ten high priests at any time). As a high priest is released from the institution, another inmate steps forward and assumes the function. The high priests are inmates who can be trusted. No inmate has been known to have gotten into trouble with the staff because a high priest "ran off his mouth." Hence, unqualified prestige is conferred upon them by the Western inmates:

> It's a great honor to be a high priest. Everybody respects you. It's a lot of work and sometimes the high priest receives gifts like food packages, and clothes.

A high priest's request to borrow is not likely to be refused—whatever the item requested.

In many respects, the marriage procedure of the Western inmates is similar to that of the Eastern and Central inmates. But the Western inmates have adapted the procedure to conform to the physical structure of the one-story cottages. In order to avoid the possibility of detection, they schedule their weddings when the cottage is crowded, especially during the weekend when it is easier to muffle the conversation of the inmates and to keep the staff member who is seated behind the desk occupied.

One of the essential requirements for a marriage is a ring for the fem. As the inmates put it: "You steal it, make it in arts and crafts, but you give a ring to the girl." (Beaded necklaces are also sometimes exchanged or given as a gift to the fem by the butch.) The butch and fem must also dress in suitable attire for a wedding.

> The man and woman get dressed up. The fem wears a good dress that you have here. The man dresses up. If on the dorm he tries to wear pants and a shirt. If someplace else, he tries to have on something that looks masculine—a tie or socks, or just your clothes in general, but not too fussy. You'd know. The two people would know.

Whenever feasible, the Western inmates also attempt to duplicate a traditional church wedding inside the institution, modifying the procedure whenever necessary; vows are exchanged, and sometimes background music is provided. The married butch and fem refer to each other as husband and wife.

Weddings need not be elaborate, especially when certain staff members are on duty; the high priest may simply take the ring worn by the butch, place it on the fem's finger and state: "I pronounce you man and wife, and now you'll be married for the rest of your lives in gay life and never be separated." Or the couple may state their vows aloud before the high priest and exchange rings.

After the wedding, the Western cultural tradition emphasizes that the couple leaves to "room hop on their honeymoon." (The term *honeymoon* was rarely used by the Eastern or Central inmates, although the behavior of the inmates after marriage was the same.)

Occasionally the Western inmates celebrate wedding anniversaries; a month is used as the unit of measurement and is equivalent to one year. Such events may be the occasion for a party, and sometimes gifts are exchanged. For example, a couple who celebrated a two-month anniversary exchanged the following gifts and proudly showed them off: the husband's gift to the wife was a heart-shaped pin (made in arts and crafts); the wife presented the husband with a poem that she had written.

Marriage changes the intensity of the interaction between the butch and the fem. The social relations expected of a married couple at Eastern, Central and Western is "constant togetherness," although the relationship between the husband and the wife is by no means an egalitarian one. At Western, the fem is expected to defer to the husband in all instances. Her contacts with butches are restricted and her letter writing is circumscribed to friendly notes; she is expected to do the butch's washing and ironing when they live in the same cottage and to comply with any request made of her. However, it is understood that they share their possessions, including all food packages received.

Although the parents are the undisputed leaders of the family groups, the butch exercises considerable authority over the fem, even during the "going together" stage. For example, the butch makes the decision about which institutional activities they will take part in and circumscribes the fem's interaction with other inmates.

With the wife's knowledge and approval, a few of the married butches exploit other fems to obtain food, clothing, makeup, shampoo, and other scarce goods, which are shared. The fem who has frequent visitors is apt to be singled out for exploitation. Although relationships of this type existed among the inmates in all the institutions, they were more prevalent at Western because the Western inmates were provided fewer personal items. Usually, the older inmates exploit the more youthful inmates. At all the institutions, I observed that inmates with no experience of homosexual behavior prior to commitment express much doubt in the beginning concerning such practices but gradually come to regard it as "normal" behavior, at least within the institution. In the words of the inmates:

> When a girl comes on the dorm and she's not interested in going together, she says: "No, I'm all for dudes." Yeah, when they first come in; but after one to three months, they change. Their attitude changes. They are all the same. Betty, who said she never would, said the same thing and after one month, she was feeling on a girl, and she let other girls feel her. Almost everybody here is involved in chick business.

> A lot of girls try it out for curiosity. Some girls have heard about it, but they've never really seen what goes on. And they'll go with a girl—to see if you feel any difference—just to make love. It's something to pass the time away.

> When you are surrounded by one environment, what alternative do you have but to indulge in the same things that are going on around it. If I see a man, I can't have him; I can't touch him. Homosexuality is the thing here. It's not real in a place like this. You're doing it because you're lonely. You want someone to be close to. You want understanding. Everyone wants someone to confide in—to talk to.

> You've gone with boys outside—everybody has had sex. You're here, and one day a girl may touch you, and you get those chills, and the next thing you know you're playing and laughing. . . . And it's only a matter of time. If she has never been in chick business, it's only a matter of time, then someone will turn her on. But it's a common thing. Like I said before, every girl has had sex. They just make use of what's available. They would be fantasizing. I've been on one of those trips, and I'd be thinking of my man. Both of us would be ladies.

> All the girls here are going together. It's just a game. I'm going back to my man. I hate to hurt the man who I'm supposed to be engaged to, but up here everyone goes with girls. I wouldn't disgrace myself on the streets by going with a woman. It's just a game.

While the inmates maintain that their participation in the informal social system is to alleviate the pains of incarceration—and they emphasize the temporary quality of their relationships—it is difficult to ascertain the extent to which this phase of their institutional experience will affect their lives when they return to civil society. The youthful inmates in all the institutions occasionally express doubts and reservations, or at the very least, maintain that their experience inside gives them a new dimension of reality. An inmate put it in this way:

> I guess if you're here in an institution—if you mess with a woman—if you kiss a woman, in some ways you look at a woman in a different way outside. When you see a woman, you just naturally look at her, and you be thinking and saying: "Gee, that's a pretty dress! You've got nice shoes," and stuff like that. After you leave a place like this, you say the same things, but it goes farther. You think: "She's got a nice body—I wouldn't mind kissing her."

> There's nowhere to turn; there's nowhere to turn but run to your room. You look in a mirror, and you see yourself; you turn this way, and you see a woman. If you scream too loud, you'll hear a woman's response.

The transition in perception from one level of reality to another is expressed in the same way by the inmates in all three institutions. An inmate who had been at Western for twenty months, summed it up: "In the beginning it seemed like a fantasy—like a fairly tale. But it seems real to me now."

DIVORCE.   Marriage is intended to be a permanent relationship until one of the partners is released, but a few inmates do utilize the infrequent phenomenon of divorce at Western. A marriage is dissolved by destroying the papers when one partner is released. At other times, the same procedure is followed for divorce. Western inmates tear up the existing copies of their marriage certificate. The butch and fem may destroy their copies of the marriage certificate together, or one of them may tear up her copy and present the pieces to the other, which would prompt her to destroy her own copy immediately. The certificate held by the high priest must also be destroyed. Each inmate is now free to go with other inmates and to remarry. If the couple discusses the impending divorce with the high priest first, the high priest may "counsel" the couple in much the same way as the preacher at Eastern. One important difference, however, is that the high priest has no power whatsoever to grant a divorce. This right belongs to the married couple.

Western inmates tend to remain married until one of the partners leaves the institution. They "separate" for a time, but their marriages are stable structures due in large measure to the fact that for many inmates, marriage is the last stage of a relationship that was first established by reciprocal naming. When one of these relationships is changed to marriage, it is after both inmates have tested the relationship. Moreover, the larger family groups established by the inmates contribute in an important way to maintaining the stability of the Western marriages.

A divorce means the loss of a nickname for the principals; names such as "Inspiration," or "Honey" are no longer appropriate, of course. If the inmates remain friends after a divorce, they eventually select other nicknames; if their relationship was defined by a special nickname before marriage, they may use the same nickname.

In somewhat the same manner that the Eastern inmate calls the numbers, a few Western inmates state their position squarely on the line: "I don't want you anymore." But the Western inmates tend to use indirect approaches to secure their ends, which are meant to provoke the other individual into tearing up the marriage certificate—a fact of life from which there is no turning back—unless the inmates remarry, which occurs very rarely at all the institutions.

Some inmates communicate their desire for a divorce to another inmate within earshot of the wife or husband. That a third party has been brought into the picture is certain to bring about the desired result without contest.

> We went to the swings, and I overheard a conversation. I overheard her telling someone: "I wish I could have my things back." So I gave the ring and beads back. I got the ring three days after we were married because she had to make it. We used Betty's for the wedding.

Another favorite device is to decrease contacts with one's mate without providing an explanation.

> When you want to break up, you ignore the person. You don't have anything to do with them. Everytime they come by, you cut the conversation short. You go in the other direction when they come near you, so the person gets thinking that you're acting funny. She gets to thinking the butch is acting funny.

If not successful at first, the girl will try until the partner may hand her the bits and pieces of the marriage certificate and exclaim, "O.K.! If you want to call it quits, you can!"

Some inmates ignore the individual altogether and go with another inmate openly:

> You just stay away from them. You don't say anything to them. Most likely, they'll get the hint. Or if they don't, you can stop talking to them completely and start going with another inmate.

The actual reasons given for a divorce may be rationalized in a variety of ways. The reasons are face-saving devices.

> I want to break up with you because you might break up with me and I don't want to get hurt.

> The staff is getting too suspicious, and I don't want to get involved. (Then they turn around and go with someone else.)

> We can't get along! (You get into a fight. This is an excuse; naturally, you break up.)

Statements such as the above also are made when an inmate wishes to terminate a relationship during the courtship phase. While public explanations may take various forms, the inmates usually sever courtship relationships when one inmate is attracted to someone else.

THE STRUCTURE OF KINSHIP TIES.   The group structure of the Western inmates is similar in structural form to that at Eastern and Central. At the outset, the differentiation of sex roles structures many of the roles defined in kinship terms that inmates may occupy. However, the principle of personal selection in the formation of kinship ties is highly developed among the Western inmates. Kinship ties are established both before and after marriage. Papers are not required to establish kinship ties.

The Western family groups span all the cottages, and they are racially integrated. Indeed, the Western family groups merge into one social unit that includes almost the entire inmate population. The inmate social system is a large network of loosely structured nuclear families, matricentric and patricentric families of varying size, and other dyadic configurations composed of kinship ties and family fragments. These structures are linked to other similar structures due to the fact that some family members have overlapping membership in two groups.

The principal basis for kinship role differentiation is sex, and to a limited extent, age is an important variable that is taken into consideration. Physical size, however, is not considered. The important contributing factors leading to the formation of kinship ties are the social and psychological needs of the individual. Inmates who are thirteen or fourteen years of age often are recruited to be children in a family. Many inmates maintain:

> If you're sixteen you prefer children thirteen or fourteen rather than fifteen. You want to feel the responsibility of a mother, and the years apart between your age makes a lot of difference. It makes it seem more realistic.

Inmates in the thirteen to fifteen age range may seek out an older inmate: "Can I be your daughter?" because she "looks up" to the individual and believes that she will "help her more" with any problems she may have.

Each cottage usually has four or five family groups. Although the Western families vary in size, the family groups typically include six to eight members: parents and children, aunts, uncles, and sometimes grandparents. In addition most of the family members acknowledge other kinship ties, both within the cottage and elsewhere in the institution. Cousins may be part of the family, but they are always looked upon as peripheral relatives. (Four of the Western families had a godmother and godfather who were related to the entire family.)

Grandparents are part of a family when the family has persisted to the extent that "generations" have been the natural outcome of the marriages of family members and the addition of children. An inmate is almost never recruited to be a grandmother. Such an invitation would be considered an insult; it would mean that an individual's behavior is not perceived as that of a mother, but of one who is not in tune with present-day happenings.

After the marriage, the Western wife "takes the butch's last name"; all the members of the family use the father's legal name as a reference term. But partial family units, such as dyads consisting of mother and child, do not have a "family name."

The Western inmates may assume the role of parent before they marry, and their children automatically are related to the marriage partner. Nevertheless, the newly married couple "starts a family" soon after the marriage by adding at least one child. This event often takes place on the wedding day or within a few days after the marriage. The couple may simply approach an inmate and say: "You be our child," or "You're going to be our son. Okay?" Because the individuals concerned already share a close relationship, it is unlikely that the invitation will be refused. Parents introduce their children to the other inmates: "This is my daughter," "my child," or "our baby."

Some inmates do not wait to be asked, however, and request membership in certain families: "I want to be your cousin," "I want to be your little girl." If the individual addressed does not want her as a daughter but does not wish to offend her, she may invite her to be part of the family in another role: "You could be something else, but not my little girl because I already have a little girl."

Nuclear family ties, made up of close friends who can be trusted, are preferably located in the cottage to facilitate mutual aid on a variety of levels.

You prefer them on your dorm because you see them more often, and you do stuff with them. You get a food package and you have a party: "Let's have tea tonight." You want a close type family that you can have fun with—share things, room hop. If no food package, the rest of the family will give you things. We try to help each other from having incidents [discipline reports], getting into trouble from jumping somebody or splitting. The things you can't go to the staff with, you talk over. I think they help more than the staff does. They're here in the cottage and they know what's happening.

Although the parents sometimes rule out an inmate as unsuitable, all members of the family may recruit inmates to be part of the family. In addition, members of the family may form isolated kinship ties, such as brother, sister, aunt, uncle, and cousin, with inmates in other cottages. They are usually acknowledged by the other family members and increase the size of the family. Parents urge their children to go with and marry other inmates, which contributes to the size of the families. A first offender sometimes joins a family group as a daughter, but after a short period of time, she begins to respond affirmatively to the buzzes that are an inevitable part of institutional life:

Of course, there are some, but not many that don't play the game. But pretty soon your parents will want you to get married. They want to keep the family going. They like to be able to say: "I want you to meet my aunt—my son-in-law."

Norms governing marriages include the provision that a child should be sixteen years of age when she marries—a norm that is more frequently violated than adhered to. When a child goes with an inmate (a "serious" relationship), the parents acknowledge the individual as an "in-law," although they are not "legally" married. If the relationship is terminated, the in-law relationship is no longer honored by the family members. The kinship ties established by all the members of a family satisfy the different needs and preferences of particular inmates.

A Western family is made up of close friends, but factors that are always taken into account include the personal and social characteristics of the individual, whether she is attractive and has a pleasing personality, and especially whether she possesses the qualities that would enable her to act according to the normative prescriptions of the kinship role, as mother, father, brother, sister, aunt, or some other kinship role.

To what extent are the reciprocal nickname friendships absorbed into the kinship structure? The nickname relationships consisting of friendship dyads may be seen to cut across the kinship network, but these relationships are on a different level of interaction from the kinship ties, and they are kept quite distinct by the inmates. Except in extremely rare cases, the nickname friendships are not the source of an inmate's *kinship* ties, but courtship partners and marriage mates often are first nickname friends. An inmate describes the process:

> It would be first as an acquaintance and then as a tight friend. You'd give her a nickname. The one that is interested is analyzing all the time. You could make little advancements. If she doesn't say anything, this signifies that she's interested. You call her "honey" or "lover," and then you more or less slide into the stage of going together. Then you will say, "Let's make love"; or, "Do you want to room hop or shower hop?" Then you will get married.

In short, one's "Crazy" is not asked to be in one's family as a daughter or a sister, but she may marry into the family.

Divorce is infrequent at Western, and the families are relatively stable. "Once you start a family, you stay a family." Divorces often come about because one of the parents is going with another inmate, which inevitably means remarriage. When there are children in a family, divorce disrupts the structure of social relationships; the children in the family may choose their "favorite" parent, and the remarriage of this parent means either a stepmother or a stepfather. Sometimes a child remains close friends with both parents. Some inmates may terminate some or all kinship ties within the family depending upon individual preference, but most inmates continue to honor their kinship ties, although a few may redefine their relationship as close friends.

Other events that may alter the structure of the Western families are (1) a change in sex roles on the part of one of its members; and (2) an inmate's voluntary departure from the family. Western inmates do not change sex roles often; ridicule serves effectively to deter most aspiring deviants. Except for those who acknowledge a commitment to a male or female role new girls are typed by the cottage population into masculine or feminine roles suggested by their behavior and appearance. This differentiation may be based on responses to inquiries about "the gay life," or the fact that the inmate happens to be wearing a pair of slacks or some other clothing to which the inmates attach a specific meaning. Later they are approached according to the implications of this definition. Not only does this procedure function to decrease instability in sex roles, but it helps to maintain a balanced sex ratio at Western.

Although inmates can choose their own roles, those who exhibit near-perfection in performance have fewer options open to them. Some inmates are so convincing in the male role that were they to assume a female role, they would be laughed at. Yet, although the practice is strongly disapproved by the inmates, a few inmates can change sex roles simply because their flexibility in both roles (demonstrated over a period of time) makes their performance both believable and acceptable. Nevertheless, very few of the Western inmates change from one sex role to another.

An individual may postpone assuming the sex role she prefers because her partner assumes one role consistently and may be a better role player. Consequently, she may wait until the inmate is released before she changes sex roles. But whatever the reason, the inmate who exhibits sex role instability may find that she no longer has a family unless each member of the family establishes a new kinship tie with her.

Once an inmate assumes a kinship tie, the bond is expected to be permanent. The families at Western are said to "stay together." Hence, when an inmate leaves her family voluntarily, the other members express considerable anger. Two reasons may justify an inmate's exit from the family: (1) She is to be released from the institution in a very short period of time; or (2) a member of her family has acted in a way that is incompatible with the behavior expected of kinsmen. For example, a mother refuses to give a child a cigarette or an inmate violates an institutional rule and a member of her family brings this to the attention of the staff. While this behavior would justify leaving the family, it is not very likely to occur as family members do not act this way toward one another.

THE SOCIAL FUNCTIONS OF KINSHIP TIES. Like the kinship ties at Eastern and Central, the kinship network at Western links individuals together by convergence of interests and social and psychological needs. The kinship ties are conditioned by the principles and values associated with the nuclear family in civil society, and such relationships enable the inmates to interact in patterned primary relations similar to those they had in the community. The social relations between members of the family are characterized by respect, trust, identification, affection, and love; the kinship bonds are also differentiated from all other relationships in that mutual aid is channeled through the family.

Although it is true that the Western inmates regard the individuals with whom they share a nickname as special friends, the few inmates who are included in this category are individuals who are potential partners in courtship and marriage alliances. This is what is meant when the inmates exclaim, "You really want a close friend, but the only way you can get it is by chick business." The nickname relationships function on a different level of social intercourse from the family relationships. The former neither serve the same needs as the kinship ties, nor are the unique rights and obligations of the kinship ties attached to them. The rights and obligations of kinship are in sharp contrast to the way in which the Western inmates relate to the rest of the inmate population (including the inmates who share the same nickname in terms of friendship). Although the inmates in all three institutions justify the exploitation of certain inmates, they make an exception for their close family members.

The social functions of the kinship ties fulfill the inmates' needs for emotional reciprocity, security, and protection against the other inmates. Located in the cottages, the family provides a secure defense against any charges made about its members during the group therapy meetings. Kinsmen can be expected to close ranks and remain silent or to minimize the seriousness of the family member's behavior. Moreover, they can join forces to apply pressure upon the inmates who take the meetings too "seriously" and voluntarily bring up incriminating topics. The family is a small circle of individuals who can be trusted and who can be relied upon at all times.

The Western parents also perform the important function of socializing the inmates to conform to the institutional rules. Indiscriminate violation of the rules is not part of the normative structure of the inmates. Children are cautioned to deviate from the rules with discretion in order not to prolong their institutional stay. Parents also function importantly in handling the many details that arise in connection with courtship and marriage. Any member of the family may be called upon to act as a lookout, especially when members of their family are "room hopping" or "shower hopping."

The brief comments below are typical of those made by the Western inmates, and they pinpoint some of the important functions of kinship:

I look at Cathy and Brenda as my own children. I love them as my own children, and I'm concerned about them. When they get into trouble, I'm hurt. When I see them getting into trouble, I pull them out of it. I send them to their rooms, or I talk to them—like if they're going to be getting into fights, arguments, cursing out staff.

The family keeps you happy, especially if you don't see your mother. It helps to know that someone cares. Maybe you're up here because you have a crummy family. Time goes by slow. It helps to make time easier.

The routine is the same. Sometimes you say to someone: "Write me a buzz so I'll have something to do tonight." Time goes by slow.

To me it's a good feeling because you can talk to them and you trust them. You don't have finks in the family. If a girl is a fink, the girls don't associate with her. It gives you a good feeling—a caring feeling for each other. It makes you feel more secure when you're locked. There's this love dormant in you and it's kind of hard.

When you have a family, you have someone to talk to. You can talk to someone when you want to. The hardest thing being here is when you're lonely and you don't have someone to talk to. If you want something you can go to your family: "Mom, give me this."

You wake up and you know today is like yesterday and tomorrow will be the same—like yesterday, the same routine. It's something to pass the time away. Chick business helps; it helps to pass the time. Your family here means a lot to you.

The parents make sure they [children] get their homework in for school; that they're neatly dressed for school. If they're cussing someone, they tell you: "Go to your room and cool it."

It seems more realistic to you. You want to make it as realistic as possible. I guess it gives you self-confidence. Staff don't really know you. It makes you feel more secure. It makes you feel more secure when you know that you can care about someone and someone cares about you.

Being part of a family means that's your family. I'd come to them [her parents] with just about anything. Anyone in the family would help you. They are like a family.

The Western inmates face the same sense of isolation as a consequence of the abrupt termination of freedom and the separation from family and friends experienced by the Eastern and the Central inmates. To resolve some of their problems, the female inmates seek a solution to the deprivation of incarceration by establishing family groups. The structuring of social relationships by kinship bonds may be viewed as an attempt to reshape and restructure the institutional experience in the image of the external world—to make it realistic. Unable to resolve their feelings of isolation in the structure of the formal organization, the inmates feel that membership in the informal social system provides a temporary solution to the deprivations of incarceration.

CHAPTER TWELVE

Deprivations, Inmate Culture, and Treatment Goals

The antecedent conditions of inmate culture are the social, personal, and material deprivations confronted during incarceration. No institution program, however idealistic, can overcome the handicaps under which these institutions labor. Although it is widely believed that an institution organized on the cottage system provides the physical environment for a homelike experience, the inescapable fact is that a cottage that houses twenty, forty, or more inmates can never be homelike, no matter how many "homelike touches" are added. No home that a youngster came from was so lacking in privacy as were the facilities at Eastern, Central, and Western. The sense of constraint, inherent in mass living under regulated authority, permeates the institutions. As Paul Tappan puts it: "It is in the very nature of institutions that life differs from that of free society outside.[1]

THE DEPRIVATIONS OF INCARCERATION. Only the separation from family and friends is equal to the loss of liberty for the adolescent female offenders at Eastern, Central, and Western. Because most of them are children, they do not view their situation as does the adult offender who is reduced to the status of a child.[2] On the contrary, children view adults as exercising legitimate authority in any setting.[3] Although the adolescent female offenders assert that they want and seek the protection of adult authority, loss of liberty is still severely depriving for a child. Indeed, the idea of freedom takes on new meaning for the incarcerated adolescents. The following comments are typical of those made by all the inmates:

> You miss being free more than anything. Going where I want to. What you hate is the doors being locked at night. When you hear that key turning, it really does something to you.

> What I miss the most is my freedom, my family, my man, and being able to do things without being supervised. You know—having responsibility for yourself. Before—at home, you do what your father wants you to do, but you still do things.

> You hate being locked in your room. Everybody hates being locked in. You miss your freedom most of all. Being able to go where you want to go. Able to take a walk—even just a little walk—whenever you feel like it. Some days, I feel like I'm going to jump right out of my skin if I can't go off by myself from everyone in the cottage, and just think by myself. *You miss your freedom.*

Although the adolescent offenders maintain that they sometimes resent the controls imposed by their parents (for example, curfew hours), they recognize that within certain limits, a measure of freedom and choice is possible in civil society even for very young children. They, like all adolescents, are preoccupied with their progress to adult status. Hence, the kind of restriction on freedom imposed by the institutional staff creates a situation for them wherein they feel they must regress to an earlier stage of childhood. The fact that the inmates joke about the necessity for their mothers to teach them "how to make change from a dollar" when they return home serves to underscore their bitterness and indicates their underlying anxiety about their future adjustment to the external world.

Closely related to the deprivation of freedom is that of autonomy. While the adolescent inmates recognize that adults have authority over their lives in the external world, they are as chafed as adult offenders by the fact that every aspect of their behavior inside is controlled by the long lists of bureaucratic rules imposed by the staff. In addition, the handling of rule violations by staff members often appears capricious to them. Staff do frequently confine inmates to their rooms and use group punishment extensively, but the rationale for the decisions is not at all clear to the inmates. They remain unconvinced by the vague arguments that assert a relationship between certain decisions and individualized treatment; they contend that many of the rules exist solely for the convenience of the staff.[4] For these reasons, the Eastern, Central, and Western inmates are united in their belief that specific penalties should attach to all the rules. To eliminate favoritism, they would go beyond a simple listing and institute a system whereby the same penalty attaches to any rule violation, regardless of how many times an inmate violates the same rule.

By contrast, the vast majority of the staff members prefer to exercise "discretion" in the matter of rule violations, not because they can demonstrate the relationship of any decision to individualized treatment, but because it clearly gives them more leverage: Everything can be justified in the name of treatment. The concept of treatment, in whatever organizational context, imbues negative sanctions with a respectability that would scarcely be possible if the sanctions were equated solely with custody.[5]

In American society, material goods are the measure of one's economic success; they not only confer status, but they are often considered to be the measure of one's moral worth. Clothing, especially, has symbolic meaning for the members of our society, and children learn this very early from their parents. It is reinforced in school, and clothes among adolescents are closely attached to popularity with both males and females. The competition regarding clothing carries over into the institutional setting, and clothes are an important means to express one's individuality *inside* as well as in the community.

Many of the so-called amenities that are lacking in institutions for adult offenders are routinely supplied to the adolescent female delinquents in order to stimulate proper grooming, especially feminine grooming. Although some items of clothing are supplied by the institutions, the inmates have no selection, and the adolescents again feel reduced to the status of mere children. The girls are at a stage when they are beginning to experiment with clothing that is suited to particular "types," and any attempt to limit their experimentation is viewed as depriving by the youthful inmates. Moreover, institutional administrators tend to be guided in their choice of clothing for the inmates according to what they consider to be "good taste" for young girls, whereas the youthful females tend to be guided by whatever is in fashion at the moment outside. Pants suits and boots, although taboo items at all the institutions, headed the list of clothing preferences for the inmates.

In their progress to the goal of adulthood, the adolescents equate the process of making choices with adulthood, and they are very sensitive to the whole spectrum of possibilities wherein they may exercise initiative. They feel keenly the fact that they have few choices of cigarette brands, candies, and the small personal items that can be purchased at the Eastern and Central canteens. The situation is considerably more critical at Western which has no canteen facilities at all. The Western inmates had to prevail upon the staff to make all their purchases in a store located nearby—an arrangement that brought forth cries from the inmates that they were "treated like kids."

Although fighting among the adolescent female inmates is a fairly common occurrence, the Eastern, Central, and Western inmates do not fear for their personal safety as do adult male and female prisoners. As a result of the temporary love affairs and the established marriages between inmates, direct confrontation on the physical level occurs fairly often at Eastern, Central, and Western, particularly when triangular situations develop. Nevertheless, most differences tend to be settled verbally. These verbal battles are anxiety-provoking for the adolescent female because of her ambivalence toward other girls, whether or not they are her friends.

Adolescent girls are competitive for the attention of adolescent boys. Consequently, interaction between them tends to be somewhat cautious. They do, however, need the companionship of other girls for friends and, by observing and noting their positive and negative reactions, to chart their own progress toward adult beauty and womanhood. Competition is not carried on aggressively among adolescent girls, but it is recognized by all of them as a fact of life. This is what the inmates mean when they say that "You can't trust another girl!"—a theme that is as valid among adolescents girls in the external world as it is for the adjudicated female delinquents.

To ascertain the extent to which the female delinquents perceive other females as trustworthy persons, they were asked to indicate their agreement or disagreement with the statement: "You can't trust most girls. One minute they're on your side, and the next minute they're talking about you." It is significant that 97 percent of the Eastern inmates, 94 percent of the Central inmates, and 96 percent of the Western inmates agreed with the statement. Moreover, only 9 percent of the Eastern inmates, 15 percent of the Central inmates, and 10 percent of the Western inmates indicated that they would like to see all or most of their sister inmates after they are released, which also suggests the low regard in which most of the inmates are held.

In our society, the female is taught from an early age to develop and to emphasize her beauty in the pursuit of popularity with the opposite sex. During adolescence, she constantly assesses her physical attributes in terms of how she appears in the eyes of everyone in her social environment, especially her male peers. Hence, the lack of heterosexual relationships during the period of institutionalization is felt to be acutely depriving by the adolescent inmates.

Incarceration may be psychologically damaging for the youthful girls because the ambivalence of the adolescents concerning their sexuality and the natural desire for new experiences combine to create conditions that may not be easy for the inmates to shed when they return to civil society. They are developing images of themselves as adult women, and they are beset with many anxieties concerning their sexuality and acceptance by males. The exclusion of males in their own age group is a source of confusion for the adolescent girls. (Only the few confirmed homosexuals fall outside this group.) Their confusion is compounded by virtue of the fact that during incarceration they are socialized to view other women as legitimate sex objects. As put by the inmates:

> There is a lot of sex play in the cottages. One girl could be playing with another girl's body. You see it and you ignore it. You're in these surroundings and you look at it every day—kissing and petting and anything else they care to do. You look upon it as an everyday thing. You don't think anything about it.

> You're surrounded by it. You hear it every day. That's all everybody talks about. Who's going with who. Who's getting married. You're not here to learn. You don't hear this: "I had a good day at school today. I got good grades." Instead what you hear is: Guess who so and so is going with? Or, she's going with so and so. Sooner or later, everyone goes with someone.

> To security, homosexual behavior is when two girls have physical contact—holding hands, arms around each other. To the dorm staff it gets a little more involved. They give us more leeway: Two girls going together, kissing and doing what they want—they go all the way after they go together! It depends on who's on the dorm; some turn their head, and another will jump the gun before anything happens.

The informal social system is functional in that it provides substitute relationships for the community ties that were severed, and it enables the inmates to experiment in new social roles. However, within a short period of time, all the Eastern, Central and Western inmates view the redefined male and female sex role differentiation as reality. Whether the inmates' experiences in the informal social system will affect their ability to develop and to keep meaningful heterosexual relationships in the future is difficult to assess.[6] Certainly, the experience of incarceration creates enormous psychological burdens about sex. (1) The adolescent female offenders have not yet established adult heterosexual relationships in the external world, and they have little or no basis for comparison; (2) the confirmed lesbians among them have considerable prestige and power, and they are important socializing agents; and (3) the ambivalence of many staff members concerning the courtship, marriage, and kinship ties leads many of the adolescent offenders to believe that these relationships are acceptable to the staff.

Another factor of institutionalization is boredom. There is little to do in the evenings, on holidays, and during the weekends. It is alleviated only rarely by home visits. Seventy-three percent of the Eastern inmates, 85 percent of the Central inmates, and 94 percent of the Western inmates had not gone home on a visit since their commitment. In addition, during the month prior to completing the questionnaire, 40 percent of the Eastern inmates, 53 percent of the Central inmates, and 56 percent of the Western inmates had not been off the institution grounds for a recreational or cultural event such as a movie, museum visit, roller-skating, or dance. (The small difference observed at Eastern is due to the fact that the Eastern inmates completed their questionnaires in January, and members of the church choir had participated in Christmas holiday activities at nearby churches.) Nevertheless, 29 percent of the Eastern inmates, 27 percent of the Central inmates, and 29 percent of the Western inmates had been away only once. Almost all the inmates complained of monotony in the food menu; however, only a majority of the Western inmates indicated that they did not have enough food to eat. As the memorandum below demonstrates, their complaints had a factual basis:

To: All Dorms:

Unfair To Kids!

People who are unfair to the kids, and, incidentally, to some of the other staff, are those who take their meals on the cottage by dipping into the bowls and plates of food sent up for the girls' meals. The food sent to the girls is based on a ration, and when any member of the staff dips into the food, it makes it that much less for the girls. Therefore, staff members are actually depriving the girls of the food they should have. It is unfair to other staff, too, who have sent their food tickets and payment for the food sent to them on their separate trays.

Adults have the choice of bringing food from home, or ordering a tray from the kitchen and paying with an employee meal coupon. The Board of Control rule is very specific that employees must pay for meals eaten at the institution, with only minor exceptions. Until the Board of Control rule is changed to permit staff who are on duty with the wards through a meal period to be served without a meal coupon, this practice is illegal. . . .

Bertha Whitehead
Superintendent

STAFF ASSESSMENT OF INMATE CULTURE. In this study, estimates of the number of inmates who participate in the informal culture were obtained not only from the inmates, as is customary in such studies, but also from the staff workers in order to assess the latter's knowledge of the inmates' institutional experience. Table 12.1 shows the number of Eastern, Central, and Western inmates who belong to family groups, as estimated by the staff members of these institutions.

Table 12.1   Staff Estimates of Inmates Who Belong to Family Groups

Number Who Belong	Eastern		Central		Western	
	Number	%	Number	%	Number	%
All of the girls are part of these groups	10	6.8	6	3.8	12	12.8
Almost all of the girls	55	37.4	41	26.0	35	37.2
Approximately 75%	37	25.2	27	17.1	15	16.0
About 50%	28	19.0	44	27.8	16	17.0
About 25%	9	6.1	27	17.1	15	16.0
Less than 10%	8	5.4	13	8.2	1	1.1
Total	147	99.9	158	100.0	94	100.1

The data make clear the fact that all the staff are well aware that the inmates establish relationships and informal groups like those I have described. It is noteworthy that 69 percent of the Eastern staff, 47 percent of the Central staff and 66 percent of the Western staff maintained that 75 percent or more of the inmates were bound up in family-type relationships. Only 12 percent of the Eastern staff, 25 percent of the Central staff, and 17 percent of the Western staff estimated that 25 percent or fewer belong to family groups; the others maintained that the number of members and nonmembers was approximately equal. Although staff members tend to underestimate the precise number of inmates involved in court-ship, marriage, and kinship relationships, the extent to which they can identify these relationships gives evidence of the pervasiveness of the groups. This is a sensitive area of correctional administration, and some staff members deny the existence of homosexuality either out of "loyalty" to the administration, or because they think outsiders would not "under-stand." I tried to overcome this problem by having all staff members com-plete the questionnaire just before the study ended; by this time, most of the staff members were aware that I was familiar with all phases of insti-tutional operation. New employees were the ones who underestimated the number of inmates involved because their information is limited.

How many Eastern, Central and Western inmates were actually in-volved in courtship, marriage, and kinship relationships? The data in Table 12.2 indicate the sex roles that were assumed by the inmates at the time they completed the questionnaires.

Table 12.2   Sex Roles Assumed by the Inmates

	Eastern		Central		Western	
Sex Role	Number	%	Number	%	Number	%
Male	74	36.1	98	28.7	66	41.5
Female	89	43.4	127	37.2	70	44.0
Female: Membership only in family group(s) or isolated kinship ties	16	7.8	63	18.5	13	8.2
Not involved in mar-riage, courtship, or in family groups	24	11.7	35	10.3	8	5.0
Not ascertained	2	1.0	18	5.3	2	1.3
Total	205	100.0	341	100.0	159	100.0

In all the institutions more inmates assume female roles than male roles. Twelve percent of the Eastern inmates, 10 percent of the Central inmates and 5 percent of the Western inmates did not participate in these relationships; the latter were mainly recent arrivals and a few inmates who had recently terminated their relationships in the racket, sillies, or chick business.[7]

The Western inmates exhibit a more evenly balanced sex ratio as a consequence of the way they define and isolate friendship pairs and other relationships of a more intimate nature through reciprocal nicknames. The Western inmates tend to restrict selection of mates to individuals who reside in their own living unit; consequently, an inmate's decision to form a sexual relationship may function to pattern a newcomer's sex role to complement her own. Table 12.3 shows data on the number of inmates who claimed membership in family groups.

Table 12.3   Number of Inmates Who Are Members of Family Groups

Family Group Membership	Eastern		Central		Western	
	Number	%	Number	%	Number	%
Yes	173	84.4	284	83.3	149	93.7
No	30	14.6	39	11.4	8	5.0
Not ascertained	2	1.0	18	5.3	2	1.3
Total	205	100.0	341	100.0	159	100.0

Eighty-five percent of the Eastern inmates, 83 percent of the Central inmates, and 94 percent of the Western inmates were members of family groups. The inmates who were not members of family groups may have acknowledged relationships of the courtship—"going with"—type although they did not simultaneously acknowledge other kinship ties. This was especially true for recent arrivals. Other inmates may, of course, have acknowledged kinship ties in the past.

It is important to ascertain the meaning of the inmates' informal culture for the job performance of the staff, because it has obvious implications for the rehabilitation of the inmates. The responses of the staff to a questionnaire item[8] that was designed to ascertain whether the family groups make their jobs more difficult are set forth in Table 12.4.

Less than 5 percent of the staff at Eastern, Central and Western indicate that most or all of the family groups are helpful to them; slightly higher proportions of the staff members responded that they view the groups as neutral categories, having no effect whatsoever on their job performance. The data indicated that education or years of service did not significantly differentiate the staff who attributed a positive function to the informal group structure. The responses included staff of all educational levels and individuals who had been employed less than six

Table 12.4   Effect of the Inmates' Informal Family Group
Structure on Staff's Job Performance

Effect on Job Performance	Eastern		Central		Western	
	Number	%	Number	%	Number	%
They have no effect at all	11	7.5	17	10.8	5	5.3
None of these groups are helpful to us	87	59.2	99	62.7	38	40.4
A few of these groups are helpful	27	18.4	29	18.4	30	31.9
Some are helpful	16	10.9	11	7.0	18	19.2
Most are helpful to us	4	2.7	1	0.6	3	3.2
All of the groups are helpful	2	1.4	1	0.6	—	—
Total	147	100.1	158	100.1	94	100.0

months as well as those who had been employed for many years. The majority of the Eastern and Central staff indicated that none of the groups were helpful to them, whereas 40 percent of the Western staff attributed a negative function to the inmate group structure. Indeed, 32 percent of the Western staff maintained that a few of the groups were helpful to them, which perhaps reflects the fact that sometimes members of the Western cottage staff delegated supervisory functions to inmates who were known to be heads of family groups.

As to the influence of the family groups on the girls themselves, the staff members generally agree that participation has a negative influence.[9] The data shown in Table 12.5 indicate that less than 5 percent of the Eastern, Central, and Western staff believe that the "families" usually or always have a good influence on the inmates.

The data in Table 12.5 also indicate that the Western staff members attribute a positive function to the family groups more often than do the Eastern or Central staff. Nevertheless, these data contrast sharply with the inmates' assessment of their kinship relationships.

STAFF–INMATE RELATIONSHIPS.   Although there is considerable pretension among institutional personnel that they are guided by the model of "individualized" treatment, the inmates are in fact handled en masse. The task of integrating individualized treatment with the other institutional goals of security and maintenance has yet to be resolved in

Table 12.5   Influence of Make Believe "Families"
on the Inmates as Reported by Staff

Influence on Inmates	Eastern		Central		Western	
	Number	%	Number	%	Number	%
All have a bad influence	19	12.9	27	17.1	4	4.3
Usually a bad influence	80	54.4	76	48.1	39	41.5
Sometimes a bad influence	41	27.9	50	31.6	47	50.0
Usually a good influence	5	3.4	5	3.2	4	4.3
Always a good influence	2	1.4	—	—	—	—
Total	147	100.0	158	100.0	94	100.1

institutions serving juvenile delinquents. Institutional personnel do not know exactly what is meant by treatment, what it is they are to treat, nor how to bring treatment about. The goals of custody and mainte- nance, however, are not only easily understood by all the staff, but activi- ties relating to these functions can be organized so that there is some observable correspondence between inputs and outputs.[10]

Certainly, the very fact that the inmates have been identified and iso- lated for "treatment" provides the formal structure for the staff to view them as inferior in some respects to the youngsters who remain at large in society. The responses of the staff to a questionnaire item seeking a "realistic appraisal of the situation" are pessimistic considering the in- mates' offenses.[11] Fourteen percent of the Eastern staff, 18 percent of the Central staff, and 17 percent of the Western staff indicated that "most of the girls here will improve." The staff's generalized view of the causes of juvenile offenses vary; the questionnaire responses of some are charac- teristic of differential association theory or they presume social environ- mental conditions, but the largest proportion of staff workers focus on the individual's, rather than the social structure's, need for treatment. Fifty-seven percent of the Eastern staff, 47 percent of the Central staff, and 49 percent of the Western staff indicate that juvenile offenses are caused by children with deep-seated emotional problems. Twenty-one percent of the Eastern staff, 17 percent of the Central staff, and 26 per- cent of the Western staff indicated that juvenile offenses come about through learning from close associates who are already delinquent. How- ever, 86 percent of the Eastern staff, 82 percent of the Central staff, and 77 percent of the Western staff expressed agreement with a questionnaire item stating that delinquents are "rejected children who need help."

Forty-nine percent of the Eastern staff, 42 percent of the Central staff and 64 percent of the Western staff indicated their belief that group and individual treatment programs are likely to have the greatest impact on a juvenile's reformation, rather than educational and vocational programs or the use of custodial management techniques; the "treatment" responses reflect the increased numbers of social service staff who socialize the other staff members to express verbally the current treatment orientation, as none of the institutional officials had evaluated any of their programs.

Institutional workers tend to give lip service to treatment responses that bear no relationship to their usual mode of operation; indeed, many of the so-called unsophisticated staff members with a grade school education or less have learned through in-service training and increased contact with social workers to parrot many of the "appropriate" treatment responses. Not surprisingly, the majority of the Eastern, Central, and Western staff indicate their agreement that *punishment* is not necessary for delinquents to "learn correct social behavior." The data presented in Chapter 8 point to the wide gap that exists between actions and expressed attitudes. In short, the staffs' socialization regarding the "ideal" treatment orientation is not yet complete; this is also apparent in that the majority of the Eastern, Central and Western staff still advocate social distance, rather than the close and friendly relationships that are said to be inherent in individual and group therapy techniques and the hallmark of effective treatment.

Notwithstanding the gaps in treatment orientation, "close" relationships were called into question by both the inmates and the staff. Although status and authority considerations were clearly important to all the staff, the meaning attributed by them to the informal social system of the inmates transcended the boundaries of the inmate groupings and influenced the quality of interaction between the staff and the inmates. Of those staff members who advocated friendly relations between staff and inmates, fewer of the Eastern and Central staff compared to the Western staff indicated that close and friendly relationships were desirable in order to "understand" the inmates. I observed, however, that in general the Eastern and Central cottage staff were more friendly and relaxed with the inmates; perhaps this was due to the fact that they viewed them as children and often responded to them as they might their own children—scolding them one moment and hugging them the next. Also, more of the Eastern and Central inmates were younger than the Western inmates, and the Eastern inmates addressed all cottage staff as "Ma." The majority of the staff members in all the institutions, however, expressed concern that the inmates would "take advantage" of them if they were "lenient." Sixty-eight percent of the Eastern staff, 58 percent of the Central staff, and 58 percent of the Western staff agreed with the statement: "If a staff member is lenient with the girls, they will take advantage of her." Moreover, almost all the staff members maintained that *firmness* will help delinquents to "learn right from wrong," but the Eastern and Central cottage staff often qualified the statement by adding "with love" or "with kindness." By contrast, the "clinical" orientation at Western (all cottage staff were therapists) set up artificial barriers to communication that were not observed at Eastern or Central. Only 38 percent of the Western inmates compared to 54 percent of the Eastern inmates and 49 percent of the Central inmates maintained that they were "very close" or "fairly close" to the cottage staff. A similar disparity emerged in the inmates' responses to the questionnaire item: "Most staff members here don't really care about what happens to us. They're just doing a job." Sixty-eight percent of the Western inmates expressed agreement with this view of the staff's job orientation as contrasted with 46 percent of the Eastern inmates and 39 percent of the Central staff.

It is clear that many of the Eastern, Central and Western inmates do not feel that the staff members are sincere in their efforts to rehabilitate, and they do not characterize the interaction between the staff and the inmates as particularly close. Moreover, the treatment process is further complicated by the fact that the staff and the inmates differ regarding the ability of the girls to avoid trouble. The viewpoint of the inmates is shown in Table 12.6.

The majority of the inmates indicate that most girls freely choose to engage in deviant acts and that they are aware of the consequences of their actions; indeed, less than one-fourth of the inmates in each institution indicated that the intervention of adults was necessary for them to "stay out of trouble."

In our discussing the organization of treatment services, I pointed out that the Eastern, Central, and Western inmates were expected to assume roles of treatment agents; they were to "help" other inmates with their "problems" and to offer them advice. A further expectation was that an inmate would voluntarily inform the staff of any inmate's rule infractions, presumably to hasten the process of rehabilitation. Notwithstanding the expectations of the staff, the inmates prefer not to turn to girls their own age to find solutions to some of their problems. The Puerto Rican and other Spanish-speaking inmates often mentioned that they considered matters that related to their parents or siblings to be personal; others questioned the sincerity of the inmates who were proffering advice, as

Table 12.6   Inmate Opinions Regarding External Help and the Ability of Girls to "Stay out of Trouble"

Help Required	Eastern		Central		Western	
	Number	%	Number	%	Number	%
I think most girls need help	41	20.0	78	22.9	38	23.9
Most girls could stay out of trouble if they wanted to	65	31.7	98	28.8	41	25.8
Most girls know right from wrong. If they wanted to stay out of trouble they would	88	42.9	154	45.3	75	47.2
Most girls don't need help from anyone	11	5.4	10	2.9	5	3.1
Total	205	100.0	340	99.9	159	100.0

the latter were often motivated by jealousy or competition in love affairs; or they stressed that they had their own problems and future to think about, and, therefore, did not feel that they could (or should) burden themselves with the home and personal problems of the other cottage residents:

> I feel funny talking to girls my own age about some of my personal problems. I don't think girls my age can help—they've done the same things I have. They're not in a position to give advice. I feel funny taking advice from girls my own age.

> In an institution, these girls are not going to help you. They can't help you. They have their own problems just like I've got mine. I've got all the problems I can handle without worrying about everybody else in this cottage.

> I couldn't talk about my parents and family in front of the girls and the staff. I think that it's personal. They can't help me as far as that's concerned. The only ones who can straighten things out are my parents and me, but I never see them while I'm here. How can you solve your problems when your folks are out there and you're a hundred miles away in here?

The concerns of the inmates have obvious implications for group therapy treatment programs. When the discussion in the group therapy sessions was not focused on the informal social system, the content tended to remain on a very superficial level.

To what extent can the inmates function as "treatment" agents? The treatment process requires communication characterized by trust. But the inmates of all three institutions hold most inmates in low regard; interaction that is characterized by trust is reserved for the inmates to whom they are bound up in courtship, marriage, or kinship ties. Only 9.8 percent of the Eastern inmates, 9.7 percent of the Central inmates and 10 percent of the Western inmates maintained that one does not have to be very careful about what one says and does around the inmates. Even if this were not the case, the inmates' ability to function in treatment roles would be problematic because the staff restrict interaction among the inmates in an effort to decrease the formation of courtship, marriage, and kinship relationships. Indeed, the majority of the inmates contend that in order to stay out of trouble with the staff, isolation from one's peers is the best procedure. Sixty-seven percent of the Eastern inmates, 63 percent of the Central inmates and 64 percent of the Western inmates agreed with the following questionnaire item: "You have to be pretty careful around the girls you get friendly with here. To stay out of trouble with the staff it's best to keep to yourself." It is interesting to note that the responses of the staff to a similar item indicated that the opposite is the case; 69 percent of the Eastern staff, 78 percent of the Central staff and 68 percent of the Western staff disagreed with a statement asserting that the inmates who "keep to themselves and don't get too close to the other girls" get the "most out of their stay." Of course, the fact that all the inmates had to congregate in the living room area unless they were restricted to their rooms rules out isolation as a logical possibility. But the staff wanted the inmates to interact with and help one another without establishing courtship, marriage, or kinship bonds.

Most of the staff's time is taken up with problems that arise from a large group of girls living in confined quarters, leaving little time for "individualized" treatment. The content of the group therapy sessions, whether small or large groups, was more often than not concerned with problems associated with the racket, the sillies, chick business, and the violation of other institutional rules. When the inmates were asked to indicate in their own words what they had to do to obtain a parole or discharge, they stressed conformity to the institutional rules; the responses of 65 percent of the Eastern inmates, 53 percent of the Central inmates, and 77 percent of the Western inmates stressed conformity to the institutional rules and compliance to the staff's demands. The responses of only 18 percent of the Eastern inmates, 16 percent of the Central inmates and 6 percent of the Western inmates could be coded as "treatment" responses, that is, indicating a gain in self-insight. Interviews with and observation of the staff indicated that the staff's generalized view of "understanding" subsumes conformity to all organizational rules. Indeed, staff members take conformity for granted as indicative of an inmate's readiness for reentry into society.

In like fashion, the Eastern, Central and Western staff members indicate that the inmates approach them about matters of institutional routines rather than the situational factors that contributed to their incarceration. These data are shown in Table 12.7.

Table 12.7 Primary Reason Inmates Usually
Contact Staff as Reported by Staff Members

Primary Reason for Contact	Eastern		Central		Western	
	Number	%	Number	%	Number	%
Change in a class assignment, such as academic or vocational school or group therapy	13	8.8	20	12.7	4	4.3
Work assignment change	7	4.8	5	3.2	5	5.3
Punishment received or loss of privileges	19	12.9	9	5.7	8	8.5
Parole or release date	18	12.2	26	16.5	4	4.3
Institutional rule violation	47	32.0	76	48.1	52	55.3
Relationships with family	27	18.4	10	6.3	15	16.0
Trial visit	—	—	3	1.9	—	—
Past deviant behavior	14	9.5	9	5.7	4	4.3
No response	2	1.4	—	—	2	2.1
Total	147	100.0	158	100.1	94	100.1

In connection with two questionnaire items—"When you talk to your cottage supervisor [or social worker] which of these things do you *usually* talk about?"—the responses of the inmates were not clustered in the categories of punishment and institutional difficulties in which the inmates may be involved. Only a few of the inmates checked trial visit as a topic of discussion because trial visits were not part of the routine program at the institutions studied; they were scheduled only in a few special circumstances at Eastern and Central and almost never at Western. Many of the inmates at all the institutions indicated that they "never see" the social workers and do not often contact the cottage staff. These inmates checked what they would probably discuss if they did contact these staff members. Observation over an extended period of time indicated that contact between the inmates and staff members was extremely limited, and when it was initiated by the staff it tended to be in connection with institutional matters. (See Table 1, Appendix B.) Generally speaking, the majority of the inmates either discussed their problems with their intimates or did not discuss them with anyone.

The older inmates have a decided advantage over both the younger inmates and the staff, as the youthful adolescents believe that unless an individual has had direct experience in such things as the "drug" or "street" culture, they cannot understand the problems involved. This is not to say that the adolescent offenders believe that adults cannot help them at all or that they do not wish to turn to adults for help and information. Indeed, the contrary is true regarding job opportunities or the educational requirements of certain jobs. Beyond this, however, the inmates are apt to turn selectively to staff members whom they perceive to be "sincere," that is, interested in their welfare. A staff person may develop a relationship of trust with an inmate over a period of time. This process is usually time-consuming, and does not often happen. (See Chapter 7 about how the staff at Western tried to avoid the issue by having the inmates "contract" to talk with a staff member at the staff's convenience.)

The staff often worked at cross-purposes; their preoccupation with the activities relating to the informal social system of the inmates overshadowed and influenced the organization and planning of all institution programs. For example, inmates sometimes requested class changes in order to be near particular individuals. Although such changes were easier to negotiate at Western where the educational program was poorly developed and the schedule more readily compromised than at Eastern or Central, the academic staff of all the institutions spent a great deal of time with this and other matters that could be traced to the inmates' courtship, marriage, or kinship relationships.

GEOGRAPHICAL ISOLATION AND TREATMENT. The physical isolation of correctional institutions from urban centers causes additional deprivation and has ramifications for treatment programs. Location helps to maintain the barrier to communication with the external world. In spite of the treatment rhetoric that characterizes institutions today, they remain as hidden from the public gaze as they were a century ago. It is difficult to recruit the staff required for routine operation, and those persons who do work at the schools have little rapport with the city-bred girls whose experience is so different from their own. The vast resources of the city cannot be utilized to accomplish the individualized treatment objectives that are officially stated as viable goals. As a rule, access to the institutions is by private automobile (public transportation is almost nonexistent, and where available, taxi service is expensive); this means that the parents, relatives and friends of the inmates cannot visit them easily or often. An examination of the official files revealed that 33 percent of the Eastern inmates, 38 percent of the Central inmates, and 28 percent of the Western inmates had received no visitors; 22 percent of the Eastern inmates, 20 percent of the Central inmates, and 15 percent of the Western inmates had received visitors only once during the entire incarceration period.[12] Hence, within a few weeks, the inmates' ties with the outside world become severely weakened.

Why do administrators of institutions for juvenile delinquents continue to stress isolation from the larger society in the planning and organizing of their services? Contact with the outside world is viewed by the staff as disruptive to the organizational routine. Institutional officials may give lip service to the notion that they would like to "expand" the use of volunteers, but they do not mean that volunteers with professional training could actually design programs that would enable them to share their special training with the inmates. However, this would seem to be implied in the philosophy of "individualized" treatment, as there are financial limits to which institution staffs can realistically be increased in order to achieve organizational goals.

At the present time, the use of volunteers as part of the "program" at Eastern, Central, and Western is confined to an evening during the week for an hour or so and is limited to activities such as knitting or crocheting. While the latter may, of course, be of interest to a few inmates, the fact remains that the use of volunteers solely for activities of this type is administratively unimaginative and wasteful of existing societal resources. Moreover, these activities are very infrequent because the volunteers must be the "right type."

Administrators are reluctant to use volunteers and other community resources because they think the latter should be adapted to the "needs" of the institution. The subject is not discussed often, but it is apparent that administrators do not want to share or relinquish their control of treatment programs for the inmates; they insist that all such programs be coordinated and controlled by institutional workers.

The staff were asked to indicate whether they thought volunteers from the community can be utilized effectively in institutional programs. Seventeen percent of the Eastern staff, 24 percent of the Central staff, and 39 percent of the Western staff indicated that they can be "very helpful"; 61 percent of the Eastern staff, 62 percent of the Central staff, and 49 percent of the Western staff indicated they can be helpful "in certain parts of the program." The remainder of the staff either selected the response indicating volunteers "probably wouldn't contribute very much to the program" or that volunteers "mean well, but they would create problems for us." The least use of volunteers was made at Western where their presence in the cottages was a rare event.

The meaning of the institutions' physical isolation from urban resources can best be understood by examining what the Eastern, Central, and Western inmates would like to do with their lives, that is, what their work aspirations are. To obtain this information, the inmates were asked to write in their own words the kind of job that they would like to have when they complete their education. The job preferences of the Eastern, Central and Western inmates are summarized in Table 12.8. (See Table 4, Appendix B for a summary of the inmates' ideal job preferences.)

From Table 12.8, we can see that the vocational aspirations of the inmates are extremely varied. The academic retardation of many of the inmates is such that they will probably never realize their vocational ambitions unless they have access to the educational and vocational opportunities afforded by the large urban centers and unless they are encouraged to put forth the extra effort that may be required. Many of the girls have never achieved because they have been led to believe that they could not do so or because they lacked the kind of experience whereby they could perceive how their present schooling was related to future goals.

That many of the inmates have truanted from school does not mean that they have no interest in education or that they have no vocational interests and ambitions. Some of the inmates did not go to school because they lacked suitable clothing or because a teacher may have made them feel awkward or "dumb." Others truanted because the routine of the school was not suited to their particular needs. For example, some of the inmates maintained that they "really liked school," but not on an all day basis; they would prefer to go to school for a period of time somewhat less than the conventional school day and perhaps work for a few hours to earn some money.

Most of the inmates actually have little factual knowledge of the training requirements for specific vocational goals. The older inmates who are ready to enter the job market or are actively seeking jobs tend to be

Table 12.8 Job Preferences of Inmates

Job Preference	Eastern Number	%	Central Number	%	Western Number	%
Nurse, nurse's aide, other hospital work	49	24.0	78	22.8	59	37.1
Stewardess	6	2.9	11	3.2	3	1.9
Beautician, hairdresser, cosmetologist	24	11.7	28	8.2	15	9.4
Cook, dietitian, waitress	4	2.0	23	6.8	—	—
Teacher (all types)	13	6.3	21	6.2	5	3.1
Social or welfare worker	9	4.4	12	3.5	5	3.1
Doctor (includes psychiatrist)	8	3.9	3	0.9	4	2.5
Secretary, stenographer, typist, bookkeeper	30	14.6	43	12.6	11	6.9
IBM or other business machines operator	12	5.8	12	3.5	1	0.6
Salesclerk	6	2.9	12	3.5	1	0.6
Psychologist	—	—	2	0.6	—	—
Scientist	1	0.5	1	0.3	4	2.5
Laboratory technician	2	1.0	2	0.6	—	—
Postal clerk	1	0.5	2	0.6	1	0.6
Treasury job	1	0.5	—	—	—	—
Telephone operator	—	—	—	—	1	0.6
Policewoman or private detective	1	0.5	1	0.3	—	—
Parole or probation officer, lawyer	1	0.5	4	1.2	4	2.5
Cottage parent in training school	2	1.0	3	0.9	7	4.4
Armed forces, job corps, peace corps	3	1.5	3	0.9	—	—
Singer, dancer, actress, musician	10	4.9	12	3.5	2	1.3
Songwriter, writer	—	—	4	1.2	—	—
Model	4	2.0	14	4.1	3	1.9
Fashion designer, commercial designer	2	1.0	1	0.3	1	0.6
Interior decorator	2	1.0	—	—	—	—
Artist	—	—	6	1.8	4	2.5
Peacemaker or religious vocation	—	—	2	0.6	—	—
Wife, mother, homemaker	1	0.5	5	1.5	2	1.3
Hippy	—	—	—	—	2	1.3
Laundry, sewing jobs, custodian	—	—	6	1.8	—	—
Bus driver	—	—	—	—	1	0.6
No work	1	0.5	9	2.6	5	3.1
Irrelevant responses	—	—	—	—	2	1.3
Uncertain, illegible, no response	12	5.8	21	6.2	16	10.0
Total	205	100.2	341	100.2	159	99.7

vocal in denouncing their institutional training. Only 31 percent of the Eastern inmates, 28 percent of the Central inmates and 13 percent of the Western inmates indicated that they had received a "lot of help" to prepare for the kinds of future jobs they would like to hold. The data in Table 12.8 clearly indicate that the kinds of jobs to which the inmates aspire bear little or no relationship to the "work training" they receive and the educational resources of the institutions.

The aspirations of the girls are frustrated in a more subtle way, too: The institutional officials and most of the staff members hold traditional conservative views of woman's place, and this contributes to the lack of diversity in program planning. However, even if the programs were actually expanded, they would essentially remain paper programs because of the locations of the institutions.

Institutions as "Solution" to Juvenile Delinquency

Commitment of adjudicated juvenile offenders has become big business: and all institutional employees (as well as ancillary professional groups) have a vested interest in keeping these facilities open, however inefficient their operation. Institutional workers have not been vocal in the community (local or distant) about the inefficiencies of their organizations, nor have they pressed for the kind of innovative change that would truly take into account the best interests of the inmates. Indeed, institutional workers have consistently presented a picture of their accomplishments that neither corresponds to the present reality nor to what one could realistically expect them to accomplish in the future, even if additional funds were put at their disposal.

The vast sums of money that have been channeled into the institutions studied over the past several decades have been used for the most part to enlarge the physical plants and to improve the exterior. A few more staff members have been added, but the actual programs of the institutions have changed very little over the years.

Not only have the institutions continued to remain isolated from the communities where the inmates live—and to which almost all will return—but each remains an island unto itself in the very community where it is situated, tolerated, at best, because the institution provides a source of employment for the local townspeople. From Table 13.1, it is clear that most staff members maintain that the people in the local community either have very little knowledge of the institution or that they have no interest in its affairs.

Table 13.1   Local Community's Regard of Institution as Assessed by Staff

Community's Regard	Eastern		Central		Western	
	Number	%	Number	%	Number	%
Most people think the institution has a bad effect on the community	20	13.6	4	2.5	7	7.4
Most people don't know very much about us	92	62.6	110	69.6	77	81.9
Most people don't care one way or the other about the institution	23	15.6	21	13.3	5	5.3
The institution is highly regarded by most people in the community	12	8.2	23	14.6	5	5.3
Total	147	100.0	158	100.0	94	99.9

The staff were prohibited from discussing the day-to-day happenings and specific details of institutional programs with nonemployees. If the question was put to them, they were expected to emphasize what the institution was "trying to do," but to sidestep "sensitive" areas which were the domain of the top officials. In effect, sometimes staff members talked about "programs" that were not actually in operation; thus they contributed to the local townspeople's lack of knowledge. Perhaps more important, they failed to take the opportunity to acquaint the public with the very real and complex problems faced by every correctional administrator. Table 13.2 sets forth the responses of the Eastern, Central, and Western staff indicating whether they will discuss institutional affairs when the subject is raised by individuals who are not employed at these institutions.

STAFF VIEWS OF EMPLOYMENT.   The Eastern, Central, and Western staff members give varied reasons for working at the institutions, but whether their reasons are specifically stated or unstated, most of them

Table 13.2 Likelihood That Staff Will Discuss Institution Affairs When Subject Raised by Nonemployees

Likelihood of Discussion	Eastern		Central		Western	
	Number	%	Number	%	Number	%
Its very likely that I will discuss things that happen here	33	22.4	61	38.6	32	34.0
It's not at all likely that I will	66	44.9	51	32.3	35	37.2
I probably won't — it's against the institutional rules	14	9.5	15	9.5	9	9.6
Although it's against the institutional rules, I probably will talk to some people about them	29	19.7	29	18.4	18	19.2
I don't have any friends who don't work here	5	3.4	2	1.3	—	—
Total	147	99.9	158	100.1	94	100.0

work there because they lack skills to work elsewhere or other job opportunities were not available in the area. Lack of other job opportunities was stressed by 18 percent of the Eastern and Western staffs, compared to only 4 percent of the Central staff. In addition, 31 percent of the Eastern staff, 23 percent of the Central staff, and 19 percent of the Western staff indicated that their main reason for working was to supplement their family's income.

It is difficult to ascertain how honest the staff are in responding to this type of questionnaire item when the array of responses is displayed before them. In this study, an open-ended "other" category was included to give the staff an opportunity to write in other reasons for working at the institution, should they choose to do so. Twenty-four percent of the Central staff wrote in statements to the effect that they liked "working with teen-agers," whereas only 3 percent of the Eastern staff and 7 percent of the Western staff responded in this fashion. Of course, the Western staff were considerably younger than the Eastern and Central staff, and this fact may well be reflected in their responses.

The proportion of the Western staff members who indicated that their "main reason" for working at the institution was due to the fact that it was their "career" or "profession" was larger than at Eastern or Central: Specifically, 49 percent of the Western staff responded in this way compared to 32 percent of the Eastern staff, and 37 percent of the Central staff. With rare exception, however, all the academic teachers, nurses, and other college-trained "specialists" looked upon their work in "career" terms. Undoubtedly the difference in the responses of the Western staff reflects the fact that the cottage staff also functioned as "therapists" and they tended to view themselves as "professional," which was certainly not the case for the Eastern and Central staff. The definition of the Western cottage staff as semiprofessionals functioned to elevate the expectations of the cottage staff regarding their own professional advancement; for example, the Western staff received higher salaries than their counterparts at either Eastern or Central. Although they expressed less dissatisfaction with salary and wages than the Eastern and Central staff, the Western staff in all occupations expressed more dissatisfaction with their chances for advancement and promotion. At Western the cottage staff competed with the social workers because they too functioned as therapists, conducted "individual" and "small group," and sometimes prepared case reports. Significantly it was only at Western that a majority of the cottage staff indicated agreement with a questionnaire item asserting that the nonprofessional staff feel the professional staff don't do as much as they can to help the inmates. However, the Eastern, Central, and Western staffs generally were in agreement as far as discipline was concerned, and in the other ways that the professional and nonprofessional staff members related to the inmates and to each other in the performance of their duties. (See also Table 5, Appendix B.)

HOME VERSUS INSTITUTIONALIZATION. Would the inmates be better off if they had remained at home? When assessing the relevance and impact of institutionalization for incarcerated adolescent offenders, the logical comparison must be with the child's home: To ask the inmates to compare the present institution with another institution seems somewhat beside the point. The question of how they felt about their institutionalization was put to the inmates. The questionnaire item read: "Girls who get into trouble are handled in different ways. Some are sent to different institutions and some are allowed to stay home. If you were back home and had your choice, which would you choose?" Eighty-one percent of the Eastern inmates, 85 percent of the Central inmates, and 85 percent of the Western inmates indicated that they would be better off at home. These data are shown in Table 13.3.

Table 13.3   Inmates' Stated Preferences between Remaining
at Home and Institutionalization

	Eastern		Central		Western	
Stated Preference	Number	%	Number	%	Number	%
I would be better off at home	166	80.9	289	84.8	135	84.9
I would feel OK about coming here	35	17.1	41	12.0	13	8.2
I would prefer to try another institution	4	2.0	11	3.2	11	6.9
Total	205	100.0	341	100.0	159	100.0

In the main, the girls saw the institutions as places of punishment. Contrary to what one might be led to expect, this assessment is not based altogether on the fact that room confinement and group punishment were widely used as forms of social control, although, to be sure, the inmates defined them both as punishment. Rather, the inmates questioned whether a solution to their problems could be provided in the institution where they found themselves, as they insisted that their problems were external to it—*outside* with their parents, drugs, and school teachers, for example. Inasmuch as little contact with their parents was possible, it was the consensus of the inmates that they had only been "sent away."

The offenses for which they have been incarcerated, together with the family background data, suggest that many of their problems stem from conflicts with parents in particular, and the social conditions within the home, in general. Given this state of affairs, the question may be raised: Is it reasonable to suppose that treatment and rehabilitation can take place if the child is removed from the home and placed in an institution a hundred or more miles away?

Instead of abandoning the isolated physical plants, correctional officials have confronted the problem of distance by creating parallel service systems to *work with* the parents or other household head while the child is incarcerated. The "field staff," as they are often called, presumably complement the institution's functions where the staff work with the child. However, the field staff usually have no more than one (if any) contact with the family while the child is institutionalized. In addition, it is necessary that they know the child to work effectively with the parents. Some inmates at all the institutions were released without ever meeting with their field workers, and when the field workers did see the inmates their contacts tended to be hurried and brief encounters after the inmate had been scheduled for release. Attempts to increase the contacts of the field staff with institutional workers and inmates are difficult to arrange because they conflict with the institutions' schedules. Institutional officials give first priority to their own organizational routine, hence field services are coordinated with the institution's routine when convenient to the staff.

Inasmuch as there is usually one state correctional facility for juvenile girls in an entire state, the geographical area that field staffs must serve tends to be quite large. However, the findings of the present study indicate that decentralization of field services into "regional offices" may not necessarily solve the problem. Even if caseloads are decreased and the geographical area served is reduced in size, the field staff's effectiveness in dealing with the problems that are an integral part of the inmate's home situation will continue to be fruitless as long as the present practice of removing the child from the home to isolated institutions continues.

The social histories of the inmates emphasize that their families are characterized by multiple problems. Nevertheless, in only a few cases is the family unit so severely fragmented and weakened in structure that the removal of the child from the home is indicated to provide the best "treatment." In fact, even in the cases where removal from the home may appear to be the only solution, the question must be raised whether court process and institutionalization is the answer. The child could profitably be diverted from institutions to the homes of relatives, friends, or a foster home. Or, for adolescents who are at least sixteen years old, a group home or an independent living arrangement whereby the individual can continue her education or work in the community could be feasible in selected cases.

A correctional system that insists it is concerned with and dispenses *individualized* treatment must be willing to reorder its programs and bureaucratic routine to find the best recourse for *each child*.

Finally, the problems involving the schools and other social institutions in the community and their relationship to juvenile "delinquency" will not be confronted until the assumption that it is the adolescent who requires attention and treatment in every case is challenged.

Notes

1. See especially Gresham M. Sykes and Sheldon L. Messinger, "The Inmate Social System," in *Theoretical Studies in Social Organization of the Prison.* New York, Social Science Research Council, Pamphlet No. 15, 1960, pp. 5–19; Gresham M. Sykes, *The Society of Captives.* Princeton, New Jersey, Princeton University Press, 1958; Erving Goffman, "On the Characteristics of Total Institutions: Staff-Inmate Relations," in *The Prison: Studies in Institutional Organization and Change,* Donald R. Cressey, Editor. New York, Holt, Rinehart and Winston, 1961, Chapters 1 and 2; Richard A. Cloward, "Social Control in the Prison," in *Theoretical Studies in the Social Organization of the Prison, op. cit., pp.* 20–48. See also Donald Clemmer, *The Prison Community.* New York, Holt, Rinehart and Winston, 1958 (reissue of the 1940 edition); Morris G. Caldwell, "Group Dynamics in the Prison Community," *Journal of Criminal Law, Criminology and Police Science,* Vol. 46, January-February 1956, pp. 648–57; Norman S. Hayner, "Washington State Correctional Institutions as Communities," *Social Forces,* Vol. 21, 1943, pp. 316–22; Norman S. Hayner and Ellis Ash, "The Prison as a Community," *American Sociological Review,* Vol. 5, August 1940, pp. 577–83; Hans Reimer, "Socialization in the Prison Community," *Proceedings of the American Prison Association,* 1937, pp. 151–55.

2. However, despite the U-shaped pattern of change, there was a tendency for inmates to move away from conformity to conventional norms with each

increment of prison experience. Thus, first offenders and recidivists exhibit the same pattern, but the recidivists exhibit lower conformity than the first offenders. Stanton Wheeler, "Social Organization in a Correctional Community." Ph.D. Dissertation, University of Washington, 1958. See also Stanton Wheeler, "Socialization in Correctional Communities," *American Sociological Review*, Vol. 26, October 1961, pp. 696–712; Peter C. Garabedian, "Social Roles and Processes of Socialization in the Prison Community," *Social Problems*, Vol. 11, Fall 1963, pp. 139–52. Similarly, Glaser found evidence that friendship with other inmates generally assumes a U-shaped pattern during imprisonment, but he found much disparity among the institutions he studied. The shape of the curve was found to vary inversely with age or prior confinement of prisoners; see Daniel Glaser, *The Effectiveness of a Prison and Parole System*. Indianapolis, Bobbs-Merrill, 1964.

3. Clarence Schrag, "Some Foundations for a Theory of Correction," in Donald R. Cressey, *op. cit.*, pp. 309–57.

4. John Irwin and Donald R. Cressey, "Thieves, Convicts, and the Inmate Culture," *Social Problems*, Vol. 10, Fall 1962, pp. 142–55.

5. Clarence Schrag, "Some Foundations for a Theory of Correction," in Donald R. Cressey, *op. cit.*, p. 342. For a more complete discussion of these two theoretical positions, see Rose Giallombardo, "Social Roles in a Prison for Women," *Social Problems*, Vol. 13, No. 3, Winter 1966, pp. 268–88; and Rose Giallombardo, *Society of Women: A Study of a Women's Prison*. New York, John Wiley and Sons, 1966.

6. Julian Roebuck, "A Critique of 'Thieves, Convicts, and the Inmate Culture,'" *Social Problems*, Vol. 2, Fall 1963, pp. 193–200.

7. Rose Giallombardo, *Society of Women, op. cit.*

8. *Ibid.*, chapters 9 and 10 for an extended discussion of the functions of courtship, marriage, and the kinship network.

9. The importance of homosexual relations as an adaptive mode to the prison situation is consistent with that reported by Ward and Kassebaum in their study of a California prison for women. David A. Ward and Gene G. Kassebaum, *Women's Prison: Sex and Social Structure*. Chicago, Aldine, 1965.

10. The persistence of these role definitions is clearly evident in that the women's liberation movement is still unfinished business, although both the extremists and the moderates have been vocal and visible for a number of years. Interestingly enough, it is the females themselves (even on the college level, as anyone who has taught a "female course" knows only too well) who are reluctant to give up the view of themselves as docile and doll-like; they feel that they have a stake in being viewed in these terms, especially, security from an economic standpoint. See Giallombardo, *Society of Women, op. cit.*,

pp. 14–17 for a discussion of the areas in which American society differentiates male and female roles.

11.   Elliot Liebow describes the function of kinship as an extension of friendship among his street-corner black men; however, the phenomena of "going for brothers" among his street-corner men is clearly defined in terms of male kinship roles. "Going for cousins" functioned to neutralize the sexual content of a relationship between members of the opposite sex. Elliot Liebow, *Tally's Corner*. Boston, Little, Brown and Company, 1967, pp. 163–74, 207. One of the functions that kinship has among the Alderson inmates is to neutralize the sexual content of roles defined in kinship terms. See Giallombardo, *Society of Women, op. cit.*, pp. 159–73; several northern and eastern blacks with whom I discussed the "going for brothers" concept were completely unfamiliar with it, and it may be that this usage is peculiar to the geographical setting of Liebow's study, or it may be common among lower-class black males but not middle-class black males. However, perhaps it is common among male prisoners, but social researchers have not been sensitive to techniques of social interaction because of the measurement instruments they have used. Questionnaires, for example, are of no help whatsoever in trying to understand such phenomena.

12.   Ida Harper, "The Role of the 'Fringer' in a State Prison for Women," *Social Forces*, Vol. 31, October 1952, pp. 53–60.

13.   These researchers were engaged in field work and collecting data at the same time but in different geographical locations. See Giallombardo, *Society of Women*, and Ward and Kassebaum, *Sex and Social Structure*, cited earlier; also, Sister Mary Esther Heffernan, *Inmate Social Systems and Subsystems: The "Square," the "Cool," and "the Life."* Ph.D. dissertation, Catholic University of America, 1964.

14.   Sheldon and Eleanor T. Glueck, *Five Hundred Delinquent Women*. New York, Alfred A. Knopf, 1934. See also Frances A. Kellor, "Psychological and Environmental Study of Women Criminals," *American Journal of Sociology*, Vol. 5, 1900, pp. 527–43.

15.   The following are typical: Henrietta Addition, "Institutional Treatment of Women Offenders," *NPPA Journal*, Vol. 3, January 1957, pp. 21–30; Emily Barringer et al., "Minimum Standards for the Prevention and Treatment of Venereal Diseases in Correctional Institutions." New York, National Committee on Prisons and Prison Labor, 1929; Zebulon R. Brockway, "American Reformatory Prison System," *American Journal of Sociology*, Vol. 15, 1910, pp. 454–77; Edith M. Burleigh, "New Use of a Clinic in a Woman's Reformatory," *Survey*, Vol. 31, 1913, p. 155; J. K. Codding et al., "Recreation for Women Prisoners," *Proceedings of the American Prison Association*, 1912, pp. 312–28; Janie M. Coggeshall and Alice D. Menken, "A Women's Reformatory in the Making, Minimum Standards," *Journal of Criminal Law and Crimi-*

nology, Vol. 23, January–February 1933, pp. 819–28; Katherine Bement Davis, "The Laboratory and the Women's Reformatory," Proceedings of the American Prison Association, 1920, pp. 105–08; Mary Dewees, "The Training of the Delinquent Woman," Proceedings of the American Prison Association, 1922, pp. 82–90; Martha P. Falconer, "Reformatory Treatment," Proceedings of the National Conference of Charities and Corrections, 1919, pp. 253–56; Mary B. Harris, I Knew Them in Prison. New York, Viking, 1936; Jessie D. Hodder, "The Treatment of Delinquent Women," Proceedings of the American Prison Association, 1919, pp. 212–23; Eileen C. Potter, "Problems of Women in Penal and Correctional Institutions," Journal of Criminal Law and Criminology, Vol. 25, May–June 1934, pp. 65–75; Dean Shepard and Eugene Zemans, Prison Babies. Chicago, John Howard Association, 1950; Katherine Sullivan, Girls on Parole. Cambridge, Houghton Mifflin, 1956; Lorraine O. Williams, "Short-term Treatment of Women: An Experiment," Federal Probation, Vol. 21, September 1957, pp. 42–51; Anne E. Lorimer and M. Heads, "The Significance of Morale in a Female Penal Institution," Federal Probation, Vol. 26, December 1962, pp. 38–44.

16. Helen Bryan, Inside. Boston, Houghton Mifflin, 1953; Kate O'Hare, In Prison. New York, Alfred A. Knopf, 1923; Elizabeth G. Flynn, The Alderson Story. New York, International Publishers, 1963; Creighton Burnham, Born Innocent. Englewood Cliffs, N. J., Prentice-Hall, 1958; Virginia Kellog, "Inside Women's Prisons," Colliers, Vol. 125, No. 22, June 3, 1950, pp. 15, 37–41; Virginia McManus, Not for Love. New York, G. P. Putnam's Sons, 1960, pp. 216–65.

17. Eugenia C. Lekkerkerker, Reformatories for Women in the United States. Groningen, Netherlands: J. B. Wolters, 1931; Helen W. Rogers, "A Digest of Laws Establishing Reformatories for Women," Journal of Criminal Law and Criminology, Vol. 13, November 1922, pp. 382–437; Helen W. Rogers, "A History of the Movement to Establish a State Reformatory for Women in Connecticut," Journal of Criminal Law and Criminology, Vol. 19, February 1929, pp. 518–41; Mary Size, Prisons I Have Known. London, Allen and Unwin, 1957.

18. Cecil Bishop, Women and Crime. London, Chatto and Windus, 1931; Frances A. Kellor, "Criminal Sociology—Criminality Among Women," Arena, Vol. 23, 1900, pp. 516–24; Otto Pollak, The Criminality of Women. New York, A. S. Barnes, 1950; Stephen Schafer, "On the Proportions of the Criminality of Women," Journal of Criminal Law and Criminology, Vol. 39, May–June 1948, pp. 77–78.

19. Margaret Otis, "A Perversion Not Commonly Noted," Journal of Abnormal Psychology, Vol. 8, June–July 1913, pp. 113–16.

20. Charles A. Ford, "Homosexual Practices of Institutionalized Females," Journal of Abnormal and Social Psychology, Vol. 23, January–March 1929, pp. 442–49.

21. Lowell S. Selling, "The Pseudo Family," *The American Journal of Sociology*, Vol. 37, September 1931, pp. 247–53.

22. Romolo Toigo, "Illegitimate and Legitimate Cultures in a Training School for Girls," *Proceedings of the Rip Van Winkle Clinic*, Vol. 13, Summer 1962, pp. 3–29.

23. Sidney Kosofsky and Albert Ellis, "Illegal Communication Among Institutionalized Female Delinquents," *The Journal of Social Psychology*, Vol. 48, August 1958, pp. 155–60.

24. Seymour L. Halleck and Marvin Hersko, "Homosexual Behavior in a Correctional Institution for Adolescent Girls," *American Journal of Orthopsychiatry*, Vol. 32, October 1962, pp. 911–17.

25. Gisela Konopka, *The Adolescent Girl in Conflict*. Englewood Cliffs, N. J., Prentice-Hall, 1966, pp. 102–03.

26. Clifford R. Shaw and Earl D. Myers, "The Juvenile Delinquent," in *The Illinois Crime Survey*, John W. Wigmore, Editor. Chicago, Blakely Printing Company, 1929, Chapter 14, pp. 720–21.

27. Ju-K'ang T'ien, "Female Labor in a Cotton Mill," in *China Enters the Machine Age*, Kuo-Heng Shih, Editor. Cambridge, Harvard University Press, 1944, pp. 178–95. See Giallombardo, *Society of Women, op. cit.*, pp. 11-13 for a discussion of the conditions for survival faced by the Chinese women and the relationship to the prison situation.

28. A. J. W. Taylor, "The Significance of 'Darls' or 'Special Relationships' for Borstal Girls," *British Journal of Criminology*, Vol. 5, October 1965, pp. 406–18.

29. *Ibid.*, p. 408.

30. Heffernan, *op. cit.*, especially pp. 156–76.

31. Stanton Wheeler, "Socialization in Correctional Communities," *op. cit.*, pp. 696–712.

32. Donald Clemmer, *The Prison Community, op. cit.*

33. Wheeler, *op. cit.*, pp. 696–712.

34. Peter C. Garabedian, "Social Roles and Processes of Socialization in the Prison Community," *op. cit.*, pp. 139–52.

35. Daniel Glaser, *The Effectiveness of a Prison and Parole System, op. cit.*

36. Hans Reimer, "Socialization in the Prison Community," *op. cit.*, pp. 151–55.

37. Lloyd W. McCorkle and Richard R. Korn, "Resocialization Within Walls,"

The Annals of the American Academy of Political and Social Science, Vol. 293, May 1954, pp. 88–98.

38. Richard McCleery, "Communication Patterns as Bases of Systems of Authority and Power," in *Theoretical Studies in Social Organization of the Prison, op. cit.,* pp. 49–77.

39. Norman S. Hayner and Ellis Ash, "The Prison as a Community," *op. cit.,* pp. 577–83.

40. Richard A. Cloward, "Social Control in the Prison," *op. cit.,* pp. 20–48.

41. Gresham M. Sykes, *The Society of Captives, op. cit.* See also Gresham M. Sykes and Sheldon L. Messinger, "The Inmate Social System," *op. cit.,* pp. 5–19.

42. Erving Goffman, "On the Characteristics of Total Institutions: Staff-Inmate Relations," in Donald R. Cressey, *op. cit.,* pp. 68–106.

43. George P. Grosser, "The Role of Informal Inmate Groups in Change of Values," *Children,* Vol. 5, January–February 1958, pp. 25–29.

44. Gordon H. Barker and W. Thomas Adams, "Comparison of the Delinquencies of Boys and Girls," *Journal of Criminal Law, Criminology and Police Science,* Vol. 53, September 1962, pp. 470–75.

45. Howard W. Polsky, *Cottage Six.* New York, Russell Sage Foundation, 1962.

46. Seymour Rubenfeld and John W. Stafford, "An Adolescent Inmate Social System—A Psychological Account," *Psychiatry,* Vol. 26, No. 3, August 1963, pp. 241–56.

47. Sethard Fisher, "Informal Organization in a Correctional Setting," *Social Problems,* Vol. 13, Fall 1965, pp. 214–22. Other papers that deal with the inmate system are compiled by Sheldon L. Messinger in "Issues in the Study of the Social System of Prison Inmates," *Issues in Criminology,* Vol. 4, No. 2, Fall 1969, pp. 143–44; the reader should note that the conclusions drawn by the later writers fail to take into account the theoretical work in connection with the female prison, thus their conclusions are of questionable value.

48. David Street, Robert D. Vinter, and Charles Perrow, *Organization for Treatment.* New York, The Free Press, 1966; see pages 325–26 for a listing of publications and dissertations connected with this study.

49. In a few instances, it will be apparent from the wording of specific questionnaire items. Since the comparative study of six institutions for boys focused on the chief executive and organizational goals, I might note at this time that soon after the field work at Eastern began, it became readily apparent that

Eastern's superintendent not only was "treatment oriented" (as the term is understood in the institutional context), but had considerable administrative experience and expertise regarding organizational analysis. Yet, despite his dedicated efforts over a period of several years to implement treatment innovations, the institutional operation emphasized custodial solutions.

50.   There is no theoretical justification for describing the inmates in terms of their most serious offense rather than to describe them in terms of the actual offenses that led to incarceration. The reader is entitled to have this information as it may be important in terms of making comparisons across the institutions. In addition, by searching the inmate's history for his most deviant behavioral act, the researchers introduce a static view of the inmate and his behavior that may bear little relationship to the present situation.

51.   Rose Giallombardo, *Society of Women, op. cit.,* Chapters 8, 9, and 10.

52.   A detailed treatment of the method of the study is given in Appendix A.

CHAPTER 2

1.   Individuals who come under the jurisdiction of the youth commission may remain under its jurisdiction until they are 21 years of age.

2.   The administrators of all the schools studied believed that some inmates would profit from a short stay of perhaps one or two months, after which release to the community would be desirable. Since the "modern treatment" could not be applied in this brief period, the main purpose of institutionalization would be that of the lesson to be learned. *Punishment* as such is altogether too unsophisticated a concept to be applied during our modern times, especially for juvenile delinquents; more probably, the "crisis intervention" concept of the mental health field would be substituted in this context by institutional administrators.

3.   The staff at both institutions had often expressed the view that such facilities should be provided.

CHAPTER 3

1.   In addition, other types of behavior that are not directly related to the inmate's present offense are often discussed in presentence reports, presumably to be taken into account in the disposition process.

2.   Since many of the Western inmates are beyond the legal age requirement for school attendance, they are not referred for school truancy.

3.   Moreover, references to dates of commitment to various facilities were sometimes recorded, but no corresponding information about the date of re-

lease was recorded; the latter were excluded from the tabulations because both the entry and release dates were not recorded.

4.   A few cases result in dismissal, with or without admonition.

CHAPTER 5

1.   The staff had no knowledge of the community schools that the inmates had attended before incarceration.

2.   The registered nurses felt that this responsibility posed a conflict of interest because it violated their professional ethics.

3.   The Superintendent's Council at Eastern consists of one inmate from each cottage, who is elected by the cottage inmate population.

4.   The informal social system of the Eastern inmates is called the "racket."

5.   The training meetings began a few weeks before the study ended.

CHAPTER 6

1.   The academic guidance counselors at Central each had a number of cottages assigned to them, but their work was confined to the inmates' academic and vocational concerns.

2.   Western had a few portable lamps that operated by batteries, but both the staff and the inmates rated their performance as unsatisfactory.

CHAPTER 7

1.   The functional responsibility for custody and control was that of the head group supervisor, together with the assistant head group supervisors and the male security staff. Facilities in the control office consisted of monitoring equipment.

2.   The pervasive power of custody is also reflected in the fact that the head group supervisor's control extended to the clothing department; the Western inmates could wear their own clothing, but they had fewer choices as to type of clothing than did the Eastern and Central inmates.

3.   During the brief hospital stay, the inmate will be spoken to by a "classification officer," who explains the school attendance policy, and the work regulations.

4.   "Volunteering" for work tasks may result in a "commendation" for the inmate; the following commendation, dated November 18, 1970, for kitchen services from 9:00 to 12:00 a.m. provides a good example:

All of my regulars were not able to come to work. I need girls that knew what to do without being watched over every minute. I asked School Department to see if Mattie would volunteer to leave her classes and come down to make pie shells and do other things that she knew to do without being told. She volunteered and helped me tremendously. She is my weekend baking girl and lots of help.

Signed: Diana Fox
Cook

5.   In Western state's correctional system, only individuals who hold a master's degree in social work are social workers, although individuals with no training may function in the same role.

6.   The superintendent maintained that the report writing justified the upgrading of the staff from youth *supervisors* to youth *counselors*. The only members of the cottage staff who were not upgraded to youth counselors were those who worked the night shift and therefore were not assigned a caseload.

7.   The training officer had been employed at Western only a few months, but he had worked for many years in other institutions in Western state.

8.   The professional staff workers were not on the job during evenings and weekends, although at this time the inmates did not attend school and were relatively free from scheduled work assignments. Western, Eastern, and Central were similar in that all treatment activities were scheduled from the standpoint of institutional convenience.

9.   The "behavior modification system program," as it was called at Western, had been put into operation in the cottage that housed the inmates who were eighteen years or older.

10.   To some extent the inmates were differentiated on the basis of age; two cottages were designated for inmates sixteen years or older, and at the time of the study, the inmates in one cottage were eighteen years or older; two cottages were for inmates below age sixteen, but the age distribution included inmates who were older than fifteen. The cottage unit designated for the "more aggressive" girls (based on I-level classification), contains inmates of all ages. The other cottage is the disciplinary unit (recently renamed "treatment center"); the two wings of this unit resemble the physical structure commonly associated with adult prisons. One wing consists of stripped cells equipped with toilets, but the water flow is controlled externally by the staff. The outer doors to this unit are always locked, and the inmates of all ages are restricted to quarters.

11.   According to interpersonal maturity level (I-level) theory of behavior, offenders can be divided into nine separate subtypes which can be predetermined and used to establish differential treatment goals. For an introduction to this literature, see J. D. Grant and M. Q. Grant, "A Group Dynamics Approach to the Treatment of Nonconformists in the Navy," *The Annals of*

the American Academy, Vol. 322, March, 1959, pp. 126–35; C. F. Jesness, "Preston Typology Study: Final Report," Sacramento, California Youth Authority, 1968 (mimeographed); C. E. Sullivan, M. Q. Grant, and J. D. Grant, "The Development of Interpersonal Maturity: Applications to Delinquency," *Psychiatry,* Vol. 20, 1957, pp. 373–85; Marguerite Q. Warren, "The Case for Differential Treatment of Delinquents," *The Annals of the American Academy,* Vol. 381, January 1969, pp. 47–59.

12. Advocates of behavior modification techniques claim that the approach generally entails less encroachment into private matters and mental states than do psychoanalytically oriented techniques. Critics of behavioral methods, however, maintain that "therapists" are manipulative, undemocratic, and deal with irrelevant symptoms. For a discussion of these and other issues involved in the controversy, see Frederick H. Kanfer, "Issues and Ethics in Behavior Manipulation," *Psychological Reports,* Vol. 16, 1965, pp. 187–96; Louis Breger and James L. McGaugh, "Critique and Reformulation of 'Learning Theory' Approaches to Psychotherapy and Neurosis," *Psychological Bulletin,* Vol. 63, 1965, pp. 338–58.

13. Official files, *"Behavior Modification System Manual."* Approximately four weeks after their arrival, the Western inmates were required to complete a "behavior checklist" to determine their "behavior deficiencies"; moreover, staff members (a teacher, social worker, and a youth counselor) also were required to fill out similar lists for each inmate. A composite profile—in the form of a computer printout—of each inmate's behavior deficiencies was prepared from them; these profiles were sent from the central office approximately five weeks after the checklists were completed. Because the teachers and social workers had limited contact with the inmates (especially at this early stage of institutionalization) the task of completing all three of the checklists was often delegated to the senior youth counselor by the social worker. On the occasions when the youth counselor could not complete the forms, the inmate's own behavior checklist was used as a guide; or the youth counselor would consult the case file and use the information appearing therein. The inmates often filled out their forms aided by other inmates—a task which evoked much merriment.

14. According to the official manual: "While the accumulation of parole points works well for the long-range treatment goals, the short-term goals often need immediate reinforcement. For this purpose, dollars are placed in the ward's bankbook to be used in purchasing immediate reinforcers."

CHAPTER 8

1. The questionnaire item read: Staff members have different problems in institutions for girls and boys. What about problems of girls running away? If you didn't supervise closely, would the girls run away?

2. None of the staff members of these institutions thought that the cottage staff could do a good job with no disciplinary power whatsoever; only 4 percent of the Eastern staff, 3 percent of the Central staff, and 6 percent of the Western staff indicated that the cottage staff could do their job well with "very little disciplinary power."

3. Concerning the reward structure, the vast majority of the staff members considered themselves to be disadvantaged; only 24 percent of the Eastern staff, 27 percent of the Central staff, and 17 percent of the Western staff disagreed with the following questionnaire item: It would make our jobs easier if we had more ways of rewarding the girls for learning good behavior.

CHAPTER 9

1. Other code numbers are used by some of the inmates, but they are not known by all the inmates. These code numbers refer to sexual practices, but the inmates also use other slang expressions to refer to the same behavior.

2. This aspect of incarceration is as depriving for the youthful inmates as it is for the adult female offenders. See Rose Giallombardo, *Society of Women.* New York, John Wiley & Sons, 1966, pp. 133–35 for a discussion of the problems faced by the adult women.

CHAPTER 11

1. A few years ago, the term *vot* was used to refer to an individual who assumed the male role. Recidivists are familiar with this term, but it is no longer used by the Western inmates, although the staff still use the term when they refer to someone assuming a male role.

CHAPTER 12

1. Paul W. Tappan, *Juvenile Delinquency.* New York, McGraw-Hill Book Company, 1949, p. 431.

2. For a discussion of the "pains of imprisonment" experienced by the adult female and male prisoners, see Rose Giallombardo, *Society of Women.* New York, John Wiley & Sons, 1966, pp. 92–104; and Gresham Sykes, *The Society of Captives.* Princeton, Princeton University Press, 1958, pp. 63–83.

3. This fact is not fully appreciated, perhaps because adolescents may refuse to acknowledge the authority demands of particular adults; however, correctional workers generally assume that adjudicated delinquents refuse to acknowledge the authority of all adults.

4. Some indignities associated with the lack of autonomy are peculiar to specific institutions, for example, the fact that the Western inmates had to use

their wastebaskets for toilet purposes during the night. In addition, the Western inmates in the behavior modification program were not convinced of any direct benefit they would derive from the program, and complained bitterly of being used as guinea pigs.

5.   The concept of *punishment* as such is no longer given verbal expression by institutional personnel. Indeed, considering the current "commitment" to treatment goals, it is too unsophistictaed for present-day usage. This does not mean that institutional routines and programs have been appreciably changed or that punishment has been eliminated. Rather, this change reflects the current approved vocabulary among institutional workers that substitutes *firm controls* for punishment.

6.   The inmates who assume only female roles in courtship, marriage, or other kinship relationships, as well as the isolates who do not participate directly in these relationships, accept and honor the differentiation regarding sex role distinctions. The official case files recorded homosexual experience in the community for 1.5 percent of the Central inmates, 5 percent of the Western inmates, and 10.2 percent of the Eastern inmates. These data, however, reflect the record-keeping policies of the institutions, rather than the actual experience of the inmates. At Eastern, information of former homosexual experience was made part of the social record, as it was called for on the official forms, whereas this was not the case for Central and Western. All the institutions resembled one another, however, in that information concerning the extent of the inmates' participation in the informal social system was virtually nonexistent. Thus, if one were to look only at the official records, one would come away with the erroneous impression that this did not constitute a problem for the administrative bodies of these institutions.

7.   Information was not available for fifteen Central inmates who had recently been committed and were housed in the orientation unit.

8.   The wording was: "In juvenile institutions, girls develop cliques and informal groups that consist of make-believe families. Would you say that these groups create problems for you; that is, do they make your job more difficult?"

9.   The questionnaire item read: "What about the make-believe families as far as the girls are concerned? Would you say that they have a good or a bad influence on the girls?

10.   For a discussion of the incompatibility of the functions that society ascribes to correctional institutions, see Giallombardo, *op. cit.,* chapter 5 and chapter 6. These comments also have relevance for institutions serving juvenile delinquents.

11.   Some forms of behavior, such as truancy from school and home, for example, are related to the inmates' youth; sex-related offenses, in the main,

merely attest to the double standard in handling females in the courts; and, with a few exceptions, the other categories relate to the subordinate status of children in American society. Moreover, as is now well known, certain groups in American society receive differential treatment in the criminal justice system because of their position in the class structure. This consideration, coupled with the ineffectiveness of the institutional setting to rehabilitate, suggests to many serious observers that commitment is justified only for the offender who poses an obvious threat to the security needs of society.

12.   The fact that the two institutions for juvenile girls in Western state now base their admissions on geographical location rather than age has meant that more inmates receive visitors. The Western inmates whose families lived in the county in which the institution is located and the one adjacent to it, however, received the most visitors, of course.

A Methodological Note

This research was designed to find out something about which little or nothing is known. It was structured at the outset to be conducted over a long period of time in order to observe firsthand the operation of these institutions on a day-to-day basis. My aim throughout was to study each institution in depth as a social system and to collect the same kinds of data in each institution that would make comparison of them possible. In an effort to accomplish the objectives of the study, data were gathered from a wide variety of sources, using different techniques, to overcome partially the inherent problems of measurement that are present and remain unresolved in all forms of social research.

I have discussed the use of participant-as-observer techniques in exploratory studies to investigate areas for which questionnaires are inadequate elsewhere.* While the same reasons apply here, in this study the data thus obtained, as well as from the interviews, provide a check on the reliability and validity of questionnaire data. The interviewing procedures that were utilized during my study of the Alderson prison for adult women guided the present study. The Eastern, Central, and Western inmates were all interviewed with the primary aim of assessing the argot roles, the structure of the family and kinship relationships, and the

* See *Society of Women.* New York, John Wiley & Sons, 1966, pp. 189–99.

meaning of these structures for the inmates. The inmates were interviewed in their own rooms to insure privacy and to keep the interview informal in the surroundings most familiar to each inmate. This also served to emphasize the fact that I was not part of the staff (none of the staff members ever talked to an inmate in her room with the door closed).

The theoretical concerns of the study indicated a research design that included institutions that vary to some degree with respect to goal orientation; hence, the organizations studied were not randomly selected, but I have no reason to believe that the institutions that make up the sample studied differ markedly from others of their genre throughout the nation (although the institutions studied are often cited as providing models for the other states to follow).

The adequacy of the data obtained from interviews with the inmates concerning their participation in the informal social system were checked out by items incorporated into the staff questionnaire to measure the existence, pervasiveness, and effect of this social phenomenon throughout the organizations studied. Other data were obtained by attending all inmate functions (group therapy meetings, classification meetings, orientation unit, academic and vocational classes, work details, movies, and other recreational events) and other formally scheduled functions to see what situations the inmates meet and how they behave in them for the purpose of assessing the meaning of these events for the formal and informal organization. In addition, data were obtained by personal observation in cottage units and on the grounds; casual and unstructured conversations were the sources of data collection to discover the interpretation of the events observed and the value structure of the group.

I examined institutional records to obtain information of the communication patterns of the inmates with the outside world, such as institutional visits and home visits; I also examined the official case files to obtain the social background characteristics of the inmates and their parents. These data were in turn cross-classified with questionnaire data and data about the inmates' participation in the informal organization to determine to what extent the kind of pre-institutional behavior or intellectual equipment of the youthful inmate is transferable to the institutional situation and whether it favors one form of adjustment over another.

Other sources of data concerning official goal statements, operating procedures, problems of implementing goals, and the like were obtained from official documents; minutes of staff meetings; attendance at staff meetings; and interviews with top administrators, institutional officials, and other staff members. The superintendents were kind enough to allow me to examine old records—minutes of official meetings and official correspondence—which enabled me to gain an historical perspective of the institutions' programs that would not have been possible otherwise; in addition, such records provide a check of sorts on the data obtained through interviewing staff members, particularly in connection with an institution's past programs and organization.

The entire study was completed over a five-year period beginning in early April, 1968, through April, 1973. The data were collected over a total period of twenty-seven months spent at Eastern, Central, and Western. (The data were coded and tabulated by the research assistants associated with the project during the short period of time that elapsed prior to entering another institution for study.) I spent approximately ten months at Eastern, nine months at Central, and seven months at Western. The institutions were studied in the order listed, but a period of approximately three months elapsed between the data collection phase of the first and second institutions and between the second and third institutions. This period allowed sufficient time for the coding of all questionnaire data as well as the time required to complete the final arrangements for the data collection in the next institution. (The selection of the institutions had tentatively been made prior to this time, and in one case arrangements had been finalized but later had to be changed when there was a personnel change in the agency that operated the state's correctional institutions.)

At Eastern, Central, and Western, the study was introduced to the staff by the superintendent who sent a memorandum (which I drafted) to each staff member stating the approximate time the study would be in progress, the confidentiality of all information received, and the fact that the study was part of a larger research project; cooperation was urged. (None of the staff members knew which institutions had been included in the study, although a few staff members in each of the schools did ask.)

The inmates of each institution completed the questionnaire during the final weeks of the study; this phase of the study was planned and scheduled at this time to maximize the possibility that the inmates would respond truthfully. The details in connection with the scheduling of inmates to complete the questionnaire were handled by each institution's academic school director. However, preliminary discussion with the superintendent was very important; the substance of this talk was to stress the importance of scheduling as many inmates as possible on a given day in order to decrease the possibility of discussion among the inmates. Cottage location was also taken into consideration. One and one-half hours were allowed between individual sessions for any unforeseen developments and to ready materials for each new group; hence we could begin almost immediately after the inmates entered.

In all the institutions the inmates filled out the questionnaire in a school classroom. They all arrived in a cottage group, and they returned to their cottage together. No staff members were present at any time. I administered the questionnaire myself, and the same preliminary remarks were made to all the inmates. I explained the purpose of the study and emphasized that their cooperation would be appreciated but that their participation was altogether voluntary. No one refused to participate. By this time the inmates knew me well, and they viewed the completion of the questionnaire as an extension of the kinds of interaction we had been having for many months in my endeavor to understand what institutional living was like for them. Although the number of inmates present at any time varied from eighteen to forty, there were no discipline problems—a fact I believe surprised many staff members. I think my experience stems from several important factors: First, I knew the inmates from previous lengthy interviews (most of them were at least one hour in length) and from my attendance at institutional functions and informal observation in the cottage units. Second, the details in connection with the actual administration of the questionnaire had all been carefully worked out prior to the inmates' arrival including unforeseen contingencies; careful attention to and organization of such details made it possible to proceed quite efficiently. Third, the cooperation of the officials in connection with the organizational details was such that their own institutional schedules were changed in order that my research would proceed unhampered.

At Eastern all the inmates completed the questionnaire in three days; there were two cottage groups at each session. At Central the inmates completed the questionnaire over a period of three days; there was one cottage group scheduled at each session. At Western the inmates completed the questionnaiare in one and one-half days; one cottage group was present at each session.

Just before the study ended, I administered a questionnaire to the staff members. I assumed that they would be more likely to respond in a truthful fashion at the end of the study than at any other time: I had gotten to know most of them quite well; they were accustomed to seeing me almost daily in the cottages, at different functions, and at staff meetings. Thus, they knew that I had an intimate knowledge of the inner workings of their institution's operation and problems.

Each staff member received a memorandum from the superintendent requesting cooperation in filling out an anonymous questionnaire for my study; the notice stated that individual answers would be kept strictly confidential and would not be available to the institution or department employees. The date, the time, and the place where the staff person was to go were stated.

The director of cottage service at Eastern and Central and the head group supervisor at Western completed all the scheduling for the cottage staff; other department heads scheduled their staff members at the time periods that had been established for the cottage staff. The teachers and social workers, however, all completed the questionnaire in separate groups.

The staff members also filled out their questionnaire under conditions that would maximize confidentiality. A classroom in the academic school was reserved for this purpose; the staff members who were scheduled to appear at specified times left as soon as they completed filling out the questionnaire.* The time varied from thirty-five minutes for a few staff members to more than an hour for some. All were completed during the regular working hours; the staff members were never interrupted for any reason at this time, and none felt pressured to return to their jobs.

An attempt was made to schedule the entire staff in as few sessions as possible, taking into account the tours of duty and the institutional needs. At Central all the staff completed the questionnaire within four days. At Eastern the staff completed the questionnaire within a period of six days. At Western the staff completed the questionnaire within five days. Some groups were scheduled at 7 a.m. and others as late as 4 p.m. At Western eight staff members who worked the night shift completed their questionnaire during the period 11:30 p.m. to 6:15 a.m.; they left their post of duty and completed it in a vacant office in the administration building. No one filled it out on the job. (For the latter group, I remained close by to answer any questions about the wording or interpretation of any item and to insure that they were not interrupted.)

The questionnaires were anonymous; neither the staff nor the inmates signed their names; a checking procedure was used to note which staff

---

* For the benefit of other sociologists who will be conducting similar research, I would like to emphasize that this procedure has a decided advantage over simply leaving questionnaires with the staff members to be filled out on the job at their leisure. Anyone who has spent any time at all in correctional institutions soon discovers that the staff, in general, and the cottage staff, in particular, discuss and compare notes on all institution-related matters.

members had completed it, however. The inmates' questionnaires were numbered to match them with the file data so that various kinds of statistical analyses could be made.

None of the administrative heads saw the instruments I used. Their willingness to adapt their routine to the requirements of the research project and the amount of time spent by the administrative staff to schedule each staff member at designated times is indicative of the kind of cooperation that I received. This enabled each of the staff members and the inmates to fill out the questionnaires under similar conditions and for me to proceed in all phases of data collection in each institution in much the same way.

Supplementary Tables

Table 1   Topics Discussed by Inmates
with Social Workers and Cottage Staff

	Social Worker						Cottage Staff					
	Eastern		Central		Western		Eastern		Central		Western	
Topic	Number	%	Number	%	Number	%	Number	%	Number	%	Number	%
Trial visit	16	7.8	41	12.0	—	—	12	5.8	20	5.9	3	1.9
Parole date	42	20.5	89	26.1	32	20.1	28	13.7	34	10.0	32	20.1
Work assignment change	6	2.9	1	0.3	—	—	9	4.4	41	12.0	2	1.3
Punishment received or loss of privileges	1	0.5	2	0.6	5	3.1	11	5.4	38	11.1	4	2.5
Institutional rule violation	5	2.4	5	1.5	6	3.8	21	10.2	21	6.2	13	8.2
Plans after release	36	17.6	84	24.6	32	20.1	27	13.2	60	17.6	32	20.1
Relationships with family	14	6.8	27	7.9	15	9.4	27	13.2	28	8.2	13	8.2
Past deviant behavior	24	11.7	19	5.6	32	20.1	17	8.3	20	5.9	24	15.1
Personal problems that concern inmate	59	28.8	68	19.9	33	20.8	51	24.9	78	22.9	31	19.5
Not contacted by social worker or does not discuss personal problems	2	1.0	5	1.5	4	2.5	2	1.0	1	0.3	5	3.1
Total	205	100.0	341	100.0	159	99.9	205	100.1	341	100.1	159	100.0

Table 2 *Secondary Reason for Referral to Court*
Classified According to Type of Offense

Type of Offense	Eastern		Central		Western	
	Number	%	Number	%	Number	%
No second offense listed	67	32.7	29	8.5	48	30.2
Assault or threat to assault	5	2.4	5	1.5	3	1.9
Robbery	—	—	3	0.9	2	1.3
Burglary (break and entry)	—	—	3	0.9	2	1.3
Car theft	—	—	1	0.3	—	—
Theft (other) or possession of stolen goods	5	2.4	16	4.7	4	2.5
Vandalism	—	—	2	0.6	—	—
Check forgery	—	—	2	0.6	—	—
Drugs or other noxious agents	3	1.5	1	0.3	11	6.9
Habitual truancy	35	17.1	73	21.4	5	3.1
Running away from home	30	14.6	73	21.4	17	10.7
Incorrigible in school	9	4.4	6	1.8	2	1.3
Incorrigible at home	17	8.3	59	17.3	12	7.6
Violation of probation/parole	5	2.4	9	2.6	32	20.1
Drinking and intoxication	6	2.9	7	2.0	1	0.6
Prostitution	—	—	4	1.2	2	1.3
Promiscuity and pregnancy	5	2.4	33	9.7	3	1.9
Association with undesirable companions	14	6.8	8	2.4	2	1.3
Incorrigible in and/or running away from child-care institution	3	1.5	3	0.9	4	2.5
Suicide attempt(s)	—	—	1	0.3	1	0.6
Miscellaneous delinquencies	1	0.5	3	0.9	8	5.0
Total	205	99.9	341	100.2	159	100.1

Table 3 Third Reason for Referral to Court
Classified According to Type of Offense

Type of Offense	Eastern		Central		Western	
	Number	%	Number	%	Number	%
No third offense listed	137	66.8	112	32.8	93	58.5
Assault or threat to assault	—	—	5	1.5	1	0.6
Burglary (break and entry)	—	—	—	—	1	0.6
Car theft	—	—	2	0.6	2	1.3
Theft (other) or possession of stolen goods	4	2.0	10	2.9	3	1.9
Arson	—	—	2	0.6	—	—
Vandalism	—	—	1	0.3	1	0.6
Check forgery	—	—	1	0.3	—	—
Driving without a license	—	—	1	0.3	1	0.6
Drugs	—	—	6	1.8	5	3.1
Habitual truancy	12	5.8	44	12.9	5	3.1
Running away from home	13	6.3	22	6.4	11	6.9
Incorrigible in school	6	2.9	10	2.9	2	1.3
Incorrigible at home	11	5.4	47	13.8	6	3.8
Violation of probation/parole	5	2.4	17	5.0	18	11.3
Drinking and intoxication	—	—	6	1.8	1	0.6
Prostitution	1	0.5	9	2.6	1	0.6
Promiscuity and pregnancy	4	2.0	36	10.6	—	—
Homosexuality	—	—	—	—	1	0.6
Association with undesirable companions	10	4.9	6	1.8	—	—
Incorrigible in and/or running away from child-care institution	1	0.5	—	—	2	1.3
Suicide attempt(s)	—	—	1	0.3	1	0.6
Miscellaneous delinquencies	1	0.5	3	0.9	4	2.5
Total	205	100.0	341	100.1	159	99.8

Table 4 Ideal Job Preferences of Inmates[a]

Ideal Job	Eastern		Central		Western	
	Number	%	Number	%	Number	%
Nurse, nurse's aide, other hospital work	43	21.0	49	14.4	19	12.0
Stewardess	5	2.4	10	2.9	2	1.3
Beautician, hairdresser, cosmetologist	17	8.3	13	3.8	5	3.1
Cook or dietitian	2	1.0	2	0.6	—	—
Teacher (all types)	12	5.8	13	3.8	6	3.8
Social or welfare worker	8	3.9	22	6.4	4	2.5
Doctor (includes psychiatrist)	13	6.3	9	2.7	11	6.9
Student counselor or librarian	1	0.5	1	0.3	—	—
Secretary, stenographer, typist, bookkeeper	21	10.2	15	4.4	6	3.8
IBM or other business-machines operator	3	1.5	2	0.6	1	0.6
Salesclerk	—	—	2	0.6	2	1.3
Psychologist	—	—	5	1.5	—	—
Scientist	3	1.5	—	—	2	1.3
Laboratory technicain	—	—	1	0.3	1	0.6
Postal clerk	—	—	2	0.6	—	—
State senator	—	—	1	0.3	—	—
Telephone operator	1	0.5	—	—	—	—
Policewoman or private detective	1	0.5	1	0.3	—	—
Parole or probation officer, lawyer	1	0.5	8	2.4	5	3.1
Cottage parent in training school	1	0.5	4	1.2	6	3.8
Armed forces, job corps, peace corps	2	1.0	2	0.6	—	—
Singer, dancer, actress, musician	18	8.8	33	9.7	14	8.8
Songwriter, writer, newspaper reporter	1	0.5	3	0.9	3	1.9
Model	6	2.9	14	4.1	6	3.8
Fashion designer	1	0.5	—	—	—	—
Interior decorator	1	0.5	1	0.3	—	—
Artist	1	0.5	4	1.2	—	—
Law-abiding or otherwise "respectable" or dependable person	3	1.5	5	1.5	2	1.3
Peacemaker or religious vocation	2	1.0	1	0.3	1	0.6
Wife, mother, homemaker	11	5.4	37	10.8	11	6.9

290

Table 4 (Continued)

Ideal Job	Eastern Number	%	Central Number	%	Western Number	%
Millionaire or wealthy woman	4	2.0	11	3.2	4	2.5
Hippy	1	0.5	1	0.3	6	3.8
Black Panther or member of similar groups	1	0.5	1	0.3	—	—
Miscellaneous homosexual roles	5	2.4	6	1.8	4	2.5
Custodian	—	—	1	0.3	—	—
No work	—	—	10	2.9	3	1.9
Irrelevant responses (e.g., staff member for one day)	3	1.5	21	6.2	15	9.4
Uncertain, illegible, no response	13	6.4	30	8.8	20	12.6
Total	205	100.3	341	100.3	159	100.1

[a] Girls sometimes think about what they would like to be, even though they do not always believe it could possibly come true. If it were possible for you to be anything you wanted, what would you like to be?

Table 5 Satisfaction with Present Salary and Chances
for Promotion as Reported by the Staff

Satisfaction Reported	Salary Eastern Number	%	Central Number	%	Western Number	%	Promotion Eastern Number	%	Central Number	%	Western Number	%
Completely satisfied	7	4.8	7	4.4	11	11.7	14	9.5	11	7.0	6	6.4
Very well satisfied	13	8.8	38	24.0	43	45.7	21	14.3	36	22.8	8	8.5
Fairly satisfied	57	38.8	70	44.3	29	30.8	42	28.6	41	26.0	19	20.2
A little satisfied	8	5.4	9	5.7	3	3.2	14	9.5	20	12.7	6	6.4
Somewhat dis-satisfied	35	23.8	21	13.3	3	3.2	28	19.0	21	13.3	20	21.3
Very dissatisfied	15	10.2	9	5.7	3	3.2	15	10.2	20	12.7	13	13.8
Completely dis-satisfied	12	8.2	4	2.5	2	2.1	12	8.2	9	5.7	22	23.4
No response	—	—	—	—	—	—	1	0.7	—	—	—	—
Total	147	100.0	158	99.9	94	99.9	147	100.0	158	100.2	94	100.0

Table 6 Current Age Distribution of the Inmate Population

Age (years)	Eastern		Central		Western	
	Number	%	Number	%	Number	%
12	—	—	1	0.3	—	—
13	16	7.8	12	3.5	1	0.6
14	47	22.9	39	11.4	12	7.6
15	83	40.5	93	27.3	27	17.0
16	54	26.3	113	33.1	49	30.8
17	5	2.4	64	18.8	37	23.3
18 and over	—	—	19	5.6	33	20.8
Total	205	99.9	341	100.0	159	100.1

A Solution to the Escape Problem

The memorandum below indicates the monetary cost associated with attempts to control the problem of escapes at Central. It is presented because the problem is generic to all institutions of this type.

Date: April 24, 1969

To: Mr. Bertrand Bettell, Director
Central State Commission

Thru: Mr. Thomas Manville, Deputy Director
Correctional Services

From: Mr. S. M. Brown, Superintendent
Central School

Subject: Central School Survey—Escapes

Enclosed is a copy of the survey made from the official daily report records of Central School. This survey includes the time period April 1, 1968, through March 31, 1969.

I.   DEFINING PROBLEM

During this period of time, Central School had 160 escapes. Of this number 45 escaped from furlough or other off-campus situations making a total of 115 actual escapes from residency of Central School. Nineteen of the girls involved in runaways ran two or more times. Of the 115 actual institutional escapes all but 27 were apprehended within a 24 hour period. The average length of time to apprehend a student was approximately one and one-half hours. Of the 88 students apprehended, our staff apprehended 76 and the other 12 were apprehended by Highway Patrol Sheriff's Department or other police officials. Seventy-three escapes (27 who were not apprehended, 38 from furlough and 8 from other) returned to the community unauthorized and represented a potential problem. This makes an average of 9.5 escapes per month from the institutional grounds during the survey period time.

There was a total of 514 man-hours involved looking for runaways at a cost of approximately $1,700.00.

A further analysis of the survey indicated that the largest number of students escaped from the cottage area. It was also indicated that most girls ran during the 7 o'clock to 11 o'clock p.m. time block.

It was equally interesting to note that none ran from either on- or off-campus organized recreational programs.

Pursuing the survey in more detail, the fact comes to light that the largest number of runs were from our Orientation Cottage and the least number of runs were from the cottage in which we had our greatest in-depth in-service training program.

While there was no pattern to the escapes at Central School, the month of October showed the largest number of escapes. This was at a time when transfers to Maximum Security School were not possible. Eleven of these runs were by girls being held for eventual Maximum Security School placement. This was also a period of time when foster care funds were low and child movement was slow.

Based on the preceding statistics one would conclude that Central School does have a runaway problem, but one that is not of major proportion. In other words, Central School's escape problem is not one of aggressive community behavior on the part of the escapees, but one that has the potential for activating processes that can negatively effect the girl's well-being. This definition hopefully focuses on what must be the institution's major concern, that is, the girl. The following are examples of the processes referred to above:

a. Escapees create problems for themselves in that they often are risking physical injury in the process of escape. They activate institutional processes of search, capture, confinement, discipline, redirection of program, and so forth. They also add to their own negative experiences as a runaway which may also have many potential socioemotional ramifications.

b. Escapes are a problem for the institution as they result in disrupting normal routine of the institution (there is no specific security staff at this facility such as found at Brightview School for Boys) and add cost of manpower for searching, replacement of materials and supplies (window screens, linen, clothing, and so forth) and vehicle wear and tear.

c. Escapes are a potential problem for the institution in that an incident involving our girls can result in inaccurate or incomplete reporting of the incident by the news media. Even factual reporting of an isolated incident involving our girls can lead the public into thinking negatively about the overall population and program.

Our analysis of the escape problem indicated that population pressures and lack of student placement were two major contributing factors in terms of escapes.

In the survey it was also borne out that the girls ran for a variety of reasons. Many of these were youngsters that had chronic runaway records and should not have been in an open institutional setting.

II. RECOMMENDATIONS

A. *Manpower.* Since the survey indicated that the largest number of escapes were between 7 o'clock and 11 o'clock p.m. and from the cottage area, we are recommending that two (2) additional night security people be added to our staff to insure two security officers on our grounds every day during this time period. We are also recommending that the security classification now being held in abeyance for our night watch personnel be approved in order that this classification be upgraded in both requirements and compensation to enable us to better recruit the calibre of individual who can give us the necessary security protection. The cost for the total package would be approximately $14,000.00; of this amount $9,600.00 would be for two (2) additional security personnel and the remainder for upgrading the security classification.

The survey indicated that during this time period 80 youngsters ran from the cottages. It is therefore recommended that those cottages required to be overpopulated and house more than 36 youngsters have an additional person assigned to them for a 3:00 to 11:00 p.m. shift. In addition to covering the cottage area during the time period we had 80 escapes, it would also provide additional personnel to supervise movement on campus in which we had 27 escapes. Currently, 7 cottages at Central School fall into this category, therefore, 7 additional Youth Leaders IV are being recommended at an approximate cost of $35,000.00 per year.

We would further recommend that we not go to the post control where we cannot schedule additional people in, and, therefore, have to depend on the availability of on-call personnel. We have no table of experience in recruiting substitute people; however, it is doubtful these people would be available and, if they are, their effectiveness would be minimal.

We must start with the assumption that each child at some time or another in in her incarceration considers the idea of escape. For this reason, we can be sure that the phenomena of runaway is as much a part of the on-going program as if it were a planned feature. We might label it a negative feature and as such, it is subject to our influence by programming. We might hypothesize that the better the program (better—more viable in terms of meeting needs) the lower the runaway rate. In other words, "beefing up" the program in terms of meeting the needs of children will cut down the number of runaways.

We, therefore, are recommending two (2) additional social workers be employed with a goal of providing greater skills in child care and meeting the needs of the children. This will give us one social worker for each cottage. Our analysis indicated there were more runs from cottages under social workers who were, by necessity, forced to cover more than one cottage (larger case loads). These additional two people would cost approximately $16,640.00 per year.

We also recommend two (2) additional recreation positions be added to the table of organization. These positions could be separated into half time positions thereby giving us greater variety in offering leisure time activities for our students during the most prone escape time period. It would facilitate a greater involvement of those cottages with the largest populations. The cost of the two positions would be approximately $9,900.00.

The total cost of Manpower changes would be approximately $75,540.00.

B. *Physical Plant.* An analysis of our escape reports as related to Central School's survey indicated that approximately 42 of the escapees went through fire escape doors and 25 went through windows that had ordinary fly screen covering them.

It is recommended that an alarm system be installed on all outside doors to alert personnel to the fact that the door is being opened. Each unit would cost approximately $80.00. While a unit on each door would be a nice feature, it would be quite expensive. In an attempt to conserve money, we are recommending 10 units for an approximate cost of $800.00 to be utilized in the most escape prone areas.

Another item which is rather costly, but is both a safety feature as well as a security feature, is detention screens on the windows. We would recommend, again keeping austerity in mind, 10 screens for each cottage, which would cost approximately $100.00 per screen. These rooms would be utilized for those students having a history of runs. We would estimate the cost of this project at approximately $9,000.00. Five of our cottages currently have this type of screen. The survey indicated these were low escape cottages.

The third highest area of escape as indicated by analysis of the survey, was movement—primarily between school and other areas. One of the reasons is the location of the present intercom system in the Principal's Office rather than in the Attendance Office. If this intercom could be moved, then a much quicker check could be made on the movement of students. The approximate cost of moving this unit would be $1,000.00.

Another area that is recommended for immediate attention is additional and improved lighting. We recommend that our present system be changed to mercury lighting and additional mercury lights be placed in the darkest areas on our campus. The cost of such a project would be approximately $10,000.00.

The last recommendation for the physical plant would be the acquisition of a radio system for our vehicles. We spent approximately 514 man-hours searching for escapees during the time period of the survey, at a cost of approximately $1,700.00. With premium overtime the cost would increase. It is our estimate that we could save approximately $100.00 of overtime if we had had such a communications system. In addition to this, the communications system would give greater mobility and flexibility in movement of personnel and no doubt expedite the apprehension of the escapees. This amount of overtime does not include anything for those people such as Principal, Deputy Superintendent, Superintendent and others who receive no compensation looking for runaways. It is also our recommendation that night security personnel be equipped with walkie-talkie radios for instant on-campus communication. The total cost of such a package would be approximately $7,000.00.

The total cost of Physical Plant changes would be approximately $27,800.00.

C. In-Service Training. In analyzing our data we find that in the cottage in which a well-defined program of in-service training was operating there were fewer escape attempts, proving to us that such a program is a deterrent to escape attempts, hypothesizing that because of in-service training the cottage staff becomes more alert to the needs of children. We are, therefore, recommending a full time in-service training officer for this institution. We also recommend our staff be included in programs offered regarding security. This position should be no lower than an Executive III at an approximate cost of $8,736.00.

The total cost of in-service training would be approximately $8,736.00.

GRAND TOTAL: $112,076.00.

S. M. Brown
Superintendent

P.S.   In addition to the escapes at Central School shown by the survey, there were 46 escape attempts.

Selected Listings of Cottage Rules

The listings of cottage rules that follow are typical of those that were in force at the time of the study. While they do not exhaust the rules that were actually operative, they indicate the way in which behavior was ordered.

I.   WESTERN: BASIC COTTAGE RULES FOR ALL COTTAGES

Welcome to Dorm_____

We are glad you came to our dorm. Staff is here to help you. We hope you will be happy and learn to get along with our group and also add something to make it better for all. Here is a list of our rules. We hope you will learn the rules and follow them.

1.   *Courtesy.*   Girls are expected to be courteous to *staff* and to each other.

   a.   No vulgar language or swearing.
   b.   No name calling or loud arguing or pressuring others for ANY reason.
   c.   No horseplay (pushing, kicking, scratching).
   d.   No fighting, ever.

299

e. No race talk—all are equal here.

f. No carrying tales. Things discussed in Community Counseling or on dorm are not to be taken on campus.

g. Quiet time means exactly that.

h. Group will be quiet in the dining room and dayroom.

i. Talking only during commercials while watching TV.

2. *Responsibility for Yourself and Belongings.* Girls are expected to take responsibility for themselves and their belongings.

a. Get things you need at the proper time.

b. Take care of your clothing, books, and personal articles.

c. Girls are expected to keep their rooms neat and clean at all times.

d. Never leave clothing on rail; leave laundry room neat after using; never leave underwear and socks in the laundry room or on the rail.

e. Take care of your own key; do not leave it in your lock or in your room. Leave key at desk ONLY when leaving the dorm to go off campus.

f. Borrowing or lending clothes is prohibited. The ONLY exception is for dances.

3. *Appearance and Clothing.* Girls are expected to have a proper appearance and to take care of their clothing.

a. No clothes too short or too tight.

b. Clothes are to be clean, ironed, mended, and have all the buttons on.

c. No extreme makeup—your own eyebrows, please.

d. Shoes, thongs, or slippers must be worn at all times. No bare feet on the dorm.

e. Robes are to be worn in the dayroom, etc. Muumuus, or your own robe, are acceptable to be worn after showering. Underclothing must be worn (panties and bra). Slips are not to be worn over pajamas.

f. We urge girls to dress properly for dinner.

g. Cutting the sleeves and/or hems of muumuus will earn a girl an "incident" *and* possible roomtime.

4. *Details.* Girls are responsible for work in taking care of the dorm.

a. No girl may refuse a job assignment.

b. Cottage details are changed each month, so all have opportunity to learn how to do a good detail.

    c. YOU are responsible for your uniform, apron, and other things necessary for your detail.

    d. You are responsible for being on time and ready to go to detail for which you are assigned.

5. *Homosexual Activity.* Terms and clothing are unacceptable. Chick business is unacceptable; please observe these rules.

    a. Absolutely no hugging, hand-holding, or any kind of physical contact.

    b. No chick terms or buzzes.

    c. No improper dress or hairdo.

6. *Desk*

    a. The desk is out of bounds.

    b. Girls are not allowed behind the desk at any time.

    c. Do not crowd around desk. If a staff member is busy with someone, wait your turn *gracefully*.

7. *Movements and Boundaries.* Girls are expected to be responsible for going to the places they are told to and to observe boundaries.

    a. Girls will move quickly and quietly when asked.

    b. Girls will automatically go quickly, quietly, and directly to their rooms in the event of a dorm disturbance when a Security Officer is called and also when told to do by staff.

    c. You are expected to follow the proper procedure when leaving and returning to the dorm for any campus activity. Stay in twos and stay in line or stay in a close group, whichever is requested by the staff member with the group; no loud yelling, horseplay, etc.

    d. You will be out of bounds if you go farther than your own door or into the opposite hall.

    e. Girls may not stop to chat at another girl's door. Do not talk to girls serving restrictions.

    f. When smokers are smoking, nonsmokers are to *stay completely away* from the area where they are.

    g. Never enter kitchen without permission from staff.

    h. Only one girl in the shower. No underwear is to be worn in the shower or washed there. Shower quickly and exit.

    i. Only one girl at a time allowed in the laundry room.

    j. Girls will not loiter in the halls, bathroom, or near ironing boards and laundry room door.

    k. Girls are expected to be in their rooms during school time unless they have staff's permission to be out.

8. *Community Counseling.* Girls are expected to take responsibility for their behavior at Community Counseling.

   a. When coming to the dorm after school for Community Counseling meeting, go directly to your room and remain in until called to the dayroom.
   b. No eating, chewing gum, sewing, reading, writing during the meeting. No combing hair. Combs will be taken.
   c. Move quickly and quietly to your room when dismissed from Community Counseling. Do not stop at desk, enter bathroom, loiter on the way, or talk to any adult.

9. *Miscellaneous Dorm Group Rules*

   a. Girls are expected to help each other and represent our group well on campus at any activity.
   b. Group will participate in planned group activities.

10. *Rules for Your Room*

    a. Nothing on door window.
    b. Drapes on wall window open and window open by 8 a.m. school call. Nothing to be hanging on drapes or wire.
    c. Closet neat, and all clothes must be hung up neatly.
    d. Shoes on top of closet.
    e. Soiled clothes in bag—not to be kept in closet.
    f. Washcloth and towel put on holder on wall—no place else.
    g. Floor clean. Dump trash before breakfast. Only rug on floor.
    h. *Nothing* attached to light fixtures or ceiling.
    i. Dresser drawers neat and clothes folded.
    j. Bed properly made. Bed pad must be on.
    k. No contraband. If in doubt, ask supervisor.
    l. Nothing stuck on closet door except calendar. Copy of Room and Dorm Rules should be on wall.
    m. Blankets, when not in use, are to be under your bedspread as well as your pillow.
    n. No pictures on mirror except family photos.
    o. Pictures on walls must be in good taste. No nudes, cigarette, liquor, or dope pictures, posters, or ads are permitted.
    p. Personal supplies will be passed to you only by the morning counselor at specified intervals. Do not ask other staff for supplies except for laundry soap and sanitary napkins.

II. CONVENIENCE BEHAVIORS: COTTAGE BANCROFT—WESTERN*

Time Management: $25.00 Fine

On time getting up
Prompt to AM washup
Prompt to and from meals
Prompt to and from classes
Prompt to room on time
Prompt to room at bedtime
Keep Bankbook in box

Ward/Ward Relationship: $100.00 Fine

No buzzes
No homosexual involvement
No chick business buzzes
Do not argue to disruptive point
Do not threaten or pressure others
No wards' addresses in room
Talking to another dorm

Ward/Staff Relationship: $100.00 Fine

No vulgar language
Do not make smart remarks or rude gestures
Follow directions quickly and properly
Be truthful
Do not interrupt staff on phone or in conversation
No yelling across dayroom at staff

Task Management

1. *Personal Grooming: $50.00 Fine*

   Do not go barefoot
   No walking on backs of shoes
   No hem in raincoats
   Do not wear Gym Clothes unless you are going to Gym
   DRESS APPROPRIATELY! ! ! ! ! ! !
   Gym clothes must be ironed for Gym class
   Hair must be combed by breakfast
   Makeup must be worn properly

* Rules that were converted to convenience behaviors and fines.

2. *Room Behavior: $25.00 Fine*

Curtains are to be open when not in room and at bedtime
Window curtains must be open by 8:00 a.m.
Do not open door without permission
Clothing is not to be left on chair
Nothing is to be on curtains or lights
Bed pads must be on bed only
Buckets are not to be in rooms
Room must be clean when viewed through window
Tape is the only thing to be used on walls
No extra linen in your room
Room must be clean when room check takes place
No loud radio after bedtime
No talking after bedtime
Wastebasket must be emptied daily

3. *Bathroom Behavior: $50.00 Fine*

No looking over or under stall
Must be in and out on time, with your group
Toilet paper must not be left in bathroom
Quiet during bathroom call
Leave no personal items in bathroom
Do not leave wastebaskets in bathroom
Do not horseplay in bathroom

4. *Dining Room Behavior: $50.00 Fine*

No passing or accepting food from another table
No gum in kitchen
No combs or brushes in kitchen
Remove silverware and paper from table when leaving kitchen
Kitchen chairs must be clean when you leave kitchen
Do not stack plates unless they are scraped
Kitchen must be kept clean when renting
Use stove and toaster properly
LOUD
Acceptable table manners
Leave kitchen with proper group
Do not horseplay in kitchen

5. *Being at the Right Place: $75.00 Fine*

Do not leave room without permission
Do not go to kitchen without permission

No loitering
Do not go to cancelled classes
Being behind desk without permission
Going off dorm without staff's O.K.
Out of bounds
Must be in sight of staff when outside

Rule Management

1. *Recreation Equipment: $100.00 Fine*

   Must return record player in good order after renting
   Go through Game Director for a game
   Take care of recreation items

2. *Community Counseling: $15.00 Fine*

   Don't eat in C.C.
   Don't sideline talk
   No smoking in C.C.
   No knitting, writing, crocheting, etc.
   No interrupting whoever is speaking
   No popping gum in C.C.

3. *Key Rules: $25.00 Fine*

   Do not leave key in room
   Do not take key off dorm
   Nothing is to be on key
   Do not deface room key

4. *Dayroom Behavior: $25.00 Fine*

   Don't sit on heater
   No white robes in dayroom
   Loud
   Not being seen from desk
   Horseplay
   Sitting on ping-pong table

5. *Desk Area and Hall Rules: $50.00 Fine*

   Having an article belonging to desk
   Do not use desk pen without permission
   Leaving closet #34 open
   Do not slam door
   Passing items in hall
   Horseplay

6. *Linen: $15.00 Fine*

   Unmarked laundry
   Linen must be in when called for

7. *Smoking Rules*

   All smoking rules are taken care of in the Smokers' Meeting. Fine not
   levied except by smoking committee

8. *Activities: $25.00 Fine*

   Taking name off list
   Not keeping in twos
   Poor sportsmanship
   Physical contact
   Inappropriate behavior at auditorium, movie, etc.

III.   CENTRAL: BASIC COTTAGE RULES

1. When lights come on in the morning, you are to get up and start cleaning your room.
2. If door has been unbolted, come out and wash up.
3. You have only seven (7) minutes to wash up.
4. Brush teeth in hopper room *only*.
5. Friday is linen day. When you come out to wash up, bring linen to center hall to be checked. *Don't forget* to turn in your washcloths and
   towels. If you fail to do so, you won't get one in the evening.
6. Monday and Tuesday are *general cleaning* days. South Hall cleans on
   Monday. The East Hall cleans on Tuesday. Take your furniture out and
   give rooms a good cleaning (windowsills, lockers, dressers, beds, wood-
   work, hampers, floors, and doors).
7. If your room "fails" more than once a week, action will be taken upon
   you.
8. Girls stay on their own hall.
9. Do not congregate on the hall or near girls' doors.
10. Do not go into another girl's room without permission.
11. Do not run up and down halls.
12. No uncombed hair is to be worn in dining room. Rollers may be worn
    on Sunday or if you plan to have visitors, but only with the cottage
    parent's permission.
13. You are only allowed two (2) packs of sugar for tea and coffee.
14. Everyone is to take turns clearing and cleaning tables. Please clean the
    rim on the table.
15. *Do not* put your *feet* on furniture.

16. Do not go into the kitchen unless you have an assignment in there or you have permission from the cottage parent.
17. We do not leave the dining room without permission.
18. We do not go into the classroom on Monday and Tuesday because of washing and room cleaning.
19. We have to have permission to turn on the TV and record player on weekends.
20. You will be placed on card restriction if you abuse the privilege.
21. Use the bathroom when called at 8:30 (before 9:00 p.m.). Nobody will be let out of their room until after eleven. Detail will be given violators.
22. Do not move furniture without permission.
23. No lying or sitting on the floor.
24. Do not sit on the arms of furniture.
25. Do not comb your hair over any sink in any area.
26. Keep your books in the coatroom in the classroom during the day.
27. Empty your ashtrays after using them.
28. Only three (3) girls on a couch at a time. One in a chair.
29. Do not talk or hang out of your windows.
30. Don't go into another area with a lit cigarette.
31. Don't smoke or get extra food when in your room.
32. Don't go to bed until nine o'clock when "in strict."
33. Don't walk on the backs of your shoes. Detail will be given.
34. No gum chewing.
35. No borrowing at any time without the cottage parent's permission.
36. Keep your shoes tied.
37. Be neat and clean at all times.
38. Turn in cigarette butts if the cottage parent asks for them.
39. Don't sleep on your bedspread.
40. When you return clothing, make sure the cottage parent knows it.
41. No card playing in the morning.
42. No boyish hairstyles.
43. No vulgar language.
44. Shave on Saturday or Sunday morning, depending on the cottage parent.
45. Have one outfit ready for an emergency.
46. No finger popping.
47. When you come into the cottage, check in with the cottage parent.
48. Do not leave any area without permission.
49. Supplies are issued only by the regular cottage parent in the evening.
50. Do not instigate fights or arguments.
51. Do not turn around, talk, or cross legs at knees in Chapel. You may cross them at the ankles.
52. Do not slouch in your seat at the movies. You may talk to girls in your own cottage when the reel changes.
53. Punishment for hunks and sillies will be taken care of by _____.

54. Punishment for catting [unauthorized campus movement] will be taken care of by _____.
55. Do not pierce your ears or let anyone else do so.
56. Do not cut your hair.
57. Have all clothes ironed by Saturday evening.
58. Please make sure your sani is tightly wrapped and put directly in the trash can in the bathroom.
59. You are called for lockup at night after everyone is in their rooms.
60. When you start your period and end it, make sure you check with the cottage parent.
61. Do not have your coat in your room at any time.
62. No talking after lights out. Radios and record players are to be turned off too.
63. If there is a special program, be ready for bed when it is over.
64. If you have a problem, take it to the cottage parent instead of a girl.
65. If you have any questions, feel free to ask.
66. Knock on the door before entering the office.
67. No tattoos.
68. Do your hair on Fridays and Saturdays unless something special comes up. Then get the cottage parent's special permission.
69. Put all cigarette butts in ashtray, not on the floor.
70. Hospital call is at 7:30 a.m., after breakfast.
71. Be on time in the dining room.
72. Empty ashtrays after every smoke break.

IV. CENTRAL—GUIDELINES FOR ORIENTATION COTTAGE

(Among the general topics discussed in the orientation cottage are the following written guidelines; however, they do not exhaust all the rules that are brought up during the orientation period.)

1. Students going from one area to another—catting—instructed to go front line (walk in front of cottages).
2. WSC boys working on grounds—why they are here—what we expect of our young ladies.
3. Clothing—no borrowing—what students are allowed to wear on and off campus.
4. Personal cleanliness: hair, razor, cosmetics, eyebrows.
5. Hospital—procedure for being on list to see doctor or dentist.
6. Room visiting.
7. Mealtime: manners; no one excused from dining room; if in strict or in bed, eat in your room—you will have a tray with a spoon only.
8. Cleaning rooms and making bed properly—one bulletin board.
9. Assignments throughout the cottage—have C.P. check them.

10. No pop bottles in room.
11. Snacks—buying while off campus.
12. Do not pierce ears or mark your person—no cutting hair.
13. Sleep properly attired—when out of room at night, wear housecoat and slippers.
14. Smoking—in designated areas only.
15. Explain fire drill procedure.
16. No cigarettes, matches, gum, or money.
17. No scissors allowed in rooms overnight.
18. Supplies—how they are issued.
19. Address all staff properly—Mr. or Mrs.—call girls by the name under which they were committed (not nicknames or "middle" names).
20. No coats allowed in rooms any time.
21. Chapel attendance
22. Canteen: saving yellow receipts and so forth.
23. Students sent back to cottage because of illness from school or training to be checked by hospital.
24. State letters—stationery.
25. Radios, cameras, and so forth.
26. Students are not allowed to use tampons, per hospital.
27. When cottatge problems arise.
28. Sillies.
29. If you need to talk to someone, go through channels.
30. Please do not use wastebaskets as pots. Knock on door at night to use bathroom.
31. Broken screens on run attempts: You do work detail until $10.00 is paid.
32. Feet on furniture.

V. EASTERN: BASIC COTTAGE RULES FOR ALL COTTAGES

1. Do not be disrespectful to any staff.
2. Do not fight in or out of the cottage.
3. Do not become involved in negative campus activities, in or out of the cottage (racket).
4. Do not bring, take out, or deliver issues in or out of the cottage.
5. Keep your room, dresser drawers, closets, beds, personal belongings clean and neat at all times.
6. Never under any circumstances enter another girl's room.
7. Do not talk or yell out of your window at any time to anyone.
8. Do not go upstairs, downstars, basement, outdoors, or to another girl's door without *first* getting permission from the staff on duy.
9. Do not swap, borrow, loan, exchange or give away any personal clothing, yours or State issue.
10. Do not at any time create any disturbance in the dining room.

11. Do not cause any trouble going to and from chapel, movies, school or on walks.
12. Never leave the group for any reason when assembled in the recreation room, dining room, and so forth without *first* getting permission from the staff on duty.
13. *Never leave your room without first getting permission of the staff on duty.* (Knock on door.)
14. Do not talk unnecessarily after prayers are said.
15. Do not use profanity at any time.
16. Do not talk to girls in room confinement at any time.

If you want to stay out of trouble please obey the above rules, and above all never let another girl take a drag off of your cigarette.

Rules in A.M.

1. Always rap on doors to get permission to go to the bathroom.
2. Do not walk barefooted in corridor and always have a housecoat on.
3. Do get up when the staff calls the *first time.*
4. Bring all your things with you like towels, soap, toothpaste and so forth so you won't go back and forth.
5. Do not borrow anything including deodorant. If you don't have your own, use the State deodorant.
6. Do not visit with any girls. Stay by your door in your room.
7. Do have your jacket or coat in case of fire drill.
8. Do not wash personals in A.M., only when they are stained.
9. Do not sleep in the nude—always have pajamas or nightgown.
10. Do not comb or brush your hair in the bathroom. Use your mirror in your room.
11. Do not wear State sneakers to school. You can wear your own.

Other Cottage Rules

1. No smoking without permission.
2. No talking when serving room confinement—rule of silence.
3. Never more than one girl in the bathroom.
4. Do not leave the dining room without permission.
5. Ask the staff's permission to get up for seconds.
6. NO CONTACTING.
7. NO ROAMING.

INDEX

Books of related interest from Wiley-Interscience. . .

SOCIETY OF WOMEN:
A Study of a Women's Prison
By Rose Giallombardo

". . .a useful contribution to the study of nonvoluntary complex organization."
—*Social Forces*

"Positioning the nature of prison culture as organically related to that of the larger society, rather than a distortion of it, the author examines the prison as a system of roles and functions which duplicate kinship. . . . This is the first systematic and comprehensive study of the adult female prison. It is also a pioneering effort to establish why kinship, marriage, and family groups are the solution to the deprivations of prison life for female inmates. . . . This is definitely a valuable and comprehensive sociological study."
1966   244 pages   —*Journal of Human Relations*

THE COMMUNITY AND THE POLICE — CONFLICT OR COOPERATION?
By Joseph Fink and Lloyd G. Sealy

Contending that effective law enforcement depends upon cooperation between the police and the public, this book takes a critical look at the problems of police/community relations and the programs being implemented to resolve them. In the process, it challenges many of the traditional approaches to law enforcement, offers a new definition of the role of the police, and will cause you to rethink about approaches to maintaining law and order.

"I welcome this worthwhile contribution to the growing literature on improving the effectiveness of our nation's police departments. . . .

"*The Community and the Police — Conflict or Cooperation?* provides a groundwork for policemen, administrators, and the general public to begin working on a better relationship. Its basic tenets are difficult to dismiss, and they must be kept in mind if the police are to continue serving the cause of democracy rather than impeding it." —*From the Foreword by Birch Bayh,*
1974   240 pages   *United States Senator, Indiana*

CRIME IN DEVELOPING COUNTRIES:
A Comparative Perspective
By Marshall B. Clinard and Daniel J. Abbott

Focusing on similarities and differences between developed and less developed countries, *Crime in Developing Countries* carefully analyzes how criminal behavior is influenced by urbanization, migration, social organization of slum areas, opportunity, poverty, and differential peer group structures. Differences in the incidence, the types, and the forces which produce crime in developing countries are discussed in detail, as are problems concerning police, prison, and the prevention and control of crime.
1973   319 pages

MAKING IT IN PRISON
The Square, the Cool, and the Life
By Esther Heffernan

Explores such questions as how the non-criminal *square* structures a system with values and roles of the "respectable" society; how the professional criminal's *cool* system is an adaptive pattern supporting amenities without endangering parole dates; how the habitual criminal builds a *life* which must provide a complete social system to function as a substitute for the rejected larger society; and how the emerging *political* prisoner of the '70's views the prison as a microcosm of the larger society which must be reformed or destroyed in the struggle for liberation and justice.
1972   231 pages

WILEY-INTERSCIENCE
a division of JOHN WILEY & SONS
605 Third Avenue, New York, N.Y. 10016
NEW YORK • LONDON • SYDNEY • TORONTO

ISBN 0 471 29735-6

365.42
G431

102403